BACK TO AFRICA

BY THE SAME AUTHOR

THE WHITE TRIBES OF AFRICA
SKETCHES FROM VIETNAM

Back to Africa

A HISTORY OF SIERRA LEONE AND LIBERIA

—————◄●►—————

by RICHARD WEST

HOLT, RINEHART AND WINSTON, INC.

New York   Chicago   San Francisco

Designer: TERRY REID
SBN: 03-086364-3
Printed in the United States of America

First stanza of 'Heritage' from ON THESE I STAND by Countee Cullen. Copyright 1925 by Harper & Row, Publishers, Inc.; renewed 1953 by Ida M. Cullen. Reprinted by permission of Harper & Row, Publishers, Inc.

We gratefully acknowledge permission to reproduce the extract from MEN AND RUBBER by Samuel Crowther and Harvey S. Firestone. Copyright 1926 by Doubleday and Company, 1925, 1926 by A. W. Shaw. Reprinted by permission of the Estate of Samuel Crowther.

Extracts from JOURNEY WITHOUT MAPS, copyright 1936 by Graham Greene, and THE HEART OF THE MATTER, copyright 1948 by Graham Greene, are reproduced by kind permission of Graham Greene, Wm. Heinemann and Company, and Viking Press, Inc.

Contents

Eight pages of illustrations fall between
pages 160-161

MAPS

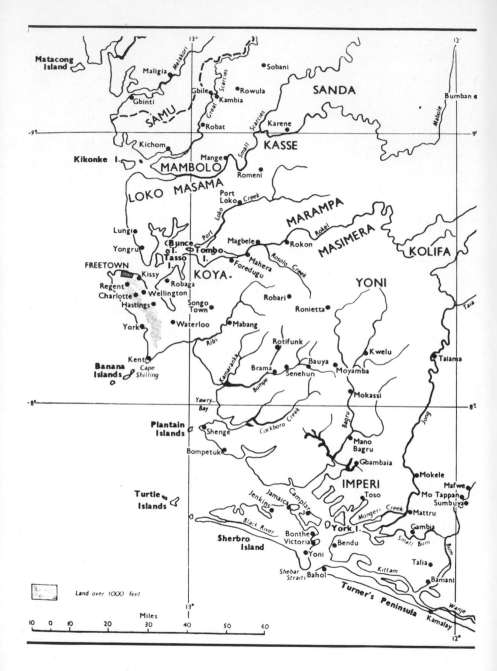

From Christopher Fyfe, A HISTORY OF SIERRA LEONE,
Oxford University Press, 1962

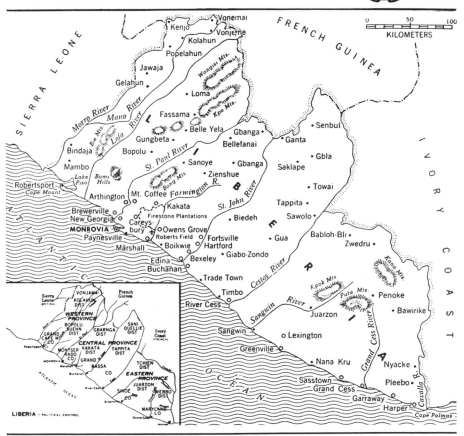

From Nathaniel R. Richardson, LIBERIA'S PAST AND PRESENT, The Diplomatic Press and Publishing Company, London, 1959

PART ONE

Chapter One

It would seem that the prejudice against colour is less strong in England than in America ... A black footman is considered a great acquisition, and consequently, negro servants are sought for and caressed. An ill-dressed or starving negro is never seen in England, and in some cases even alliances are formed between them and white girls of the lower orders of society. A few days since, I met in Oxford Street a well-dressed white girl who was of a ruddy complexion, and even handsome, walking arm in arm and conversing very sociably, with a negro man, who was as well dressed as she, and so black that his skin had a kind of ebony lustre. As there are no slaves in England, perhaps the English have not learned to regard negroes as a degraded class of men, as we do in the United States, where we have never seen them in any other condition.
(From *A Journal of Travels in England, Holland and Scotland in the Years 1805 and 1806*, by Benjamin Silliman, 1820)

A pamphlet published in England in 1772 declared that 'the public good of this kingdom requires that some restraint should be laid on the unnatural increase of *blacks* imported into it'. The author, Edward Long, accused these Negro immigrants of being idle, dissolute and a drain on the poor-rate which was used for the maintenance of their children. The pamphlet went on to warn that:

The lower class of women in England, are remarkably fond of the blacks, for reasons too brutal to mention; they would connect themselves with horses and asses, if the laws permitted them. By these ladies they generally have a numerous brood. Thus in the course of a few generations more, the English blood will become so contaminated by the mixture, and from the chances, the ups and downs of life, this alloy may spread so extensively, as even to reach the middle, and then the higher orders of the people, till the whole nation resembles the *Portuguese* and *Moriscos* in complexion of skin and baseness of mind.

Most of the Negroes in England during the mid-eighteenth century had been brought as personal slaves from America and the West Indies. Jack Beef, the slave of John Baker, a former solicitor-general of the Leeward Islands, was entrusted with messages and commissions to London, rode with his master to hounds, and was given tickets, along with the free white servants, to performances at the theatre. Although decent owners felt responsible for the welfare and happiness of these slaves, others treated them as a mere commodity. 'For sale, a Healthful Negro Boy'—ran a typical advertisement in a Liverpool newspaper for February 17th, 1758—'about 5 feet high, well proportioned, of a mild, sober, honest disposition; has been with his present master 3 years, and used to wait on a table and to assist in a stable.'

When Justice Mansfield ruled, in 1772, that slavery was illegal in England, these Negro servants became free men with the right to leave their employment. Some owners, peeved by the Mansfield decision which they saw as a threat to slavery in the Americas, dismissed their ex-slaves and then blamed the new law for the poverty of these unemployed Negroes. The malevolent pamphlet by Edward Long was published just after the Mansfield decision and it illustrates the slavers' thesis that free blacks were a danger to the country. These sentiments had support even among Lord Mansfield's legal colleagues, one of whom, Mr Justice Powell, decreed that 'the Laws of England take no notice of a Negro'.

The black community and the problem that it afforded were much increased during the seventeen eighties when thousands of Negro soldiers and sailors, who had fought for the British in the War of American Independence, were given refuge in England. The British army, having found Negroes useful as spies, pioneers and even as front-line soldiers, felt obliged not to let them return to slavery. Although, by the terms of the peace treaty, the British were pledged to hand over to the Americans all captured property, including slaves, many thousands of Negroes were granted sanctuary in Canada or in England. There are no good statistics on the Negro community in England, but by 1785 it almost certainly numbered between twenty and thirty thousand. Although some of these blacks were in Bristol, Liverpool and the other west-coast ports, the majority had assembled in London, especially in Paddington and around the Mile End Road. Their colour and their inclination to congregate made blacks conspicuous and gave an inflated idea of their number.

The Negroes in England, two centuries ago, were an object of interest and discussion but not of disdain or dislike. The views expressed in the Edward Long pamphlet, although all too common today, were rare, unfashionable and even outrageous when written in 1772. Most English people, especially the poor and the women, regarded the Negroes with sympathy and affection. In rich society, black servants were modish and therefore petted. The Duchess of Kingston delighted to dress up her black boy, who accompanied her to a box at the opera almost every night. A visitor to the same Lord Mansfield's house wrote that 'a Black came in after dinner and sat with the ladies, and after coffee, walked with the company in the garden'. This Negress, Dido, although 'neither handsome nor genteel', appears to have held great influence on the judge, and was blamed by the planting interests for the abolition of slavery. Black servants, because so chic, were also extremely expensive, hence the joke in Paris a few years later that Dumas the novelist, who was part Negro and wholly mean, used to dress up in livery and stand beside his coach, to make the passers-by think that he could afford a black footman. The handsome wages earned by black servants may explain the scene in the farce *The Divorce*, written by Isaac Jackman in 1781. The Negro Sambo asks the white lawyer Qui Tam how he can get divorced:

QUI TAM. Divorced?
SAMBO. Yes, Massa—me want to marry a pretty white
    woman.

QUI TAM. You do? Timothy, hand me my cane—I'll break this scoundrel's sooty noodle for him.

SAMBO. Pretty white woman, Massa—and here, I have brought you my year's wages—ten guineas (*gives him a purse*).

QUI TAM. Here, Timothy; you may lay by the cane—So then, Sambo, you want to be in the fashionable world, I see?

SAMBO. Oh yes, Massa. I should like to be a Man of Fashion of all things.

QUI TAM. Call in a week, Sambo, and I'll tell you. Timothy, show the black gentleman downstairs.

Off-stage, few Negroes aspired to be in the fashionable world. But there is evidence of their popularity in the social world of poor white Londoners. The Negro dances, called 'Balls of Blacks', drew many hundreds of revellers. The fondness for blacks of some white women was remarked at the time even by Dr Johnson whose black servant, Francis Barber, was pursued by an ardent girl haymaker from Lincolnshire down to London. The male whites, far from resenting these Negroes who must sometimes have taken their girls and jobs, appear to have regarded them as exotic but worthy comrades. When a planter tried to kidnap his former slave for shipment back to the West Indies, the London mob rose to protect the Negro. When two black servants fought a duel with pistols in 1780, two white servants acted as seconds.

The black soldiers and sailors, as well as the less proficient servants, found it hard to get jobs in London, so that many begged in the street or lived in a poor-house on government money. These 'poor blacks' or 'indigent blacks', as they soon came to be called in the newspapers, were an object of special concern and sympathy to that famous group of religious people known as the 'Evangelicals', the 'Clapham Sect' or, derisively, as the 'Saints'. These men and women championed the 'poor blacks' not only from sympathy with their poverty but because they opposed the slave trade and slavery. The Evangelicals were against strong drink, swearing, lewdness and breach of the Sabbath, but their fiercest, most famous and most successful campaign was against the blasphemous practice of slavery. Incidentally to this major campaign, they took up the cause of the poor blacks in England, they thought up the plan for repatriation to Africa and went on to found Sierra Leone.

The greatest of the Saints was William Wilberforce, who devoted his life to the anti-slavery movement. A public agitator of genius, a personal friend of statesmen like Pitt, a humorous and attractive man, he yet did not escape the absurdities of the Evangelical movement. Wilberforce took a tear-stained delight in long and unconvincing stories of sinners who turned to God on their deathbed; he thought Lord Castlereagh committed suicide because he had broken the Sabbath; he rolled in the muck of his own small sins, of which gluttony was the worst. 'Strange that the most generous men and religious', he wrote in his diary, 'do not see that their duties increase with their fortune, and that they will be punished for spending it in eating etc.' Neighbouring entries recount feasts of duck, asparagus, turtle and venison, with the brief, penitent wail—'ate enormously'.

One of the first 'bluestockings', Hannah More, had been London's foremost playwright and wit before she was overcome by a rush of piety to the head. She renounced 'sarcastic humour', gave up writing plays and declared in 1793: 'I should derive more gratification from being able to lower the price of bread than from having written the *Iliad*.' She railed at the smart society she had once adorned, at their talk of 'gallantry' when they meant adultery, at making the servants announce 'not at home'. (Muriel Jaeger writes in *Before Victoria*★ that 'Wilberforce's servants found the reverse policy extremely inconvenient; and so did he.') Like Thomas Bowdler, another Saint, Hannah More campaigned against impropriety in the theatre.

Hannah More and her equally pious sisters founded schools for the godless poor. Some of the funds were given her by Henry Thornton, a banker M.P. and the richest among the Saints. A dry,

★ Full bibliographical details for this book, and any other not cited in full, are given in the Bibliography.

precise and unlikable man, Thornton revelled in morbid piety, and his fondness for deathbed repentance tales was thought excessive even by Wilberforce.

Some modern zealots resemble the Saints in solemnity, priggishness and obsessiveness, but most of the causes for which the Saints fought have gone out of intellectual fashion. Only occasionally do their tracts have a modern ring, as for instance when Thomas Clarkson, published an *Essay on Slavery* in which he declared that the Dutch at the Cape were 'more savage than the brutes themselves, not only murder their fellow creatures without any provocation or necessity but even make a diversion of their sufferings and enjoy their pain'. After reading this essay at the Cambridge Senate House, where it won first prize, Clarkson was riding back from Cambridge to London when it occurred to him that the arguments he had used for the sake of an essay were true, and that slavery was a real abomination. The shock of this discovery was so strong that he had to dismount and sit by the side of the road to think things over. These thoughts made Clarkson a life-long anti-slaver and Saint.

The most important of the Saints for the history of Sierra Leone was the philanthropist Granville Sharp, who not only conceived the idea of colony in the 1780s but had already led the legal fight that ended with Lord Mansfield's judgment. He was a humbler and much more lovable man than the rest of the Evangelicals. Descended from a line of clerics, he had served apprenticeship as a draper but later went into the civil service. He spent his leisure studying Hebrew and Greek and he dabbled in arcane disputes on Socianism, Revelations, the Anglo-Saxon system of Frankpledge and Jewish theology. He was a thin, bustling, kindly, inquisitive man with a multitude of enthusiasms. Some of his causes were typical of the Saints, such as his protest against the *Beggars Opera* in drag, or his remonstrance to the Archbishop of York, whose son had acted the part of Thaïs in Terence's comedy, *The Eunuch*. Yet many of Sharp's campaigns had nothing to do with the Clapham Sect. He was against duelling and the press-ganging of sailors; he corresponded with the King of Prussia on introducing English liturgy into the Prussian Church; he wrote pamphlets on the pronunciation of English, the administration of workhouses, Catholic Emancipation, the use of draft-oxen, predestination and the encroachment of the Thames. He was a crank but a crank of genius.

Sharp's concern with slaves was caused—literally—by an accident. A black slave, Jonathan Strong, had been beaten and almost blinded by his master, who then turned him out into the street as a piece of worthless property. One day in 1765, Strong went to the surgery of Dr William Sharp, whose brother Granville had just been paying a visit. The British philanthropist, who always walked in a day-dream, and the Negro slave, who was partially blind from his injuries, collided outside the house. As soon as the good-hearted Sharp saw the broken face of the Negro, he resolved to help him back to health.

Granville and his doctor brother got Strong admitted to hospital and then found him a new job as a servant. As Strong afterwards wrote in gratitude: 'All the while I was in hospital, the gentleman find me in clothes, shoes and stockings, and when I come out, he paid for my lodging, and a money to find myself some necessaries, till he got me into a place.'

There was no political motive in Sharp's charity. He would as readily have taken pity upon a man of any race whom he found in the same condition. For two years Sharp did not even know that Strong was a slave with a legal owner. Then one day in 1767, this owner, David Lisle, who was a lawyer from Barbados, saw Strong attending his new employer behind a hackney coach. Perceiving his slave now restored to health, and therefore to proper value, Lisle had Strong traced and arrested by two of the Lord Mayor's officers. The frightened Strong, knowing Lisle's ferocity, got a message to Sharp who complained to the Lord Mayor of Strong's wrongful detention. It was the start of a great legal wrangle.

Sharp had never opened a law book, 'except the Bible', and most of the lawyers he spoke to were unsympathetic. The august Dr Blackstone, the greatest writer on British law, at first agreed to act for Sharp but later decided that slavery was admissible.

Complaining that even his own lawyers opposed him, Sharp resolved to plead himself and started a frantic study of law. Strong's owner, Lisle, who was a man of psychopathic temper, at first resisted by legal means, then challenged Sharp to a duel and threatened him with violence. But for all his gentleness, Sharp was a stubborn and brave man; he persisted in his work and produced a long memorandum to prove that a slave who set foot in England became at that moment a free man. The document was so well received at the Inns of Court that Lisle's lawyers dropped their case and Strong was allowed to go free. However, Sharp would not be content until slavery in England was declared against the law by a decision in the High Court. He took up the cases of other black slaves; he wrote many pamphlets and argumentative letters; and finally, after a five-year struggle, obtained Lord Mansfield's historic decision regarding the slave James Somerset.

An act of kindness had first involved Sharp in the sufferings of the Negroes but as soon as his interest was aroused he became passionately opposed to slavery. He made alliance by letter with Anthony Benezet of Philadelphia, the leading opponent of slavery in the New World. He read newspapers for information on slavery and the slave trade; he searched the Bible for evidence that both were against God's will; he pestered statesmen and bishops with his tracts. Always he was ready to spring into legal action. In July 1786, he heard that a Negro, Harry Demane, had been kidnapped by his master and put on a ship for the West Indies. Sharp obtained a writ of Habeas Corpus and had it served when the ship was leaving the Downs with its anchor up and sails set. Demane, who was later to emigrate to Sierra Leone, told Sharp 'that he had intended to have jumped into the sea as soon as it was dark; choosing rather to die than to be carried into slavery'.

It scarcely seems credible that Sharp can have found time for a job as well as for so many private campaigns and hobbies. But until 1775 he held a clerical post in the Ordnance Office, providing ammunition and arms to His Majesty's forces. The War of Independence in America faced Sharp with a problem of conscience, since the rebels included his friends like Anthony Benezet; but

20

the Ordnance Office, with admirable generosity, allowed him leave of absence for over two years. When they at last felt obliged to fill the post, Sharp was subsidized by two of his brothers. 'Dear Brother Granville,' wrote James Sharp, '... if you should think it proper to give up your employment—I will now speak for my brother William as well as for myself—we are both ready and willing, and, God be thanked, at present *able*, to take care that the loss shall be none to you.'

Sharp's generosity always outreached his money. In particular, he was overwhelmed with appeals from the poor blacks.

An obituary notice later recalled:

> As Mr Sharp was their known patron they had all flocked to him, in their turn, for support: he had considered them as orphans, who had some title to his care; and he had occasionally relieved them. But their number being great (about four hundred), he found that he could not relieve them daily, consistently with his engagements to others. He had many private pensioners, to whom annual sums, and these to a considerable amount, had been promised, and regularly paid.

In January 1786, a committee of City businessmen put out an appeal to help the poor blacks. This soon raised eight hundred pounds which went to a hospital for the Negroes and for daily distributions of food at Paddington and Mile End. Sharp had helped in the appeal, although with characteristic modesty he was not a member of the committee; but he knew that hand-outs of money and food would not settle the problem of the poor blacks.

As early as 1783, Sharp had discussed forming a colony in West Africa, and his memorandum contained most of the plans that were later to be used for Sierra Leone. Other writers too had discussed plans for an African colony in which trade in merchandise would replace the trade in slaves. Two free Negroes, Ottobah Cuguano and Gustavus Vassa, wrote with all the authority of their colour on the economic potential of the West Coast.

The suggestion to start a colony in Sierra Leone was made by Henry Smeathman, a botanist and sometime merchant, who had spent three years on that part of the coast. The 'Flycatcher', as he called himself, had withstood the murderous climate of West Africa and had gathered a rich assortment of bugs, but had failed in his main ambition of winning a fortune. Back in Europe and deep in debt, he was anxious to capitalize on his knowledge by starting a cotton plantation in Africa. Early in 1786, Smeathman approached Jonas Hanway, the chairman of the Committee for the Black Poor, to outline his proposal for a colony. A few weeks later, he had this proposal published in booklet form.

The Plan of a Settlement portrays Sierra Leone as a fertile and salubrious land. Here cotton, rice, sugar, tobacco and indigo could be grown as fine as anywhere in the world. Excellent brandy could be distilled out of local sweet potatoes and grapes; the site was ideal for a whaling station. The previous year, Smeathman had told a House of Commons committee discussing plans for a prison colony, that if two hundred convicts were landed in even the healthiest part of Sierra Leone 'one hundred would die in less than a month and that there would not be two people alive in less than 6 months'. Now he described it as 'very healthy to those who live on the productions of the country'.

The Committee for the Black Poor was much impressed by Smeathman's plan of settlement, as were those of the poor blacks who had originally come from Sierra Leone. The committee passed Smeathman's plan to the Treasury, which was paying a subsidy to the Poor Black Hospital and was anxious to get them out of the country. Neither the Lords of the Treasury nor their civil servants bothered to read their copy of Smeathman's plan— I found the pages still uncut—but they gave the settlement their backing. The Committee for the Black Poor then printed handbills inviting 'those desirous of profiting by this opportunity, of settling in one of the most pleasant and fertile countries in the known world'.

It was not an honest prospectus, as Smeathman at any rate knew. Malaria, yellow fever, typhoid and dysentery killed a large proportion of visitors to Sierra Leone. Its soil had never proved good for plantation agriculture; its honest commerce was not as profitable as the slave trade; no attempt had been made to buy land from the local chiefs. Smeathman's motives remain unclear, although Joseph Hanway, the chairman of the committee, came to suspect that he planned to traffic in slaves. It is my view that Smeathman was just irresponsible. One of his obsessions was the improvement of air balloons; his plan of a settlement, like his balloons, had a gaseous, airy quality. Smeathman's character was not put to the test, for he died in July 1786 before the start of the colony inspired by his rash prospectus.

With Smeathman dead, the committee lost interest in Sierra Leone and looked around for other sites for a colony of black poor. First the Bahamas were suggested; then a merchant wrote to the Treasury praising the Gambia, adding that two of his vessels would sail there within three months; one Turnbull Macaulay, with Highland directness, claimed that New Brunswick was the ideal place and offered to take the 'poor wretches' at nine guineas a head. The blacks themselves objected to these proposals because slavery was still legal in the first two territories while New Brunswick was even colder than England. They said in a petition that 'no place whatsoever would be so agreeable to them as Sierra Leone to which their attention had been peculiarly directed by the late Mr Smeathman's humane plan.' They requested that Joseph Irwin, another white man, should be their agent or leader.

The Treasury was still favourable to the plan and commissioned the Navy to find the transport vessels for the emigrants. By October the number of blacks wanting to sail to Sierra Leone had increased from 250 to 500; and when one of the black leaders predicted a further 250, the Navy commissioned a second ship. In November many blacks suddenly opted out of the enterprise, leaving less than 300 to sail in two ships that could take twice that number, whereupon the Navy Board asked the London authorities to round up black vagrants to join the settlers. In December 1786 the two transports left London for Portsmouth where they were joined by a naval sloop, under Captain T. Boulden Thompson. The voyage was cursed with bad luck from the start. It had been hoped to get to Sierra Leone well before the

23

rainy season that generally starts in May. But after a wait at Portsmouth, where fever killed off fifty passengers, two of the ships were damaged by storm and had to put in at Plymouth. The long and frustrating wait off shore affected the confidence of the settlers. The Negro author Gustavus Vassa, who had been put in charge of the expeditionary stores, quarrelled with Captain Thompson, with Joseph Irwin the agent, and Patrick Frazer the luckless man who had offered to serve as chaplain. Irwin, who was incompetent according to Captain Thompson, threatened to leave ship and go to London. The Navy Board sacked 'the turbulent and discontented' Vassa, and was much relieved when, early in April 1787, the fleet at last sailed for Africa.

Once out to sea, the Negro settlers 'behaved themselves remarkably well'. The 411 passengers included some three hundred Negro men, maybe forty Negresses, a few white artisans and officials with their families, and a group of white women of doubtful number and character. Most history books about Sierra Leone, and almost all newspaper articles, state that the first black settlers were accompanied on their journey by seventy London prostitutes. Frequently it is said that the women were made drunk and press-ganged on to the ships. The enemies of Sierra Leone in the first forty years of its history even suggested that Sharp and his Evangelical friends had planned and executed the kidnapping.

The solitary evidence for this story is a book by Anna Falconbridge, who went to Sierra Leone in 1791 and met some white women survivors of the original expedition. Shocked by the filth and wretchedness of these women, Mrs Anna Falconbridge questioned one of them on her history:

> She said, the women were mostly of that description of persons who walk the streets of London, and support themselves by the earnings of prostitution; that men were employed to collect and conduct them to Wapping, where they were intoxicated with liquor, then inveigled on board of ship, and married to *Black men*, whom they had never seen before;

24

that the morning after she was married, she really did not remember a syllable of what had happened over night, and when informed, was obliged to inquire *who was her husband?* After this, to the time of their sailing, they were amused and buoyed up by a prodigality of fair promises, and great expectations which awaited them in the country they were going to: 'Thus,' in her own words, 'to the disgrace of my mother country, upwards of one hundred unfortunate women, were seduced from England to practice their iniquities more brutishly in this horrid country.'

Mrs Falconbridge was a lively writer who relished scandalous or sensational anecdotes but she was too shrewd to accept them all as the truth. Although the other women confirmed the tale of the kidnapping, Mrs Falconbridge had doubts—'for it is scarcely possible that the British government, at this advanced and enlightened age, envied and admired as it is by the universe, could be capable of exercising or countenancing such a Gothic infringement on human liberty.'

The story told to Mrs Falconbridge is riddled with implausibilities. Had the women been kept on ship, against their will and in English waters, throughout the four months delay at Portsmouth and Plymouth, it is inconceivable that their protests would not have been heard and heeded by Captain Thompson, by Irwin the agent, by Frazer the chaplain or by some of the white or black settlers. They may indeed have got drunk at Wapping, as travellers often do before sailing, but four sober months at Portsmouth and Plymouth would have allowed them ample time to change their minds. The suggestion that Sharp or any Evangelical could have given consent to the kidnapping is a theory too ludicrous for discussion. In a search through the relevant documents of the Admiralty and the Treasury, I found no reference to those prostitutes, who in most of the popular history books are the most important feature of the founding of the colony. In July 1787, two months after arriving in Africa, Captain Thompson wrote to the Admiralty that white women had suffered badly from fever but these could have been the legal wives of white or Negro settlers. This is, in fact, the best explanation of Mrs Falconbridge's story. Since there were few Negro women in England, the men looked to white women for wives or girlfriends. From contemporary reports we know that many white women were eager to marry or live with Negroes. It therefore is likely that seventy white women chose to go to Sierra Leone as the wives or mistresses of the settlers. It is likely that some of these women had once been prostitutes. It is likely that four years later, now kicking themselves for coming to Africa, the survivors would claim that they had been kidnapped. It is likely that these survivors, their tempers raw from fever and hunger and heat, should accuse each other of having once been 'that description of persons who walk the streets of London'.

Before the expedition sailed for what Sharp dubbed 'the Province of Freedom', he had furnished the settlers with fussy advice on the laws and government of the colony. 'The most certain and effectual mode of securing peace, right and mutual protection, for any community is the old English system of mutual Frankpledge, or free suretyship, given by all the householders, for themselves and each other, in exact numerical divisions of tens and hundreds.' Each Hundred was divided into a hundredor, two chiefs-of-fifties, one town clerk, eight head-boroughs, eight assistant head-boroughs and eighty decimers. As well as the hundredors, there were to be 'tythingmen' with a judicial function. The settlers were to work an eight-hour day, and those who refused because of superior wealth were to pay a tax on pride and indolence.

The Book of Judges, the *Anglo-Saxon Chronicle*, and seventeenth-century Leveller tracts all helped to flavour this ideological stew. Sharp's busy benevolence and eager imagination planned the colony from its fundamental laws to such details as the special wing in Sierra Leone penitentiary 'for the married persons of either sex, that they may not be separated from their spouses, or families, in case they should desire to attend them'. Poor, generous, kindly, dreaming Sharp ... his settlers in Sierra Leone were going to have more to worry about than Frankpledge, sex in prison, or taxes on pride and indolence.

26

Chapter Two

The colonists left Plymouth on April 8th, 1787, stopped nearly a
week at Tenerife and reached the Sierra Leone river on May 10th.
Encouraging news of the voyage came back to Sharp who wrote
on June 23rd:

> I had the pleasure of hearing this day of the safe arrival of the
> African settlers at the Madeira islands; and that all the
> jealousies and animosities between the Whites and Blacks had
> subsided, and that they had been very orderly ever since Mr
> Vassa and two or three other discontented persons had been
> left on shore at Plymouth. Schools are established on board
> each ship, as I had proposed; and they have daily prayers.
> The account is from the chaplain, Mr Frazer.

He apparently had not heard that fourteen passengers had died
even before the ships reached Tenerife.

On May 15th the settlers put ashore at what is now Freetown,
on the northern side of a peninsula in the mouth of the Sierra
Leone river. They cut through the bush to the crest of a hill,
hoisted the British flag and named the settlement Granville Town,
after Granville Sharp, the bay St George's Bay and the hill St
George's Hill. They marked out streets and divided the colony
into 360 lots of about one acre, on which each family raised its
tent. In deference to Sharp's political principles, they elected
Richard Weaver, a Negro settler, as chief-in-command of the
Province of Freedom.

Captain Thompson, who had been ordered to purchase land
from the local chief, started negotiations with King Tom, a sub-
chief of the Temne tribe. After a few days' discussion King Tom
put his mark to a fine-sounding treaty: 'Know all men by these

presents, that I, King Tom, chief of Sierra Leone on the Grain Coast of Africa, by and with the consent of the other kings, chiefs and potentates subscribing hereto ... do grant, and for ever quit claim to a certain district of land for the settling of the said free community of theirs, their heirs and successors for ever ... ' In return King Tom was presented with goods worth nearly £60— 24 laced hats, 3 dozen hangers with red scabbards, 10 yards of scarlet cloth, 8 muskets, a barrel of gunpowder, 25 iron bars, 117 bunches of beads, one cask and one puncheon of rum. These were normal trading presents, but King Tom probably thought it strange that the white men wanted no slaves in return. It was soon to grow clear that the Temne did not respect, or probably even understand, the territorial treaty to which King Tom had put his mark.

Catastrophe struck the settlers within a few days of pitching their tents. The expedition had been planned to arrive in January, during the dry season, but it had been delayed until the start of the rains that hit Sierra Leone with colossal violence. They had come too late to grow rice; the seed they had brought would not thrive; and the shattering rain swept the soil from the hillside. Wet, miserable and half starved, the settlers sold their guns to the Temne for food. Fever and dysentery swept the settlement, killing Joseph Irwin the agent of the society, Gesau the town-major or engineer and, worst of all, Riccards the gardener, 'on whose skill in the cultivation of vines and other produce' Sharp had built great hopes of a thriving economy. Captain Thompson accused the settlers of obstinacy and laziness while even Sharp had to admit by October: 'I have had but melancholy accounts of my poor little ill-thriven swarthy daughter, the unfortunate colony of Sierra Leone.' But he tried hard to see the bright side of things, such as the physical loveliness of Sierra Leone:

They have purchased twenty miles square of the finest and most beautiful country (they all allow) that was ever seen. The hills are not steeper than Shooter's Hill; and fine streams

28

of fresh water run down the hill on each side of the new township; and in the front is a noble bay, where the river is about three leagues wide: the woods and groves are beautiful beyond description, and the soil very fine.

Moreover, Sharp insisted that the colony could not fail because it was founded on true principles: 'The code of regulations which I drew up for the settlement ... was adopted by the Settlers before they sailed: and, if they would be careful to maintain it, they would become the freest and the happiest people on earth ... ' But soon news came from the colony of its total political breakdown.

The society's agent, Irwin, never established authority over the settlers, who also refused to build a church for the chaplain, Frazer. Captain Thompson had no responsibility for the settlers once he had seen them safe on land, and he wanted none (though on one occasion he took the law into his own hands and had two settlers flogged). The elected chief-in-command, Richard Weaver, fell ill and wrote to Sharp accusing John Reid, his successor, of stealing and selling most of the stores. The accused man, Reid, wrote an even more plaintive letter to blame almost everyone but himself:

There was sixty-three muskets stolen by our people, by whom I know not. And after that, Mr Weaver and Mr Johnson held with the people, and told them that I had made away with them myself, and got them under arms against me; and they rised on me, and seized my house, and took it from me, and all what little I had in the world, and sold it, to pay for those things that were lost ...

The most poignant letter to Sharp came from another Negro, A. Elliot (' ... You will not recollect who I am ... I am the young man that you lent the £1 6s. for which I am in duty bound to pray for your goodness') who wrote from Sierra Leone on July 20th, 1787:

Honoured Sir, I am sorry, and very sorry indeed, to inform

you, dear Sir, that this country does not agree with us at all; and, without a very sudden change, I do not think there will be one of us left at the end of a twelvemonth. Neither can the people be brought to any rule or regulation, they are so very obstinate in their tempers. It was really a very great pity that we ever came to the country, after the death of Mr Smeathman; for we are settled upon the very worst part. There is not a thing, which is put into the ground will grow more than a foot out of it ...

Sharp refused to be downhearted. When he heard, early in 1788, that only 130 people still remained in the colony, he decided, rather than wash his hands of the project, to send out reinforcements. He dispatched the brig *Miro* with thirty-nine settlers, most of whom were white.

Although the Treasury and some friends contributed to the cost, Sharp reckoned that by the end of 1788, he had spent more than £1,700 on Sierra Leone. The letters he sent with the *Miro* were full of his usual assurance. 'The climate of Sierra Leone is not chargeable with this great mortality of the Settlers', he told the 'worthy inhabitants of the Province of Freedom', but rather 'the imprudence of those who daily consumed their full allowance of salt provisions, as well as of rum, against which I repeatedly warned them before they sailed.' (For nearly a century in Sierra Leone, death from dysentery and malaria was attributed to some kind of moral delinquency.) He advised them on how to care for the livestock, which had not been put on the ship, and on how to run their bank, which had not been founded. In another letter, addressed to the passengers on the *Miro*, Sharp showed equal concern for moral issues and for minute practical details. He warned them to water their rum if they must drink; he explained how a thicket of lemon trees could be made into a barricade against leopards; and, of course, he remembered Frankpledge: 'I must also request, that, as soon as the ship leaves the port of London, all the male passengers, above sixteen years of age, will form themselves into dozens; and that each dozen will elect a head-borough, and an assistant head-borough, whose authority must be controlled by the majority of votes in each dozen ... '

Soon after the *Miro* sailed, Sharp received a dispatch from Sierra Leone that taxed even his trusting and kindly temper. He learned that 'the greatest part of the people had left the settlement; and (to my great concern and surprise) that some of them were gone in the slave-ships, to trade for slaves, and that others were gone to the neighbouring slave-factories!' There were several of these depots, or factories, on the coast near by, and the trade offered good money to those who could take the climate. Merchants in other produce complained that the slavers got four times as much wealth in return for the spirits and iron bars they gave to the chiefs. Those Negro settlers at Sierra Leone who were literate and knew some simple arithmetic could command tempting salaries as clerks or agents for the slavers; some set up in business on their own. Since agriculture had failed at Sierra Leone, it was understandable, if lamentable, that some settlers looked for a living to trade.

The white settlers sent out by Sharp and his Evangelical friends, proved even more unscrupulous than the blacks. The passengers on the *Miro*, whom Sharp had instructed to choose their 'boroughs' and 'hundreds' went almost immediately into the slave trade, headed by the doctor. 'All the white people whom I sent out last year, to assist in supporting the settlement,' Sharp wrote in 1789, 'have been wicked enough to go into the service of the slave trade at the neighbouring factories, having been enticed away, I suppose, by high wages.' The perfidy of the Negroes, although less widespread, was even harder for Sharp to bear. The most flagrant example of this was Henry Demane, whom Sharp had himself rescued from kidnapping in 1786. On hearing that Demane had become a prosperous slaver, Sharp wrote to the settlers to remind Demane of his feelings under the horrors of slavery, 'when he turned his face to the mast of the ship into which he was trepanned by his wicked master ... he is now in danger of *eternal slavery!*' If Demane heard this reproach it did not bother him for he was still a prosperous slaver twelve years later.

This ingratitude shook even Sharp's belief in the kindness of

31

human nature, as one sees from his little essay called 'Comparison of Brute Animals with Man':

> When a schoolboy I had various animals, at different times, under my protection, as favourites: and the affection even of the meanest of them, a jack-daw, cannot possibly be described in words, so strongly as it was expressed in the bodily exertions of the little animal, when he heard my foot upon the steps of the house returning from school, that he might hasten to meet me ... But by ingratitude for the Divine favours, inconsiderate men degrade themselves far below the brute creation, even of dogs and jack-daws, which are never ungrateful.

By 1789 there were scarcely two hundred citizens of the Province of Freedom at Granville Town, where most lived in ramshackle huts or tents. Agriculture had proved a disappointment. Some settlers traded up the neighbouring rivers where they often came into conflict with other trading companies, especially an American slaver, Captain Bowie, who resented this upstart black colony with the high-falutin name, and who called the settlers saucy and troublesome. Meanwhile King Tom had died and the new local chief, King Jemmy, refused to adhere to the pledges made by his predecessor. Bowie, disliking both Granville Town and King Jemmy, egged on both sides in their mutual hostility. When the British naval vessel *Pomona* arrived in the bay in May 1790, its captain, Henry Savage, was pestered both by the settlers and by Bowie with furious accusations against King Jemmy and one another. After much confused bickering, Savage requested King Jemmy to come aboard and, on being refused, sent a party of settlers and marines, who burned down Jemmy's village.

As soon as the *Pomona* sailed away, King Jemmy issued an ultimatum, giving the settlers three days to leave Granville Town. Then he burned it down. Since Granville Town was no more than a few poor huts, one should not exaggerate this sacking. It did, however, mean the end of a physical colony. Some of the settlers stayed in the neighbourhood but most drifted to other villages on the coast.

As soon as Sharp heard the depressing news he wrote to the Prime Minister, William Pitt, appealing for a naval vessel to reinstate the settlers. But in 1790, with revolution raging in France, the British had little time to waste on the bothers of West Africa. Even Sharp's sly suggestion that Sierra Leone might be attacked by the French did not arouse any interest in Westminster. The four letters that Sharp wrote to Pitt did not even receive a reply.

However, Pitt was a friend of the influential Wilberforce, who had not yet lost his interest in the Sierra Leone experiment. Early in 1790, even before the news of the burning of Granville Town, certain prominent Saints had formed a commercial enterprise, called the St George's Bay Company, to provide financial support for the colony. The directors included Sharp and two of his brothers, Wilberforce, Henry Thornton the banker M.P., and Samuel Whitbread the liberal brewer, who had already given money to Sharp—and casks of beer to the Sierra Leone settlers.* The stated purpose of this company was 'the opening and establishing of trade in Africa' from which the directors hoped for considerable profits. However, it would be unfair to suggest that philanthropy was merely a cover for business interests. If anything the reverse was true. The directors, all enemies of the slave trade, wanted to prove that honest commerce was possible in Africa. They were all astute businessmen. They knew from recent experience that any venture in Sierra Leone was likely to run into difficulties. When offering shares in the company, Thomas Clarkson wrote:

I should not permit anyone to become a purchaser, who would not be better pleased with the good resulting to Africa than from great commercial profits to himself; not that the latter may not be expected; but in case of a disappointment, I should wish his mind to be made easy by the assurance that

* Whitbread's brewery provided beer for Sir Francis Chichester in his voyage round the world in 1966–7. Their philanthropy was well publicized.

he has been instrumental in introducing light and happiness into a country where the mind was kept in darkness and the body nourished only for European chains.

The slaving interests tried to stop the company getting a Royal Charter but, thanks to the influence of Wilberforce and Thornton, an Act was put through Parliament in 1791, setting up what had been renamed the Sierra Leone Company. The new company was given a new chairman when the banker Thornton replaced the philanthropist Sharp. As a contemporary put it, 'the philanthropic object of the settlement had by many been deemed so highly visionary, that it was judged advisable to elect a chairman, whose ordinary connections with concerns of more acknowledged substantial foundation might seem to authorise the expectation of success.'

Not only Sharp but two of his fondest ideals had been dropped by the Sierra Leone Company. From now on the directors in London, and not the settlers in their Hundreds, were to exercise government in the colony, since Frankpledge and the ancient Israelite laws did not interest Henry Thornton M.P. It had been one of Sharp's purposes to prove, through his colony, that Negroes were the equals of whites, just as the Scriptures had declared that 'God hath made of one blood all nations of men'. The directors of the Sierra Leone Company no doubt agreed with this view in principle but they did not approve it in practice. From now on they preferred to send white rather than Negro settlers to the colony; the officers of the company were to be white; the Negro Hundredors would become just an advisory body.

Early in 1791, the directors of the Sierra Leone Company sent out an agent, Alexander Falconbridge, to find the survivors of the original settlement and to gather them under his government. Falconbridge was an odd choice for the assignment. A former ship's surgeon, who had worked mostly on slaving vessels, he was now hotly opposed to that trade from religious principle. He was not only belligerent but, like most ship's surgeons in fiction if not in fact, a devotee of strong liquor. The combination of these two

34

failings is dangerous even in temperate climates, but normally disastrous on the West Coast of Africa. It was fortunate for historians, if not for Falconbridge himself, that before going to Sierra Leone he married a Bristol girl, Anna.* We have already quoted from her account of her travels. Her racy, humorous and very intelligent book, *Two Voyages to the River Sierra Leone*, is an acute and generally accurate narrative. The fact that Anna Falconbridge was clearly a bit of a bitch served only to improve the wit of her writing.

Anna, her husband and his brother went to Sierra Leone on a ship of the Anderson slaving company which had a depot on Bance Island, where twenty years earlier Smeathman had relished the Anderson hospitality and tried his hand 'at Goff, a game only played in some particular parts of Scotland and at Blackheath'. Falconbridge disliked having to fraternize with slavers and he began to row with the Anderson men even before they left England. On arriving at Sierra Leone he insisted on sleeping in a ship rather than lodge in the comfortable slaving fort on Bance Island. At dinner one evening, discussion turned to that *abominable* trade. 'The glass went quickly round,' Mrs Falconbridge reported, 'and the gentlemen growing warm, I retired immediately as the cloth was removed.' Their attitude to the slavers split the newly-wed couple. Anna detested sleeping aboard a hot, cramped ship, eating beef so tough that it could hardly be cut, and listening to the grievances of a grumpy husband. She yearned for the comfort and company of Bance Island, where she had made friends with both Africans and the slavers. One morning, she recounted: ' ... I feigned sickness, and begged to be excused from attending Falconbridge; he therefore set out, reluctantly leaving me behind: when he was gone, I went on shore, and spent the day in comfort and pleasantry, under the hospitable roof of Bance Island house; where I related the adventures of the preceding day, which afforded much glee to the company.' Her husband meanwhile was trying to round up the settlers.

* A recent biographer, Averil MacKenzie-Grieve, failed like other historians to discover Mrs Falconbridge's maiden name or her later history.

Some refugees from Granville Town had taken shelter on Bance Island; one party of fifty had gone up-river and lived in an African town. Several had taken jobs on passing ships or had made their way back to England. Before trying to refound the Granville Town colony, Falconbridge had several palavers with Naimbana, the overlord of the Sierra Leone peninsula, who was both more intelligent and more friendly disposed towards foreigners than his sub-chief King Jemmy had proved. Mrs Falconbridge was impressed by him but her housewife's instincts were offended by the holes in His Majesty's stockings. King Naimbana renewed the former treaty with the settlers in return for the usual gifts of rum, tobacco and iron bars. Treaty or no, Falconbridge thought it unwise to risk offending King Jemmy by founding another colony on the same spot, so he shifted Granville Town about two miles to the east, choosing a village of fifteen good huts which the natives had abandoned for fear of ghosts. The fifty or so settlers who gathered at this new Granville Town included the so-called prostitutes who were mentioned in the last chapter.

Within a few weeks at Granville Town the settlers had built additional huts, a strong-house for arms and ammunition, and had cleared and planted four acres of land before the heavy rains set in. The men were determined to defend themselves; they were loyal to the society that had sent them out but had lost the taste for self-government and they asked the company agent to rule them. The report that Falconbridge brought back to London in summer 1791 encouraged the company to make an ambitious investment of £100,000, which was afterwards oversubscribed to £235,280.

The Falconbridges took home King Naimbana's eldest son, who came to be known in England as the 'Black Prince'. The king had a curious and receptive intellect and was keen to learn of the world beyond the rain forest. He had sent another son to be educated in France and a third to be taught the Muslim faith by the Mandingo tribe to the north. The King had taken one of the Granville Town settlers, Elliott Griffiths, to act as a secretary and interpreter in his dealings with foreign traders. Griffiths, a protégé of Sharp, no doubt told good things of him to the king. He phrased and may have composed the letter that Naimbana wrote to Sharp and sent on the ship with his son. The king asked Sharp to help him trace three relatives who had been kidnapped in a Danish ship and asked him to send out settlers worthy of taking the care and command of the place:

> then you need not be afraid of their prospering in this country. Mr Falconbridge, during his time out here, I approved much. I ever was partial to the people of Great Britain, for which cause I have put up with a great deal of insults from them, more than I should from any other country. My son, I hope, you will take care of, and let him have his own way in nothing but what you think right yourself.

The son, John Naimbana, who left with the Falconbridges in June 1791, was aged between twenty-four and twenty-nine. On reaching England he was introduced to Thomas Clarkson, Henry Thornton, and other directors of the company. 'I could not help secretly smiling,' wrote the irreverent Mrs Falconbridge, 'to see the servile courtesy which those gentlemen paid this young man, merely from his being the son of a nominal King.' There is no record that he actually met Granville Sharp, but he showed his respect by taking the names Henry Granville at his christening. The Black Prince emerges from the accounts as a shy, studious man with a diffidence, sometimes erupting in anger, that frequently marks young Africans in Europe. He studied the Bible and Hebrew, and when he had no special tasks would read for eight to ten hours in a day.

> He had few advantages of person [says a rather censorious report], but he was uncommonly pleasing in his behaviour, showing much natural courtesy and even delicacy of manner … He was quick in all his feelings, and his temper was occasionally warm; some degree of jealousy also entering into his character: in particular he was indisposed to answer questions put to him by strangers concerning the state of his own

37

country; for he was apt to suspect that they meant to draw comparisons unfavourable to its character; and he would therefore, on such occasions, often turn the conversation, by remarking, that a country so unfavourably circumstanced as Sierra Leone had hitherto been, was not to be supposed capable of having made any attainments worthy of being the subject of conversation in Great Britain.

Once, when somebody mentioned the name of a man who had said degrading things of the Africans, the Black Prince 'broke out into violent and vindictive language'. On being reproved for this unchristian behaviour, he replied: 'If anyone takes away the character of Black people, that man injures Black people all over the world; and when he has once taken away their character, there is nothing which he may not do to Black people ever after ... *Oh, they are only Black people—why should I not make them slaves?*'

The old king died in February 1793, and his son, the Black Prince, set sail for Africa. Somewhere in tropical waters the young man fell ill, and by the time the ship neared home was close to death. 'In one of his lucid intervals he desired the person who gave this account to assist him in making his will ... and he introduced into the will an earnest request that his brother would exert every endeavour to put an end to the slave trade.' He died shortly after the ship put in at Sierra Leone. That the Saints had made a true convert of the Black Prince is shown by these extracts from his diary on the voyage: 'I shall take care of this company which I now fallen into, for they swears good deal and talked all manner of wickedness. Can I be able to resist that temptation, no I cannot, but the Lord will deliver me.' This apparently had been written at Plymouth. At sea the Black Prince wrote on a leaf of his pocket book: 'I have this day declared that if Sierra Leone Company's vessels should all be like the *Naimbanna* or have a company like her, I will never think of coming to England, though I have friends as dear to me as the last word my Father spoke when he gave up the ghost.'

His brother who had been to France for an education, said that the Black Prince had been poisoned by the British. For generations afterwards the Temnes held his death against the Sierra Leone settlement. But other chiefs sent their sons to be educated in England, starting the long West African tradition by which the British first educated then tamed the potentates of the rain forest. It was the start of that system of government that Lugard called 'indirect rule'.

The tale of the Black Prince, with its suitable deathbed piety, whetted the appetite of the godly in Britain for African missionary work. Henry Granville Naimbana is one of the heroes of *True Stories of Young Persons distinguished for Virtue and Piety who died in Early Life*. It recounts in language much more polished than Naimbana's how 'the profligate manners and licentious language of the ship's company shocked him exceedingly. The purity of his mind could not bear it.' The cover of another tract, entitled *The African Prince*, showed Naimbana spurning a lewd book.

Chapter Three

The settlement in Sierra Leone was regarded with special interest by the three thousand Negroes who had gone to Nova Scotia after taking the British side in the War of American Independence. Probably most were former slaves who had deserted their rebel masters, but some had been free, even wealthy men. 'When the American War of Independence broke out,' one of the Nova Scotian émigrés was to claim years later, 'I held a farm of 300 acres in one of the southern states; my cotton and coffee plantations succeeded well; I was comparatively rich, and thriving prosperously. The Americans, then called rebels, called upon me as a free proprietor, to join them in the cause of freedom; but I would not.'

The Treaty of Paris which ended the war in 1783 obliged the British to give back American property, but few black troops were in fact returned to servitude. More than 3,000 Negroes joined the 25,000 white Loyalist troops in exile in Nova Scotia. The British had promised land to all the veterans, black and white, but the promise was difficult to fulfil. Farmers used to the black cotton soil of the south or to lush New England pastures were offered patches of bush and scrub pine. The Negroes complained, very likely with justification, that the whites were given preference in the apportionment of lots. Obliged to work as hired hands, the blacks discovered that Nova Scotian landlords were scarcely more kind than the Americans; indeed slavery was still legal in the province. The Negroes suffered even more than the whites from the fierce, Canadian winters.

The Nova Scotia Negroes found an advocate in Thomas Peters, a millwright, who had served in the Guides and Pioneers as a sergeant. After six years waiting for land in Nova Scotia, Peters crossed the Atlantic to London to make his complaint. The journey was hazardous because if the ship had been forced by storm to shelter in a United States port, Peters was subject to arrest as a runaway slave. In London, Peters met Sharp, who in turn presented the Negro's case to the Sierra Leone Company and to the government. When Thornton and Pitt agreed that Negroes in Nova Scotia would make good settlers for the distressed Sierra Leone colony, the directors of the company decided to send a representative to Nova Scotia to find out how many Negroes really wanted to emigrate.

John Clarkson, the man they chose, took up the job with pleasure, indeed with zeal. Now twenty-eight, he had served as a junior officer in the Royal Navy, but had resigned his commission when he became a pacifist, as a result of reading the Bible. He was emotional and excitable but neither impractical nor unworldly. His brother Thomas, the then-famous writer and Saint, provided the underpinning of fact and information to support the moral crusade of the anti-slavery movement: visiting Liverpool and other slaving ports, inspecting the slave ships and measuring their cramped holds, and interviewing scores of sailors, he built up a dossier on the trade. John, though less of a scholar than his brother, shared his passionate hatred of slavery as well as his respect for realism and detail. He was emotional and excitable, but neither impractical nor unworldly, and although he is sometimes portrayed in the histories of Sierra Leone as a weak and lachrymose hysteric, it should in fairness be said that without his drive and administrative skill there might not have been a migration of Negroes from Nova Scotia.

Clarkson arrived in Halifax in October 1791 and promptly became an enthusiast of the Negro cause. He was one of those Englishmen, and the breed is still common today, who not only espouse the cause of some foreign minority but fall in love with the people concerned. He wrote of those Negroes who wanted to go to Sierra Leone: 'I have every reason to believe that the majority are men of good moral characters. I remarked how fearful the whole were of getting into debt and that they questioned me closely relative to the assistance to be given them to support their families at Sierra Leone without borrowing money.' In particular he was charmed and impressed by the Negro village of Preston:

> I can assure you' [he wrote to Henry Thornton] that the majority of men are better than any people in the labouring line of life in England. I would match them for strong sense, quick apprehension, clear reasoning, gratitude, affection for their wives and children, and friendship and goodwill towards their neighbours. If I speak more favourably of these men than the rest, it may be because I have seen more of them, as they live in the neighbourhood, but I have good grounds for having formed a favourable opinion of the whole.

Having become an enthusiast for the cause of migration to Africa, Clarkson got carried away into making unwise promises. The Nova Scotia Negroes, as the material we have quoted from Clarkson's report shows, were anxious about the economic prospects of life in Sierra Leone. They thought they had been ill-used in Nova Scotia and did not want to make another journey unless they obtained an assurance of free land. Above all they wanted to know if they would have to pay rent for their land to the Sierra Leone Company. Clarkson assured them, over and over again, that any money they might have to pay to the company would not be rent but a tax for schools and the poor. The Negroes were sceptical—and rightly so as it turned out. In dealing with refugees—the oppressed, the disillusioned, and the suspicious—it is rash to make assurances on behalf of the authorities. Clarkson repeatedly did so. For instance, he promised that all those Negroes who did not travel to Africa would be quickly given their share of land in Nova Scotia. The Negroes replied, with good reason: 'Massa Governor no mind King, he no mind You.' They knew very well, and even Clarkson suspected, that 'Massa Governor' of Nova Scotia had neither the power nor the will to provide them with land.

In spite of their misgivings, 1190 Negroes elected to sail with Clarkson for Sierra Leone. Whatever his faults as a politician,

Clarkson was masterly as an administrator. He acted as banker for the new emigrants, helped them to sell their property, and saw that the ships were ventilated and dry. The British Treasury was paying for transportation but Clarkson warned the ships' captains that if they did not treat the Negroes as fare-paying passengers he would refuse to sign the documents at the end of the voyage. If Clarkson was too kind and permissive towards his beloved blacks, he was tough and aggressive towards the authorities. The transports sailed on January 15th, 1792.

The voyage of these Nova Scotian blacks was bleak even by eighteenth-century standards. At least sixty-seven passengers died on the way under the care of a surgeon, Dr Taylor, whose medical treatment was limited to emetics. Clarkson himself sailed on the hospital ship and was grievously ill of a fever caught in Halifax. In his journal he mourned the loss of

my poor servant who from great attention to me during the days that I was delirious is supposed to have caught the fever off me. His death affects me greatly. I was this day brought upon deck on a mattress as I was not able to walk or to be moved in any other way ... This was the first time I had been on deck since the 21st of January. Had my cabin and bed place cleaned out and washed with vinegar as well as fumigated with tar and gunpowder balls. From my poor servant's illness as well as Captain Coffin's, I experienced great neglect in the latter part of my illness, as previous to the latter being taken ill, all the crew were sick on board except himself and the mate, and I certainly should have been killed during the gale of wind on the 29th January, when the vessel was pooped, if it had not been for that accident, which providentially obliged the captain to come down into the cabin to secure the deadlights which had been stove in, when he found me rolling from side to side quite exhausted, covered with blood and water, and very much bruised, for I had at that time four blisters upon me.

The ships with the Nova Scotia immigrants reached Sierra

Leone during the end of February and the first weeks of March. For most of the voyagers it was a happy arrival and one man 'when he landed, found himself on the same spot from hence he had been carried off, and pointed to a particular part of the beach, where, as he relates, a woman laid hold of him, he being then a boy, and sold him to an American slave ship in the river'. For Clarkson, exhausted by fever and work, the arrival meant only fresh problems to face. When agreeing to bring over the Nova Scotia Negroes, he had assumed that his job would end on arrival at Sierra Leone. But in the meantime the company had changed the administrative structure and had replaced the governor (one had proved a failure) by seven councillors from the white community. They now expected Clarkson to take charge of the colony, not as sole authority, but as superintendent of the councillors. These were a rum bunch. They went on board the ships from Canada wearing swords, cockaded hats, and epauletted coats, and vaunting their new title of 'Honourable'. One of their number, the surgeon, Dr Bell, was outstandingly alcoholic, but most of these senators would get 'beastly drunk' and exchange blows in the council meetings. No wonder that Clarkson, after meeting the councillors had to be carried to bed, where he lay 'in violent hysterics for nearly two hours'.

Clarkson settled his Nova Scotian charges on the site of the first, or 1787, Granville Town, which he renamed Freetown. The pious new citizens gathered under a giant cotton tree to sing hymns of gratitude for their safe arrival. The cotton tree is still standing—flanked by the Law Courts, the Intra Bank and the Tropicana Night Club—but many of the Nova Scotian immigrants died within the year. Thirty-eight died in the first few weeks. On April 1st, even before the start of the rains, Clarkson wrote in his diary:

If putrid fevers do not break out amongst us, unsheltered as we are from the rain, crowded and living upon salt provisions, it will be owing to a particular interposition of Providence. Nothing made of steel can be preserved from rust. Knives,

44

scissors, keys etc. look like old, rusty iron. Our watches are spoiled by rust and laid aside useless.

When the rains began in May, the 'putrid fevers' killed 98 more of the new black settlers and almost half of the 119 Europeans who had come to Sierra Leone that year. Anna Falconbridge, who had returned with her husband, wrote: 'It is quite customary of a morning to ask "How many died last night?" ' Those whites who survived were almost without exception useless to Clarkson. The surveyor neglected to plot the land for the Nova Scotia immigrants. The surgeon, Bell, was drunk. The company agents swindled unmercifully on supplies. 'You appear to have been cheated in every department,' Clarkson wrote the directors, 'ships, stores and cargo. Very few of the things of any kind are near what they ought to be for the money they cost you.' Even Falconbridge, who had once been a capable fellow, was now rendered useless by liquor. 'Mr Falconbridge talks of making a trip to purchase stock for the Colony,' wrote Clarkson in his diary, 'but from his constant drinking he has rendered himself incapable of being trusted and I do all I can to amuse him, in order to keep him quiet, if he had not one of the strongest constitutions in the world, he might have been dead long ago.' He died a few months later unlamented by his widow. 'I will not be guilty of such meanness', she wrote, 'as to tell a falsehood on this occasion, by saying I regret his death, no! I really do not.' And a fortnight later she married one of his colleagues. The drunk Dr Bell died of delirium tremens and, much to the fury of Clarkson, was given a military funeral by his scarcely more sober fellow councillors who ordered minute guns to be fired from the ships, blowing an arm off one of the gunners.

The white women were even more troublesome than the men. 'The ladies in the colony,' Clarkson complained, 'by their mutual jealousies and absurd notions of their rank and consequence, give rise to many private piques, which often cause open dissensions among the gentlemen, and the mischief they have occasioned since the ships left the Downs to the present day cannot be

45

estimated.' He implored the directors: 'Pray let no more captains who have passengers bring out their wives. Be very circumspect whom you suffer to come out in future, either as settlers or artificers. Those already here, as well black as white, are too generally immoral, idle, discontented, ungovernable people, whose example and conduct has done us much harm already.'

As if the resident whites were not trouble enough, the colony was visited by strange ships and even stranger white passengers. 'I am continually exposed to the shameful intrusion of strangers,' Clarkson wrote, with the characteristic twang of hysteria, and the unexpected arrival of more whites from along the coast, 'filled my mind with gloomy ideas, for I cannot calculate the consequences from so many people of mixed character, coming to us at the present time.' When three white sailors insulted the Nova Scotia settlers, Clarkson had them flogged by a Negro in front of the assembled colony.

If Clarkson was exasperated by life in the little colony, he disliked even more his contacts with neighbours. The palavers with King Naimbana were a particular irritation. 'The fatigue and unpleasantness of such a visit is not to be described. So many people jabbering together, others speaking to you through an interpreter, and the whole drinking to excess.' No wonder that he complained in a letter to Henry Thornton that 'fainting and hysteric fits frequently close the mortifications of the day'. He seems to have been one of those men who cannot relax and calm the brain. There was always something to upset him. Once he went to meet some slavers on the Bananas Island, where after dinner he lay down to rest on a sofa. 'Shortly afterwards,' he records, 'two female slaves were sent to fan me while I slept but the very idea of having slaves "to fan me while I sleep, and tremble when I wake" prevented me from enjoying that repose.'

Hysterical and fussy he may have been; but Clarkson's gentle good nature always reasserted itself in dealing with the Nova Scotian settlers. Through all the miseries of that first year, he kept his respect and affection for his black charges. The directors of the company agreed with his high estimate of the Nova Scotians:

46

'Marriage is extremely general among them,' says the report referring to 1792, 'drunkenness is by no means common: swearing is hardly ever heard: their attention to the Sabbath is also great.' This last virtue made a special appeal to the Saints in London. Trial by jury was established from the start, although few of these black immigrants possessed the financial and social qualifications required from jurymen in Great Britain. The directors reported that the 'verdicts have been in general very just, and, on the whole, the Nova Scotians have served on the juries in a manner that sufficiently proves the propriety and prudence of extending them a privilege which they so much value'. These black jurymen were to remain an object of interest, and more frequently of abuse, to generations of visitors to the colony.

Even Clarkson had to recognize that the Nova Scotia blacks were a very litigious lot, whose snarling, cantankerous feuds divided the thousand settlers. Indignant men, and even more often furious women would pester him with semi-literate pleas and complaints against each other, the company and himself. The directors admitted this failing:

> If an additional sixpence be not added to their wages, they declare that they shall then conceive themselves to be treated as slaves. If the Governor be not dismissed for having ordered water to be mixed with the rum before it was exposed to sale [which he did to obtain the right proof of spirit] it is intimated in like manner that the whole colony is about to be reduced to slavery.

This litigiousness and this eager spirit of grievance were typical of a refugee mentality. The Nova Scotian settlers, just like modern refugees, had been induced to leave the security of their temporary camps for a most uncertain and unkind life abroad. In the first few months, thanks to the lethargy of the white officials, the land that had been promised them had not even been surveyed. They had no proper shelter against the torrential rains, and no proper medical care after the death of Dr Bell.

The malcontents among the Nova Scotians found a spokesman

in Thomas Peters, the elderly Negro who had first sailed from Canada to petition the British Government. Even in Halifax, Peters had sulked when Clarkson not he had been chosen to lead the exodus. On April 8th, Clarkson received a warning that Peters was plotting to get elected as governor. He records in his diary:

> As soon as I had read this letter, I went on shore, and that no time might be lost, I called upon Mr Peters, one of the council, on my way to the centre of the town, and desired the great bell to be rung immediately to summon all the settlers together. They soon assembled, officers and people, not knowing what was the matter, and many of them appeared much agitated. I placed myself under a great tree, and, addressing myself to Peters, I said it was probable either one or other of us would be hanged on that tree before palaver was settled ... *

This gesture was no doubt over-dramatic, for Peters had small support among the Nova Scotia settlers. Those who had sided with Peters informed Clarkson later that they intended no disloyalty. But Clarkson, usually gentle, showed no compassion towards the wretched old man, and subjected him to a strict shadowing: 'He (Peters) is a man of great penetration and cunning,' wrote Clarkson, after the showdown under the great tree, 'and from the attention shown to him in England, he thinks himself vastly superior to his countrymen ... I shall feel it my duty not only to keep an eye on him myself but also to have his actions watched and reported to me in private.' A few weeks later, Peters was brought to court on a charge of embezzling money, found guilty and harshly rebuked. His following gone, and his pride brought low, Peters caught fever and died on the night of June 25th. One cannot help feeling sorry for Peters. He was not a man of learning or skill at

* Describing the same incident in his retirement, Clarkson wrote: 'I addressed T. P[eters] and told him what I had heard of him and that if I found he could not clear himself I should instantly hang him on the tree over our heads as it was always better at the beginning of a new government to hang three or four who might be the cause of future misery to the place.'

leadership; he may not have been quite honest, but he had first planned the exodus to Africa, and he had seen his vision adopted by a white Englishman, who had also become an enemy. It was the first but far from the last time in the history of Sierra Leone that an able Negro saw the leadership of his people pass into the hands of a white man.

Clarkson worked himself to the edge of death on behalf of his Nova Scotians. By the end of the year he saw them housed, healthy and starting to gain a livelihood from the soil. With great diplomatic skill, he managed to merge his own Nova Scotia blacks with the residue of the first Granville Town settlers. It gave him 'heartfelt satisfaction to find that we are likely to get into some kind of order, and hope that we may begin under the blessing of God to date our happiness with that of your "the Granville Town" posterity from this hour.' He was tireless in persuading the settlers to work hard and to accept his leadership; and when persuasion failed he made fervent appeals to their consciences. 'I dwelt a long time upon the consequence likely to arise from their extreme suspicion of white people,' he said in a sermon in September, 'and I asked them how they would like it if they were in my situation to be treated in the way that some of them had treated me.'

When remonstration and pleading failed, Clarkson would threaten to sail to England as a punishment for the blacks' ingratitude. Whereupon, as another Englishman remarked, 'they took the alarm and begged him ardently not to desert them'. The factiousness of the blacks, the drunken incompetence of the whites, the fever, the rains and the heat combined to make Clarkson's job a torment. On top of this he was pestered by uncomprehending advice from England. His brother Thomas wrote sanctimonious letters; Thornton's instructions became increasingly stern; and of course Sharp wrote about re-introducing hundredors. Mrs Falconbridge, a ruthless assessor of character, thought Clarkson the only man fit to govern the settlers he had brought with him, and she took his side against the envious whites: 'He is an amiable man, void of pomp or ostentation, which his senatorial colleagues (the white commissioners) disapprove of exceedingly,

49

from the ridiculous idea that their dignity is lessened by his frankness.'

The questions of land and tax made Clarkson unpopular with the Sierra Leone Company. He had promised free land to the Nova Scotian settlers; the directors maintained that there was not enough land to go round. He had promised the settlers they would not have to pay rent (though they would have to pay the company a tax for schools and the poor). The company wanted to introduce a quit-rent, or tax on land. Clarkson's letters to Thornton became increasingly irritable and emotional. Thornton's letters to Clarkson were all the more odious for their frozen politeness. 'But let me begin, my dear Sir,' Thornton began on September 14th, 1792, 'with requesting your kind construction of what I shall say in the same manner as I am used to construe in the most friendly manner everything in your dispatches however strongly you may write.' He goes on to warn Clarkson that he was only a temporary superintendent at Sierra Leone. 'If you will look into your appointment, I believe you will find these were the terms of it—we had no idea that you would accept the superintendence for any period longer than a few weeks or possibly months.' This statement was not just churlish but untrue, for Thornton's letter appointing Clarkson (December 28th, 1791) quite clearly implied that the job would be permanent.

At the end of 1792, the company sent two more officials to Freetown, ostensibly to replace Clarkson should he fall sick or go on leave. Both William Dawes, an officer in the Marines, and Zachary Macaulay, who is discussed in the next chapter, were nearer to Thornton than to Clarkson in temperament and ideas. When Clarkson left Freetown to marry in England, on December 30th, 1792, he expected soon to return with his bride to continue in office as governor. But the directors who had welcomed Clarkson on his arrival back in London, informed him in April, a few days before his wedding, that his services would no longer be required.

This news was received with fury in Freetown. During Clarkson's absence the acting governor, Dawes, and his aide Macaulay,

50

had provoked unrest in the Nova Scotian settlers, who complained of racial discrimination. They claimed that the company had broken its word on the distribution of lots, on surveying new land and on prices charged in the company stores. 'Why are not all the Company's promises to us fulfilled?' the settlers demanded on February 7th, 1793. 'We have a high regard and respect for Mr Clarkson, and firmly believe he would not have left us without seeing every promise he made performed; if gentlemen here had not given them the strongest assurances they should be complied with immediately.' To which Dawes replied 'that it was not uncommon for Mr Clarkson to make prodigal and extraordinary promises without thinking of them afterwards ... '

The Nova Scotian settlers sent a petition to London asking that Clarkson be reinstated. Others said they would leave the colony or, much to Mrs Falconbridge's approval, 'harassed Mr Dawes with insults, in hopes he may take it in his head to be disgusted and march off'. They even went so far as to remind Dawes of the recent fate of Louis XVI of France. Threats and pleas were equally vain. The colony was to be ruled for years by hard, unsympathetic men like Dawes and Macaulay.

Clarkson settled down in Cambridgeshire as a banker, sometimes easing his feeling against the Company with long, self-pitying letters to his friends. Anna Falconbridge, also leaving Sierra Leone for good, accused the company not only of foul ingratitude but of stealing her first husband's pension. After a vicious row with Thornton, whom she detested, Anna got the money and went with her second husband to the West Indies. In the last of the letters that compose her delightful book, she compares them most unfavourably with the Barbados slave traders.

Chapter Four

> Mr [Zachary] Macaulay was admirably adapted for the arduous and uninviting task of planting a Negro colony. His very deficiencies stood him in good stead; for in the presence of the elements with which he had to deal, it was fortunate that nature had denied him any sense of the ridiculous. Unconscious of what was absurd around him, and incapable of being flurried, frightened or fatigued, he stood on a centre of order and authority amidst the seething chaos of inexperience and insubordination.
>
> (From *Life and Letters of Lord Macaulay*, by George Otto Trevelyan, 1876)

If Zachary Macaulay had not been the father of the historian, few people today would have heard his name. Yet he was one of the most influential Saints, second only to Wilberforce in the battle against the slave trade, and first in the campaign for moral purity. As a character he was more intriguing, because more riven by guilt, even than Wilberforce or Hannah More; and as deputy governor and at last as sole governor of Sierra Leone, between 1793 and 1799, he reformed and gave a destiny to the settlement. He ranks with Stanley, Lugard, Johnston, de Brazza and Rhodes as one of the great white colonialists in Black Africa. His colony may have been small and his colonists black, but Macaulay's vision of civilization spread through trade and Christianity was at last to subdue the whole continent. He was a dour and most unattractive person, one of those puritans whose self-delusion came dangerously near to hypocrisy, but in strength of will and in sheer God-driven ruthlessness, he matched the later, more famous Victorian colonialists.

The Macaulay clan come from the Hebrides, but when Zachary was born in 1768, his father was the minister at Inverary. There were too many mouths to feed in the manse so Zachary, at the age of fourteen, went to work in a merchant's office in Glasgow. Our knowledge of Macaulay's early life comes from a brief and breast-beating essay in autobiography that he wrote in 1797, when Governor of Sierra Leone. At the age of fourteen, so we learn from this memoir, Macaulay was an accomplished little sinner: 'I remained in Glasgow upwards of two years; and during those two years I improved indeed in the knowledge of useful learning [he read widely in many languages] but I made much more rapid progress in the knowledge of evil.' His fellow students used their flattering friendship to demolish Macaulay's religious beliefs, and his leisure hours were spent with drunken profligates. 'Taught by them, I began to think excess in wine, so far from being a sin, to be a ground for glorying; and it became one of the objects of my ambition to be able to see all my companions under the table. And this was the more surprising as I really disliked, nay even loathed, excessive drinking.'

Young Zachary did not escape from sin even among his father's respectable friends. 'Being tolerably accommodating I fell into the predilections of the ladies of the family, which were entirely for new plays and marble-covered books. When I was not draining the midnight bowl, I was employed in wasting the midnight oil by poring over such abominable, but fascinating works as are to be found under the head of novels in the catalogue of every circulating library.'

Macaulay, like several opponents of slavery, had personal know-ledge of what he opposed, for when only sixteen he had gone to Jamaica and worked as under-manager on a sugar plantation.

What chiefly affected me at first [he later confessed in his memoir] was that by my situation I was exposed not only to the sight, but also to the practice of severities on others, the very recollection of which makes my blood run cold. My mind was at first feelingly alive to the miseries of the poor

53

slaves, and I not only revolted from the thought of myself inflicting punishment upon them, but the very sight of punishment sickened me. The die, however, was now cast; there was no retreating. I should gladly indeed have returned to Europe, but I had not the money ... In the West Indies, I was bound, if I would not forfeit the regard of all who were disposed to serve me, even to give no vent to those feelings which would have seemed to reproach them with cruelty. As the only alternative, therefore, I resolved to get rid of my squeamishness as soon as I could, as a thing which was very inconvenient. And in this I had a success beyond my expectations.

The rapidity with which Macaulay overcame his squeamishness does not surprise the student of his life. There are hints both in his writing and his actions that he took a secret pleasure in physical cruelty. A letter to a friend from Jamaica about this time expresses more pity for its author and his financial plight than for the unhappy Negroes:

But far other is now my lot, doomed by my own folly to toil for a scanty subsistence in an inhospitable clime ... You would hardly know your friend, with whom you have spent so many hours in more peaceful and more pleasant scenes, were you to view me in a field of canes, amidst perhaps a hundred of the sable race, cursing and bawling, while the noise of the whip resounding on their shoulders, and the cries of the poor wretches, would make you imagine that some unlucky accident had carried you to the doleful shades.

Many plantations were run on more gentle, humane, principles. Macaulay, from his own account, was a vicious slave-driver.

Later enemies of Macaulay pointed out that his virtue never prevented him from earning a great deal of money. Here he describes a card game on the ship coming back from Jamaica:

I had the misfortune to fall into the company of two amateurs of play. One, a son of the late Governor Winch, had already thrown away £30,000 on the turf and at gaming-tables ... I played at first very cautiously, and never permitted myself to be tempted to bet. But as my winnings increased, which they generally did, I was exposed to the danger of becoming attached to play, and the miseries which I felt would naturally follow such an attachment. I heroically resolved, therefore, to break the chain, and adopted some strong determinations on the point, which I have since, with few deviations, been able to keep.

It takes a strong man to beat the gambling instinct; it takes a Macaulay to beat that instinct just when he is well ahead of the game. One can but pity those 'amateurs of play' who had the bad luck to fall into Macaulay's company.

When Macaulay returned to England in 1789, he went to stay with his sister Jean who had married Thomas Babington, a rich Leicestershire squire. The meeting was so important for Macaulay that he named his first son, the historian, Thomas Babington Macaulay. Although little older than his brother-in-law, Thomas Babington was already a Saint and his home, Rothley Temple, was so popular with the Evangelicals as to be almost a country Clapham. The arrival of Macaulay, brash and coarse after his years in the sugar plantation, offered a challenge to Babington's pious enthusiasm. Discreetly at first, then with missionary directness, he strove to win Macaulay's soul. Perhaps Macaulay was ripe for conversion; perhaps Babington was irresistible since even among the Saints 'he was acknowledged to be unrivalled in the art of reproof and exhortation'. Within weeks Macaulay became an Evangelical who could never afterwards think of Babington 'but my thoughts are drawn to that Saviour with whom he first brought me acquainted'.

One of Babington's daughters heard her parents say that when Uncle Zachary first returned from Jamaica he was a disagreeable, conceited youth, with a self-sufficient, dogmatic manner—but that before long he was wholly changed. Perhaps not the man himself but the object of his ambition had changed: where before he had sought only pleasure and wealth, he now sought wealth and salvation. The new convert turned against slavery, made the acquaintance of Sharp, Thornton and Thomas Clarkson, and soon became an enthusiast for the Sierra Leone project. His experience among Negroes and his proved resistance to tropical climates and disease were thought good recommendations for getting a job with the company. He went to Freetown in 1792 and in April 1793 was appointed deputy governor to Dawes.

With Clarkson gone, Dawes and Macaulay brooked no foolish complaints from the Nova Scotia settlers. They put up the price of goods in the company store; they refused to make the settlement a haven for runaway slaves; they imposed stern punishments for any breach of discipline. 'The Quarter Sessions began,' wrote Macaulay on August 18th, 1794. 'A case of adultery was tried and proved. The woman was punished by flogging, and the man by a fine of five pounds.' Such a barbarous punishment for a mild offence would not have been countenanced in Clarkson's time, nor indeed in contemporary England, but Macaulay's attitude to the Negro race had been brutalized by his experiences in Jamaica.

It was part of Macaulay's job to visit and come to terms with the local slavers—Tilley at Bance Island, Renaud at Gambia Island, Cleveland on Banana Island and Aspinall in the mouth of the Scarcie River. While Clarkson had endured these visits as a distasteful part of his duty, Macaulay actually liked the slavers. In fact one gets the impression that he enjoyed the company of the slavers far more than that of the ex-slaves. Sometimes, on reading Macaulay's journal, one begins to suspect that his horror of slavery—like the horror he later felt for indecent literature—was mixed with fascination.

Early in 1794, Dawes went to England on leave and Macaulay, at twenty-two, became acting governor of the colony. He soon proved himself just as tough as Dawes by dismissing two company servants who had insulted the captain of a slave ship. The hundredors and tythingmen—impotent relics of Sharp's political system—met to protest at the dismissal and offered their resignation. A riot started and threatened the governor's mansion but Macaulay was not perturbed. He set up cannon at the gate, addressed the mob and brought it to its senses.

The settlement could be proud of its progress during the two years since the Nova Scotians arrived. There were nine streets running north-west to south-east, laced by three smaller cross streets. The carpenters, who formed a large proportion of Nova Scotia immigrants, put up four hundred wooden houses tiled with wooden slats and fixed on foundations of laterite stone. Thanks partly to better shelter, the sickness and death rate had decreased; indeed the company remarked, with a hint of displeasure, that the settlers 'entertained the sick Europeans from the slave-ships, many of whom have been attracted to Freetown by the known salubrity of the air, or the expectation of getting good medical advice'.

The economic progress was far from enough to enrich the directors in London, but at last they began to see some returns on their capital expenditure. The settlement was now self-sufficient in rice and vegetables, and had started to grow a few export crops. A new commercial agent had started trading along the coast and had opened a factory in the Sherbro estuary.

It had long been the intention of the company to found plantations in Sierra Leone where free men would produce sugar, cotton and rice to rival the export of slaves. In 1792, the company bought a square mile of land on the other side of the estuary and started a plantation with local Temne labourers. These hired hands were paid three dollars a month, a pint and a half of rice and two or three ounces of meat a day and a 'small glass of rum if they turn up promptly at sunrise'. The manager, James Watt, who was a former West Indian planter, watched the operation from his window and occasionally walked among the men. The company reported that the men's labour 'is thought equal to about two-thirds of a common day's work in the country, and it is tolerably steady, although they show no great exertion in it'. The labourers 'sold' their dollars in Freetown for clothes and household utensils.

The plantation was almost everything the company could wish. It proved that cotton, sugar and rice could be grown by free, paid labour. It provided an agricultural industry for the colony. It created a new demand for European goods and it introduced pagans to Christianity.*

The settlers, however, refused to work as agricultural labourers, work they thought fit only for slaves. Some, like Macaulay, the governor, started small farms; but these were subsidiary to the real work of the colony, which was trading to the interior.

Macaulay, in 1794, was proud of the little colony which he began to refer to as 'my family'. He wrote in December 1793:

> Our schools are a cheering sight, three hundred children fill them, and most of the grown persons who cannot read, crowd to the evening schools. We have made a schoolmaster of almost every black man in the colony who reads or writes well enough, and the business of instruction proceeds so rapidly within the colony, that in the course of a year or two, we expect there will be few within it who will not be able to read their bibles.

England could not compete with its colony either for literacy or for piety. 'I never met with, heard, or read of any set of people observing the same appearance of godliness,' wrote Mrs Falconbridge of the Nova Scotians, 'for I do not remember since they first landed here, my ever awaking (and I have awoke at every hour of the night), without hearing preachings from some quarter or another.'

The intellectual life of the colony centred on Adam Afzelius, a Swedenborgian Swede and pupil of Linnaeus, who had been sent out by the company to study botany. Two gardens were laid out for him and he started to send back reports in 1794. His curiosity was wide ranging and his journal is full of interesting details. He noted that the arrival of slave ships from Europe dried up the flow of trade goods from the interior. He ventured boldly and wrongly into an argument that was still going in Freetown more than

* Watt died in 1797. The plantation did not survive him.

150 years later: 'It is wrong what Matthews says [describing an inland tribe] that the women cut off their clitoris, it is never done nor can it be.'

The affairs of Sierra Leone during its early years went almost unreported in England. This was not out of indifference to Africa, for Sierra Leone was constantly in the news during the nineteenth century, but because the British at that time had more important things to worry about. The early years of the colony coincided with the French Revolution, which later developed into a European war. News of these great events reached West Africa and in 1792 Clarkson wrote to Lafayette to use his influence 'to obtain an order that our colony may not be disturbed by any of your vessels' should England 'be wicked enough' to interfere in the French war against Germany. In 1793, England joined in the war while in France such liberals as Lafayette were replaced by left-wing Jacobin sans-culottes. Even after the Jacobin leaders were overthrown in 1794, ships manned by Jacobin sailors roamed the high seas in search of revolution or plunder.

Seven of these arrived off Sierra Leone in September 1794. Some were captured English ships and all were rigged in the English way, so that at first the colony did not take fright; but when they came nearer on September 28th, Macaulay saw that men in one of the frigates were aiming a gun at his piazza. The settlers, knowing they could not fight such a fleet, struck colours and put out a flag of truce, but the French replied with a fusillade of musket and grape-shot that killed a Nova Scotian woman and child. At ten in the morning the French ceased fire and came ashore with an American slave-trader, Newell, who nursed a grudge against the settlers. Macaulay wrote in his journal that Newell 'came to my house attended by half-a-dozen sans-culottes, almost foaming with rage, presented a pistol to me, and with many oaths demanded instant satisfaction for the slaves who had run away from him to my protection'. Ignoring Newell, Macaulay approached the nearest French officer and asked to meet the Commodore, who invited Macaulay to dine on board but explained that he had no control over his crew. The appearance of these sans-culottes both shocked and angered Macaulay: 'The Frenchmen who had come ashore in filth and rags, were now many of them dressed out with women's shifts, gowns and petticoats ... The scene which presented itself on my getting on board the flagship was still more singular. The quarter-deck was crowded by a set of ragamuffins whose appearance beggared every previous description, and among whom I sought in vain for someone who looked like a gentleman.'

The French stayed for more than a fortnight, in which time the sans-culotte rabble caused £50,000 worth of damage. The sailors concentrated their revolutionary rage on the offices and homes of the company staff, even cutting down those plants in the Governor's garden that looked either beautiful or useful. To every protest from Macaulay, the Commodore simply replied: 'Citoyen, cela peut bien être, mais encore vous êtes Anglais.' 'They began immediately to break open the houses, and plunder,' wrote Dr Afzelius to the Swedish Ambassador in London, and 'what they did not want they destroyed, burned or threw into the river. They killed all the cattle and animals they found in the fields, streets, yards, or elsewhere, not sparing even asses, dogs and cats. These proceedings they continued the whole succeeding week, till they had entirely ruined our beautiful and prospering colony.' Poor Afzelius found that the French had not only looted his own clothes, money and furniture, but even worse:

> The rest, which was of no use to the enemy, but on which I myself put just and great value, I had the mortification to find so totally destroyed, that the sight almost drew tears from my eyes. My neat and beautiful little garden I found entirely ruined, the trees cut down and the plants pulled up by the roots. My living animals and birds were partly eaten, and partly thrown out of doors with their heads cut off. My library and collections of animals, fruits and flowers (preserved in spirits of wine), or birds, insects, shells, herbarium fruits, and seeds, together with all my manuscripts, all were thrown down and spread over the whole floor, where they

were mixed with offals of victuals, treacle, rum, beer, and other things of the kind.

The Commodore had protested his friendship towards the Negro settlers, and even the sans-culottes at first reserved their threats for the white men; but blacks in the end suffered as much as whites from the pillage. 'As they took away all the clothes from everybody, whites and blacks, so they stripped me among the rest of all my clothes,' wrote David George a Baptist pastor from Nova Scotia. '... They did not leave me a second shirt to my back. My wife and children were almost naked.'

The French attack, in material terms, was a catastrophe for the colony, but it does not seem to have hurt its morale. On the contrary, the Europeans behaved with unusual fortitude under the sans-culotte occupation. 'We found', wrote Macaulay, while prisoner in his own house under the guard of savage sans-culottes, '... that we had lost very little by the change. We were free from pain; we felt neither cold, nor hunger nor thirst; in short, we found out that happiness does not consist in the number of things we possess ... we now found out, too, how much better the mind of man is fitted to bear adversity than prosperity.' After the French had gone, Macaulay wrote that the Negro settlers had behaved 'with great outward kindness to all of us, and there was no instance of any of them, even of those who were most disaffected, showing a disposition to insult any of us. I was indeed much better pleased with their conduct than I had yet been.'

But shortly after the French had gone, the colony returned to form, with various Nova Scotians accusing each other of having stolen their property and Macaulay accusing others of having robbed the company. Macaulay realized that he needed a rest after a long and gruelling stay in Freetown. 'I have enjoyed moderate health,' he wrote in a letter to England, 'but I am already so metamorphosized that you would scarcely know me were you to see me. My face has remained its tropical colour, and my hair is cropped close to my head. I fear that if my exile continues for five years longer, that I shall be unfit for the society of any woman who will not ... attach little value to a bow.'

By May 1795, Macaulay was ready to sail to England on leave. Any other man, feeling tired and homesick after so long in the tropics, would have chosen to sail in one of the fast and fairly comfortable ships of the Sierra Leone Company; Macaulay chose to sail home via Jamaica, doing the first leg of the journey in a slaving ship. The vessel he chose was the *Anna*, bound for Barbados, whose captain promptly protested that since he carried a full cargo of slaves, there was no room for a passenger, let alone the governor of Sierra Leone. He should have known better than to dispute with Macaulay. By May 5th, Macaulay had paid his passage and boarded the ship in which a hammock was slung for him. The captain, who may have enjoyed Macaulay's discomfort, 'said he hoped I should not find any inconvenience from a few small slaves sleeping below it. "The smell", he said, "would be unpleasant for a few days; but when we had got into the trade-winds it would no longer be perceived".'

No leading anti-slaver had ever before sailed the infamous 'middle passage' from Africa to America, and Macaulay made the best of his chance to gain evidence and statistics. He took constant notes, using the Greek script to disguise his thoughts from the eyes of ignorant slavers. The captain of the ship did his best to disguise the cruelties, but Macaulay was hard to deceive:

> *May 7.* I observed one woman handcuffed, and enquired the cause. I found she had lately attempted to drown herself, and for this misdemeanour she had received a severe punishment and was still handcuffed as an example to the rest. *May 23.* I observe the slaves reject their food. The officer on duty threatened them with the cat. *May 24.* The captain wanted the slaves to dance but they showed no inclination till the cat was called for.

The captain may have been brutal towards his slaves but he showed an understanding of Evangelical prejudice, for Macaulay had to admit that: 'The captain's behaviour towards me was very civil and attentive. He paid me the compliment never once to swear when I was on board, and he also repressed the practice among the officers and seamen. I observed, however, when we went ashore, that he was much addicted to the vice.' Indeed, Macaulay found life in Barbados almost as bad as life on the ship. Before continuing home to England he wrote in his diary that the Barbados morals were 'νερι βαδ'.

Macaulay spent most of his leave with his sister and Babington, also paying long visits to Clapham where Thornton and Wilberforce shared their pious villa and entertained those enemies of the slave trade whom Pitt laughingly called the 'white Negroes'. While Macaulay had been in Sierra Leone, the Clapham Sect had formed a still closer alliance with Hannah More and her equally Evangelical sisters, who ran a school for girls near Bristol. After a single visit, Macaulay became a close friend of the More sisters and soon was a frequent guest at their houses in Bristol and Bath. He fell in love with a Miss Selina Mills, who lodged with the Mores, had been taught by them and was looked upon as a sixth sister. By 1796, Macaulay was most unhappy in love. He was due to sail for Sierra Leone in February; he had no idea whether Selina returned his feelings; and if she did there was no question of taking her as a bride to the West Coast of Africa. He had decided to slink away without even saying goodbye but the More sisters insisted that he visit them once again.

The man who could handle rioting settlers, or impose his will on a cannibal chief, was awed by this houseful of bluestocking ladies and did not know how to deal with them. He had learned that Hannah More knew of his love for Selina but did not realize that Patty More also regarded the girl with a 'jealous affection' that must have amounted to love. Since Hannah did not want to cause pain to her sister, she set out to prevent Macaulay paying suit to Selina. The guileless man, who could not anyway believe that Selina returned his love, went to Hannah 'requesting a few minutes conversation on a subject ... that concerned him very nearly ... '. 'I think it might be better not', Hannah replied, 'for your uneasiness will be, I fear, increased instead of lessened.' However, Macaulay insisted on hearing the truth, even unwelcome truth. Whereupon Hannah said that Selina was entirely indifferent to him and that her feelings 'did not exceed the limits of ordinary friendship'. Since Selina was much in love with Macaulay, this statement by Hannah More was a shocking lie. But the Evangelicals, like other puritan thinkers from Calvin to Lenin, were not afraid to lie for the sake of righteousness.

Dinner that evening was a lugubrious meal. Convinced that Selina did not love him, Macaulay avoided talking to her; the More sisters, one assumes, were feeling a twinge of guilt for their duplicity; poor Selina found herself ignored by the man she loved on the eve of his journey to Africa. But Cupid (or, as Macaulay preferred to think, Divine Providence) contrived to upset the sisters' plot. Macaulay, just before leaving the house, chanced to catch sight of Selina weeping bitterly in a downstairs room. He rushed to her comfort, confessed his love and heard to his joy that she returned it. They became engaged on the spot. During his absence in the next three years, their deep love survived both the lassitude of the tropics and the unabated spitefulness of the More sisters.

Macaulay sailed from England with some Wesleyan Methodist missionaries who were bound for the interior of Sierra Leone. Their work was dear to Macaulay's heart. He had devoted much of his leave in England to missionary work among the poor, encouraging Hannah More to write her *Stories for Persons in the Middle Ranks of Society* and *Tales for the Common People*. But Macaulay could not praise the six missionaries on the *Calypso*. One he described as 'vain, empty, assuming and ... his disputatious temper has disgusted even his associates'. On board, Macaulay prophesied that the missionary wives' bad tempers would make them unsuitable for their work and, sure enough, as soon as the ship reached Freetown, these women burst into 'doleful lamentations or bitter complaints. To their astonishment, Freetown resembled neither London nor Portsmouth; they could find no pastrycooks' shops, nor any gingerbread to buy for their children.'

Few of the missionaries stayed more than a few weeks up

country. One of them, Jacob Grigg, came back to Freetown without even the usual excuse of bad health. He allied with a nonconformist schoolteacher, John Garvin, in a nagging campaign against the Anglican Church and Macaulay, its temporal representative. When some of the missionaries left for England in May, Macaulay was shocked by their shameless dereliction of duty, but on being thanked by a missionary artisan Macaulay was glad to perceive that 'Antinomianism had not quite erased natural affection.' Anglican social prejudice may have coloured Macaulay's view of these missionaries, who were mostly of nonconformist and humble backgrounds, but nevertheless most were by all accounts weak characters. Two missionaries who had been sent to the Bullom Shore, quarrelled so fiercely between themselves that they had to call on the local chief as an arbitrator. One Duncan Campbell brought out his wife, 'a hard-featured woman, with a hideous Scottish twang', whom he set to work barefoot among the African women. When she died after a few months, Campbell married an African girl and became a slave-trader. The Negro preachers too were often fractious and troublesome. When Macaulay tried to regularize the civil laws about marriage—bringing them into line with the British system—the Nova Scotians interpreted this as a plot to dissolve the dissenting sects.

The settlers' fears of religious persecution were mixed with well-founded complaints against the payment of tax. The Nova Scotians, in 1791, had heard Clarkson promise that they would never have to pay rent for their land in Sierra Leone. They remembered this when, in June 1796, the company announced that it would start a quit-rent, in fact a land tax, of one shilling per acre per annum. Although the Baptists agreed to pay this quit-rent, the Methodists and the smaller sects refused, bringing the major part of the colony into opposition. Macaulay harangued, threatened and pleaded with the settlers, but no quit-rent was paid in his time as governor.

Macaulay's rule was an unpredictable mixture of the reasonable and harsh. He was quite prepared to push through unpopular measures such as the marriage laws and the quit-rent, although the first was unnecessary and the second could yield only a marginal revenue. Yet he would skip outside the law to break a personal enemy. He seized Garvin's letters without authority, had him tried on a trumpery charge and then shipped him off to England. When there was talk of revolt over the quit-rent, he threatened the ringleaders with summary hanging at 'the risk of holding up my hand at the Old Bailey'. Unlike Clarkson and Sharp, he did not really believe in self-government for the settlers. 'Poor people,' he wrote, 'one cannot help loving them. With all their trying humours, they have a warmth of affection which is really irresistible.' The tone is unpleasantly patronizing. There is evidence that he said in private harsh things of the Negro race that he would not have dared to put down on paper.

Yet Zachary Macaulay could not be accused of colour prejudice. He put black officers over white other ranks in his Sierra Leone militia and his comments upon delinquent whites are even harsher than those on the Nova Scotians. Perhaps, guilt-ridden and hating himself, he felt no love or compassion for other people. In the present century, he would have made an intellectual communist, ruthless, devious, priggish, domineering, humourless and zealous, leading people he despised against the system that had created him. His self-discipline was prodigious: up before dawn; solitary prayer; the Greek Testament; communal prayer; then work from eight till seven; more prayer and Greek Testament until ten at night; then an hour or two of 'some amusing book' until he slept.

Even allowing for the intensity of Macaulay's Calvinist guilt, there was something rank and unwholesome in his character. In a letter to Selina, written in February 1797, he described how he had gone to visit a dying Englishman:

What struck me as the most lamentable proof of the man's ignorance, was that though he was continually reiterating his cries for mercy, and declaring himself a wretched sinner, when I came to ask what were the sins which lay heaviest on his conscience, he said he could not fix on any particular sins. I was at no loss, however, to remind him of numberless particular sins of the commission of which I myself had been a witness. I set them before him with all their aggravations. 'You know not even how to offer up a prayer to God,' I said to him. 'You say you have never prayed, but how often in my hearing have you blasphemed His Holy Name, and how often have I rebuked you for it?' He was not backward in acknowledging this and many other sins I mentioned to him, but they had wholly escaped himself…

After giving these words of cheer to the dying man, Macaulay left for his house on the hill before the approach of dusk.

I was proceeding along [he continues] … heaving a sigh on the recollection of the poor man I had left, and uttering occasionally an ejaculatory note of thanksgiving as I retraced seasons, during which while I was, even in my own apprehensions, sinking into the grave, I presented to the eye of sober reason a spectacle which made his case an enviable one, when I found myself, without being at all able to trace the progress by which I had got there, by one of those magical spells which our lawless imagination amuses itself with forming, stretched on what I conceived to be my own deathbed. 'Why, my Selina, should one tear dim those eyes? Lift them up to yon bright abode where myriads of the blest are surrounding their Redeemer's throne. Is there room for mourning? No, my Selina! There is all love and happiness and joy. But is it Babington I see? My dear friend, you have come in time to close my eyes, and to receive from my hand a precious deposit. By the protector of my Selina—of my—' Whether it was that I gave an involuntary sob, or what, the little native boy who walks behind carrying my shot-bag, asked me, 'My master, are you tired?' 'No, Jack, I am not tired; what makes you ask?' Before he had time to reply a parcel of humming-birds, whose beautiful plumage reflected the rays of the retiring sun, struck his eye. He pointed them out to me. I levelled my piece with murderous aim, clanged the steel, and flashed destruction. Two of them lay prostrate on the ground. I was at first pleased with my feat, my dexterity and the prize; but I recollected I had no means of preserving them at my mountain, that before I reached town they would be putrid, and that I should not gain by what I had done even the gratification of an idle curiosity. 'And how do I know,' I reflected, 'but that at this very moment the callow young of these two murdered animals are stretching their little throats to heaven, demanding food of which I have deprived them, while their shivering limbs in vain expect the genial warmth of their mothers to protect them from the cold?'

This grim, lugubrious man was not the kind who enjoys West Africa. His departure in 1799 delighted both him and the colony.

Chapter Five

By the end of the eighteenth century, more than twenty years after the founding of the colony, the original settlers of 1787 had merged with the Nova Scotia immigrants. In 1800 Sierra Leone received a third wave of settlers, the Jamaican Maroons, whose history was both sinister and strange. When Cromwell's soldiers threw the Spaniards out of Jamaica in 1655, the slaves took refuge in the mountains and dense bush of the interior of the island. The 'Maroons', a term meaning escaped slaves, became a disciplined and efficient guerrilla army who resisted all the forays of the British. In 1739, the Jamaica Government came to terms with them. The Maroons were allowed to keep their territory and their laws, in return for helping the Government to track down escaped plantation slaves at a rate of three pounds a head.

The Maroon republic prospered at first, and its captains, distinguished by silver chains and cockades, were regularly commissioned by the governor of the island. They suffered, however, when in 1769 the British lowered the prize money for recaptured slaves from £3 to £2 a head, and there were other signs of Maroon degeneracy. In his *History of Jamaica*, published in 1774, Edward Long remarked that: 'These Negroes, although inhabiting more towns than at first, are diminished in their number by deaths, and cohabitation with slaves on the plantations, instead of intermixing with each other.' In 1795, when two of their people were unlawfully flogged by the Jamaican authorities, the Maroons went to war, attacked several plantations and chopped down the redcoat troops who were dispatched against them. The British general George Walpole, eventually called in mercenaries from Cuba to track down and subdue the Maroons, who surrendered on condition that they were not deported. A contemporary writer,

R. C. Dallas, repeated the story popular at the time that the Maroons surrendered in fear of the mastiff dogs that the British had sent in against them, but from Dallas's own book we know the Maroons themselves had dogs and did not hold them in terror. Years later, the Maroons maintained that only shortage of ammunition had forced them to surrender.

The Jamaican House of Assembly broke its promise and exiled the Maroons to Nova Scotia. Like the Negro veterans of the War of American Independence, the Maroons complained of the Nova Scotia weather and stoutly refused to regard the land as a home. They sent many petitions to General Walpole, who had resigned his commission when the Jamaican Assembly did not honour his promise, and still protested their loyalty to England. When Prince Edward, son of George III, visited Halifax he asked to meet the Maroons and was most impressed by their smart bearing and dress. They told him that they were anxious to take part in the war against Napoleon, and they afterwards helped to build some of the fortifications for Halifax. The Duke of Kent, as he later became, joined General Walpole as a champion of the Maroon cause and made their grievances known in London.

The Maroons sent one petition to Henry Thornton, asking if his company would take them to Sierra Leone. Although fearing that the warlike Maroons might have a disturbing influence on the colony, Thornton also understood that since they were an embarrassment to the Government, the Treasury might provide money to send them to Africa. And so it proved. The Government agreed to ship the Maroons to Sierra Leone, to donate £7,000 from the vote for the Gold Coast Forts, to furnish troops and an annual grant of £4,000 and, finally, through a special charter, to give the company all juridical rights over the residents of its colony.

In August 1800, the 550 Maroons who had volunteered for the journey left Halifax in the *Asia*, a transport ship. A detachment of British troops was sent with them but the Maroons, under their own officers, kept their usual impeccable discipline.

Meanwhile, in Sierra Leone protest against the quit-rent

introduced by Dawes and Macaulay was growing. The dissidents complained that the rate of tax was five or six times greater than had been heard of elsewhere, and fifty times greater than in the Colony of New South Wales, which had been founded about the same time. The better the land was farmed, the more the rate was increased, so that even the new governor, Ludlam, estimated that of the settlers who were not full-time farmers, the actual majority gave up their plots rather than pay the quit-rent. The worst effect of the quit-rent was on the morale of the colony. Both the original settlers and the Nova Scotians had gone to Africa with the assurance that they would own their own land. To former slaves, still anxious about their freedom, the possession of land meant even more than it did to free-born white men. Faced with this stiff tax on their land, the settlers understandably felt that they were no more than tenants of the company.

Anger about the quit-rent provoked a more general unrest among the black settlers. The hundredors and tythingmen, who had been ignored in the Macaulay era, started to agitate for real power. They demanded that Nova Scotians should be made J.P.s and judges, that none but the hundredors and tythingmen should make the laws and that foreigners, meaning the white English settlers, should pay a tax to the blacks. In vain, Ludlam pointed out to the black settlers that none of them had the legal knowledge to act as a judge at law, and reminded them of their present right to serve as jurymen in the courts. His pleas ignored and his arguments dismissed, Ludlam thought it prudent to temporize until the Maroons arrived.

The Maroons did not arrive in time. On September 3rd, 1800, the hundredors and tythingmen went into open revolt by publishing an illegal code of laws relating to property, crime, morals and debt. They ruled that any Nova Scotian who refused to obey this code should forthwith leave the colony and that: 'the Governor and Council shall not have anything to do with the Colony no farther than the Company's affairs, and if any man shall side with the Governor, etc, against the law shall pay £20.'

Governor Ludlam ordered the employees of the company and

those few Nova Scotians who were loyal to form an armed camp on Thornton Hill. On September 25th, the loyalists marched on the rebels to try and capture their ringleaders. There was a fight in which several were wounded on both sides. The more militant rebels, amounting to one-sixth of the settlers, spread into the suburbs to plunder the outlying farms of the whites and loyal Nova Scotians. The majority of the settlers, although not yet prepared to fight, were nonetheless favourable to the rebels against the Governor.

Unpopular and outnumbered, Ludlam knew that he would have to use armed force or for ever lose his authority. Meanwhile, King Tom issued a declaration that he would shortly be forced to intervene to stop the dispute among the settlers. Just as Ludlam was preparing his men for the battle, a large vessel, the *Asia*, appeared on the horizon. The Maroon troops, eager for combat after the boredom of the journey, soon routed the settler insurgents and brought their leaders to trial. They then hunted the stragglers through the bush as they had once hunted escaped slaves through the mountains of Jamaica.

In November 1800, the charter arrived from London, establishing Sierra Leone as a colony, governed from England, with the same legal status as other colonies except that the company and not the British Government was the executive authority. The abolition of hundredors and tythingmen meant the end of the last vestiges of Sharp's ideals. The old man in retirement in England continued to offer advice to the company on the working of Frankpledge, the best way to make maple sugar and how to ensure monogamy among the Maroons. But most of the Saints were sick of their troublesome colony.

The Nova Scotians, according to Wilberforce, 'have made the worst of all possible subjects, as thorough Jacobins as if they had been trained and educated in Paris. Nothing but the greatest firmness and wisdom and temper in our Governors could for 9 years have prevented their ruining the colony.' Wilberforce and the other directors begged the Government to take over control of the colony, which they claimed had already cost the company

£200,000. This constitutional change was made in 1807, when Sierra Leone became a Crown Colony. The company was wound up in the following year.

This period of transition from private to government colony was a dismal time for Sierra Leone. A series of governors faced their unenviable job either with apathy or with fits of misdirected enthusiasm. 'No place in the world could be better suited to check an excess of ardour,' wrote Ludlam, who stuck out eight years on the coast. The testy Dawes, who had preceded Macaulay, returned for another bout in office. Captain William Day, a half-pay naval officer, built a martello tower, tried to start a sugar plantation and died after three unfruitful years. The first governor of the Crown Colony, Captain Thomas Perronet Thompson, changed the name of the capital from Freetown to Georgetown—as sounding less insolent and republican*—at the same time, and for the same reason, changing the local dollars to sterling. 'There is much that is very doleful,' he wrote after only three days in the colony. 'The state of European manners is bad beyond description. The black subjects are infinitely more orderly and decent. So much for this religious colony. And while the white inhabitants are roaring with strong drink at one end the Nova Scotians are roaring out hymns at the other.'

During these early years of the nineteenth century, several white officials and at least twenty black settlers abandoned Sierra Leone for the affluent life of a slave-trader. The quit-rent was dropped but the settlers still shied from farming. The Maroons also rejected agriculture, of which they had no experience; but they respected the laws of the new community, they made friends with the earlier settlers whom they had recently beaten in battle, and if they persisted in taking more than one wife, they did not mind hearing this habit denounced. Their military skill proved invaluable in guarding the colony from its enemies. In 1801, when the Temne attacked the settlement, the Maroons struck back, destroyed King Tom's capital, and terrorized the Temne with a bayonet charge. One of the vanquished Temne complained: 'You don't

* The next governor changed the names back.

73

fight like men, fire and have done, but you poke 'em, poke
'em.'

The little Crown Colony might have faded into oblivion but
for the abolition of the slave trade, which was to populate Sierra
Leone with its fourth, largest and most significant wave of settlers
—the slaves set free by the Royal Navy.

Chapter Six

A woman said this evening: 'Me the same like a goat; yes, me worse like a goat. I see the goats walk together, they eat a little here and a little there, and they are satisfied. But me always troubled and me no like this and that—me not satisfied, and my heart worse past everything. You see me bad past goat; the wicked be called goats in the Bible, and me worse than the wicked.'
(From the Journal of William Johnson, a missionary to the recaptured slaves in Sierra Leone. May 28th, 1821)

After twenty-five years of lobbying by the Saints, Parliament passed a bill in 1807 forbidding the slave trade within the British Empire. Since most of the trade had been carried in British ships, this Act was a triumph for the cause to which Wilberforce, Sharp, the Clarksons, Macaulay and Thornton had given most of their adult lives. The slavers and plantation owners had put up a stout resistance: the planters were our kith and kin who had fought by our side against the French; the slave trade was a nursery for the British Navy; the West Indian planters would be driven by impoverishment to emigrate to the Spanish or Portuguese territories; since other countries would break the blockade, the Act would impoverish Britain without improving the lot of the Negroes.

The Saints enjoyed a second triumph in March 1808, when an Order in Council set up a Vice-Admiralty court in Freetown for the trial and adjudication of slave ships brought in as prizes. The colony that had caused so much worry and disappointment was to come into its own at last as a base for the battle against the slave trade and as a haven for the recaptured slaves, who increased the population of the colony from only two thousand in 1807 to almost fifty thousand in 1850. Sierra Leone also became a debating point in the argument over slavery that raged with ever-increasing heat until the end of the American Civil War. The Evangelicals held up the colony as an example of how Negroes could live as free, Christian citizens, while the friends of slavery denounced it as a place of corruption, depravity and disease. Journalists of the two opposing factions gave accounts of Sierra Leone that were so unlike that one finds it hard to believe they had visited the same colony. Like Cuba, South Africa or South Vietnam today, little Sierra Leone was unwillingly dragged into a larger, distant quarrel.

As soon as the slave trade had been made illegal, the Royal Navy ships set up a blockade at the mouths of the trading rivers from Guinea to Gabon. The Royal Navy officers were not always personally hostile to the slave trade they sought to suppress. The greatest naval man of the age, Lord Nelson, wrote: 'I was bred in the good old school, and taught to appreciate the value of our West Indian possessions, and neither in the field nor in the Senate shall their just rights be infringed whilst I have an arm to fight in their defence or a tongue to launch my voice against the damnable, cruel doctrine of Wilberforce and his hypocritical allies.'

Avarice, rather than altruism, inspired the Navy's hunt for the slave ships.* Any captain who arrested a slave ship, brought it to shore and got its owners judged guilty before a Vice-Admiralty court, could claim the value of the slaves as prize. Between 1807 and 1816, the Treasury paid out nearly £200,000 as prize money to captains. By 1818, when Spain, Portugal and the Netherlands had also outlawed the slave trade, each authorizing others' navies to intercept slave ships, the hunt became still more lucrative. International Courts of Mixed Commission were set up in Freetown and in corresponding Portuguese, Spanish and Dutch ports, to adjudicate on the captured ships. The commissioners of the four countries were well paid for their labours. The British Commissary

* The debate on the slave trade found a distant echo in the recent debate on Rhodesia. One wonders whether the British Navy would have exercised a more efficient blockade in support of Britain's sanctions policy had a bounty been paid on each captured cargo.

Judge at Freetown got £3,000 a year, his junior colleague £2,000 and the Registrar £1,000 with handsome allowances for expenses, and a pension after six years. These enormous salaries, like the prize money, were paid out of the monies voted by Parliament.

Even the slavers profited from the Act. While slavery existed on the plantations of America there remained a demand for slaves, so that partial blockade merely bumped up the price of the merchandise. The governor of Sierra Leone wrote in June 1817 that:

> There appears to be at present a greater number of vessels employed in the traffic in slaves to the North of the Line, than at any point prior to the abolition ... I have found from the unanimous reports of the Masters of Merchant Vessels employed on the Coast, that they have made bad voyages, a circumstance they all attribute to the Coast being infested with slave purchasers, for, the Natives will not be at the trouble of procuring any articles of exchange for European produce, when they can do it more easily with them.

When the blockade became too dangerous on the West Coast and the Congo, the slavers went down to Angola and Mozambique from where they sailed to America by the longer, southern route. Far from decreasing the cruelty of the 'middle passage', the Act encouraged the slave traders to pack more human beings on board. Some of the slaves set free at Sierra Leone had been so cramped in the villainous holds that they never again walked upright.

British advocates of the slave trade, who affected a deep concern for the happiness of the Negroes, argued that slaves suffered less in the holds of the slave ships than they did on the naval ships that freed them. The slave ships being built to sail fast and thus escape from the British cruisers, could cross to Brazil or the Caribbean in four or six weeks, speeded along by the prevailing currents and winds. The slow British vessels, so it was argued in *Blackwood's Magazine*, took ten or twelve weeks 'to beat up to the Sierra Leone den of death'. Even arrived at Sierra Leone, the slaves had to stay on board for as long as three weeks until it had been proved in court that the ship was a lawful prize. The slaves, who had been told by the Portuguese that the British would sell them to cannibals, often jumped off and drowned rather than land at the 'Province of Freedom'.

The slaves set free in Sierra Leone were fitted out with cotton clothes and lodged in the King's Yard, near to the present hospital, which served as a kind of refugee camp. The liberated Africans, or recaptives, as they were called, were often indifferent or even ungrateful in the aftermath of release. But they remembered and appreciated anyone who had shown them real kindness, as one sees from this account by a sympathetic witness:

> A visit of some of the English prize officers to the yard had evidently given pleasure to several of their late charges. It happened, however, that when the ship-stock of yams and peppers were brought to the King's Yard, one of the black boatswains, a most ugly Kroo, named 'Bottle of Beer', who had superintended the slaves in their voyage, accompanied the sailors who brought the food. No sooner was the good-humoured merry face of the hideous Bottle of Beer perceived, than a general rush took place from all quarters of the yard. All gathered round, laughing and shouting his name. The women and children pressed upon him; at least a dozen seized him at once by the hands, arms and knees; a little girl climbed up his back to kiss him; the women tenderly wiped the perspiration from his face, and the throng threatened to suffocate him with fondness. Even the invalids, hearing the name of their friend, rose from the mats, and tottered from their sheds to greet him. He had been kind to them when kindness had little power to lessen their misery. Such gratitude, in such a place, was touching.

When Sierra Leone was appointed a depot for liberated slaves, the government intended that they be citizens of the colony. However, this new wave of immigrants lacked the education and skills of the first settlers, the Nova Scotians and the Maroons. Most had been sold into slavery from the village, spoke no English, were

78

unused to a town and almost entirely ignorant or illiterate. Many had been enslaved for crimes against tribal law, although this did not justify the accusation—popular with foes of Sierra Leone—that all recaptives were criminals.

The greatest effort was made for the young recaptives, who were sent to school to learn English. Many went to live with settler families as apprentices or servants. Still more were recruited as soldiers into the Royal Africa Corps. Although some remained in Freetown itself, most recaptives were grouped into villages near by. Often these new communities grouped together according to the tribal origins of the slaves. There was a Congo Town for example, and several villages for the numerous Ibos and Yorubas. The Ashantis, from what is now Ghana, were welcomed as fellow nationals by the Maroons, who claimed that their ancestors had come from this region.

The prize money offered for captured slave ships, the servicing and supply of the Royal Navy vessels, the provision of clothing and food to the recaptured slaves, and the consequent upsurge of trade in the colony, brought riches and opportunity to many adventurous Englishmen. It was unfortunate for the friends of the colony, but a cause of delight to its foes, that the men who made most money out of the efforts to stop the slave trade were Zachary Macaulay and his family. The former governor of Sierra Leone, now the editor of a pious monthly, the *Christian Observer*, was the principal London agent for those Royal Navy captains claiming prize money. His cousins George and Kenneth Macaulay, who ran the Freetown end of Zachary's firm, Macaulay & Babington, were two of the principal agents on the spot. Whether or not they used the influence of the Saints to win these pleasant contracts, all three grew rich from the commissions they charged on negotiating the bounties. Furthermore, Kenneth Macaulay held the lucrative job of collector of taxes and superintendent of captured Negroes, a job which during his leaves he would pass to his brother George. As superintendent of the recaptured Negroes, both men had influence on the purchasing of provisions, which very frequently came from the firm of Macaulay & Babington.

Kenneth Macaulay, especially, was inclined to use his public position to further his private ends. He applied for the judgeship of the Commissary Court in which he and his colleagues were acting as advocates; he encouraged a native war as a way of extending commerce; when he took over the acting governorship in 1826 he assumed the power of awarding all contracts in a colony where he was the leading contractor. Even the corpse of the former governor was embalmed in Macaulay & Babington rum. Quite apart from abusing their influence and their office, the Macaulays employed very questionable business practices. Owning mortgages on as many as fifty properties in the Freetown area, they were able to inflate the market rate of housing. Their near-monopoly in the retail trade of the colony meant that a shirt selling for 5s. in London, cost 15s. in one of the Macaulays' stores.

Friends of the slavers, enemies of the Saints and disgruntled officials or traders in Sierra Leone, combined with gusto to bait the Macaulay clan. The first and most telling attack was made in 1815 by a hot-tempered Irish lawyer, Robert Thorpe, who had just been sacked from his job as Chief Justice in the colony. In an open *Letter to William Wilberforce* he charged that Zachary Macaulay, 'the great shopkeeper of the colony', had gained his position and wealth on the strength of the services he had rendered to the Sierra Leone Company and its successor the Africa Institution. As to Kenneth Macaulay, the superintendent of the recaptured Negroes, Thorpe charged that he did 'coerce and chastise the same Negroes most cruelly, that he allowed them at one time, to be almost starved and at other times suffered their hospitals to be most neglected'. He added that Kenneth Macaulay neglected Christian instructions, that he flogged Negro women, allowed them to go about naked, and put them as apprentices to a bawdy-house madame.

The directors of the Africa Institution printed a long reply to Thorpe's accusations, quoting his own self-damaging letters, and arguing that he had not stayed long enough in the colony to speak with authority on its problems. In a reply 'point by point' to the reply of the directors, Thorpe hit back effectively on particulars but ignored those points where his own arguments had been weak. Later in the same year, Zachary Macaulay joined in the argument with some plausible attacks on Thorpe's character and conduct. He was not so plausible in defence of his own business etiquette. 'My profession is that of merchant,' he wrote, with rather suspicious pomposity, 'and I know of no principle which forbids of my exercising that profession in Africa, or in any other quarter of the globe where I can do it with a fair and reasonable prospect of advantage … I have had the prize-giving undoubtedly of several ships; but neither for that, nor for the agency of the Governor and Garrisons, had I made the slightest application.'

The attacks on the Macaulays and on Sierra Leone in general continued in various newspapers during the next ten years. One James M'Queen was paid fifteen thousand pounds by planters in the West Indies to write attacks on Sierra Leone.* In a series of articles in *Blackwood's Magazine* published in 1826 and 1827 he portrayed Sierra Leone as a corrupt, disease-ridden hole where 'flagellation, without any law to limit the application, is the common punishment for Negroes offending in the place. They are tied to a cart's tail, and whipped through Freetown, or bound to a stake at particular spot, and generally with an enormous cat-o-nine-tails.' Kenneth Macaulay published an answer, *The Colony of Sierra Leone Vindicated*, pointing out the countless lies and distortions contained in M'Queen's attack. The colony was as healthy as any place on the coast and if missionaries tended to perish there it was due to their morbid temperament.

From 1823, Zachary Macaulay left the effective management of the company to Kenneth and to his nephew Thomas Babington. These two were so profligate that by 1826 the firm was practically bankrupt. Masses of unsold goods were heaped up in Freetown; new factories were built and left unused; wasteful credits were given and never collected. At last the company fell with a

* M'Queen did not declare his interest in writing about Sierra Leone. In this he resembles those modern public relations consultants who write to the newspapers on behalf of some foreign government, while pretending to be merely disinterested citizens. M'Queen, had he lived today, would have thrived in this infamous trade.

crash and Zachary was obliged to pay for the damage. The editor of the *Christian Observer*, the founder of the Society for the Suppression of Vice, former Governor of Sierra Leone and the only one of the Saints who was liked by the Duke of Wellington, fled abroad to escape his creditors. He died in 1838.

A colony as small as Sierra Leone always depended much on the character of its governor. The settlers gained confidence from a kind man, like Clarkson; they cowered unhappily before a stern man, like Macaulay; they defied and took advantage of a weak man, like Ludlam. From 1814 to 1824 they enjoyed the rule of Sir Charles MacCarthy, a just and delightful man, who is still remembered in Freetown today as the best and wisest of governors. His background was quite untypical for the governorship of the colony. In spite of his name, MacCarthy was born in France, of French parents, but crossed to the British side in the Napoleonic War. In 1811 he went to the Royal Africa Corps and was in Senegal when he was given his new appointment at Freetown. His way of life was far from that of the Saints. He liked parties, was very jolly and, although he asked people in London to find him a suitable wife, he in fact preferred his several black mistresses.' Strangest of all, in that Evangelical colony, MacCarthy was a Roman Catholic, who remained true, at heart, to Rome.

MacCarthy believed that the best way to civilize the recaptives was to form them into villages under the tutelage of a missionary. The men he obtained for this work came from the Church Missionary Society that had been founded in 1799 by Wilberforce, Thornton, Macaulay and other Evangelicals. The Church Missionary Society (it did not actually take this name until 1813) began its work in Africa with the natives of the interior. These efforts were not very rewarding and the C.M.S. turned to the liberated slaves as a more likely and easy field for conversions. As an Anglican body, the C.M.S. was richer and more influential than the earlier nonconformist groups. After a nudge to the Treasury, and much agitation from MacCarthy, a deal was arranged by which the C.M.S. found the missionaries, while MacCarthy paid for them as government servants. The men

82

would act not only as ministers of the faith but as schoolteachers, administrators and magistrates to the villages of free slaves.

Most of the early missionaries of the C.M.S. were of German origin, since suitable British people dreaded Africa's feverish reputation. Of the first fifty men sent out by the C.M.S., twenty-five died within five years. One missionary, Thomas Heighway, died within a week, which may have been because he was chasing around in a tight suit all one Sunday to make sure that nobody broke the Sabbath. Those missionaries who survived the fever reaped plentiful harvests of souls, giving widespread inspiration to the devout in Britain. Many an Evangelical, every year, paid five pounds to the C.M.S. to have one of the newly converted slaves baptized with his own name. Tracts and histories of the C.M.S. told heart-warming tales of the black men's piety. '"How is it with your heart?" one liberated was asked. "Massa," was the reply, "my heart no live here now; my heart lives there", pointing upward!'

One of these missionaries, William Johnson, became a legend of piety through the churches and Sunday Schools of Britain. A German, in spite of his name, he spoke such atrocious English that even MacCarthy could scarcely understand him; but he went out first as a schoolmaster. He settled in Regent, one of the new recaptive villages, whose people were mostly of Ibo origin. Their pious frenzy sometimes alarmed even Johnson, who wrote one day in his journal:

In the evening whilst engaged in prayer, crying and praying became general, so that I was obliged to leave off and give out a hymn, but all to no purpose; I exhorted them to silence, and gave out the text, then gave out another hymn, but all to no use. The greatest part of the congregation were on their knees, and crying aloud for mercy ... From that period, I was obliged to use means to prevent further disturbances, for sometimes when I only mentioned the name of Jesus, cries were heard immediately.

Friends of the Negro people heard with approval and awe how Johnson's village respected the Sabbath, and how shocked the

83

inhabitants were one Sunday to see white people out for a ride. 'I told them [the visitors] I was glad to see them at any time,' Johnson wrote in 1820, 'but was exceedingly sorry to see them break the Lord's day. They did not answer anything but one complained much of my young horse, which came out of the meadow and kicked his horse. Mr Bull [another missionary] being present, said, the horse was very religious and did not like to see gentlemen break the Sabbath.' This was the kind of joke that made even the Evangelicals laugh. But better than any jokes were the stories of Negro piety, told in comical, Babu accents.

Business as well as piety flourished under MacCarthy's rule. Each shipload of recaptives required more food, clothing and shelter, and these the tradesmen offered at an inflated price. The officials of the Commission Court and the officers of the Royal Africa Corps which had recently formed in Freetown, paid many times the London rate for imported food and luxuries. As more traders heard of the opportunities, the white population of Freetown rose from 20 to 120. The timber trade up river needed 50 ships to carry to London produce worth £40,000 a year. The new rich created a social improvement. Hairdressers and tailors set up shop. A hotel, a club, a newspaper, theatricals and race meetings helped to divert the Freetown fashionable world.

The number of stone buildings increased from six to sixty, thanks to MacCarthy who fancied himself as a patron of architects in the Gothic style. His public works include a depot for the recaptive slaves, storehouses, a town hall complete with clock, a flight of stone steps from Water Street to the dock, and the beginning of St George's Church, later the hideous cathedral. He persuaded the government to increase his annual building allowance from £4,000 to £10,000 and by the end of his governorship he had spent £150,000 on public building. The Government grumbled but it respected MacCarthy, and rewarded him with a knighthood in 1820.

By temperament an expansive, active man, MacCarthy hoped to build empires as well as a city. As governor of Sierra Leone he looked after British interests everywhere on the West Coast of

Africa and he often travelled to crush native uprisings and safe-guard the interests of the British settlements. In 1824, he sailed west to Cape Coast in what is now Ghana and found the garrison preparing war on the Ashanti. Gallant and careless, MacCarthy joined the campaign in which the British force was annihilated. The Ashanti cut off MacCarthy's head and kept his skull as a fetish, to be shown at the annual Yam customs.

The news of MacCarthy's death caused lamentations in Free-town. The Europeans had respected him as an able, effective governor who gave new life to the economy of the colony. The Negroes respected him for his justice, his sympathy for their feelings and his freedom from colour prejudice. He had always given government jobs to Negroes of ability; he mixed with them socially; and he loved more than one black girl.

Years later, a visitor to Sierra Leone met an African from the Sherbro territory who spoke this simple epitaph on Sir Charles MacCarthy's governorship: 'MacCarthy live, I come live here too; good man too much; everybody have much work, much dollar, much laugh. MacCarthy dead, I go away—back to Sherbro country.'

PART TWO

Chapter One

The first difference which strikes us is that of colour ... Is it not the foundation of a greater or less share of beauty in the two races? Are not the fine mixtures of red and white, the expressions of every passion by greater or lesser suffusions of colour in the one, preferable to that eternal monotony, which reigns in the countenances, that immoveable veil of black which covers all the emotions of the other race? Add to these, flowing hair, a more elegant symmetry of form, their own judgment in favour of the whites, declared by their preference of them as uniformly as is the preference of the Oran-ootan for the black women over those of his own species.
(From *Notes on Virginia*, by Thomas Jefferson, 1782)

The Back to Africa movement started in England, but the plight of free blacks was both more pressing and the problem they presented more complex in the new United States, where the Negro population amounted to hundreds of thousands. Many Americans, even before the Revolution, feared the social consequence of the growing number of slaves. The Virginia House of Burgesses, in 1772, had petitioned the Crown to check the trade in Africans as 'we have too much reason to fear [this] will endanger the very existence of your Majesty's American dominions.' Nothing was done, since the northern states grew rich in the actual trade while the southern states needed slaves as cheap plantation labour. Delegates of these interests quashed an attempt to prohibit slavery in the Declaration of Independence. As Thomas Jefferson, who drafted it, recalled:

The clause ... reprobating the enslaving of the inhabitants of Africa, was struck out in complaisance to South Carolina and

89

Georgia, who had never attempted to restrain an importation of slaves, and who on the contrary still wished to continue it. Our Northern brethren also I believe felt a little tender under these censures; for though their people have few slaves themselves, yet they have been pretty considerable carriers of them to others.

Jefferson erred in his figures. Before independence, there had been as many slaves in the North as in the South, while as late as 1790 only Massachusetts forbade the practice of slavery. But many Americans, pleased with their new-won liberty, sensed the paradox and injustice of subjugating the blacks. Many masters manumitted their slaves or allowed them to purchase their liberty so that soon a new class of free blacks was formed and increased five-fold in the forty years after independence. Many tended to congregate in the Northern towns where, just as today, they made ghettoes of poverty and disgruntlement; but their numbers also multiplied in the Southern states. There were three thousand free blacks in Virginia in 1780, ten thousand in 1790, and thirty thousand in 1810. The Southern whites regarded these free blacks as a mischievous influence on the slaves, while in the North, even quite kind-hearted whites called the free blacks 'a living pestilence', complained of their 'insolent' manner and their habitual 'ignorance and crime'. The free black leaders argued with reason that they were poor, they had few schools and were generally the object of white exploitation. Without the respect accorded to poor white workers, without the free lodging and food given to slave blacks, the lot of these people was miserable in the extreme.

Anti-Negro prejudice at this time was just as entrenched in the North as in the South. A fine historian of the revolutionary period wrote that Northern newspaper advertisements of slaves for sale and of runaways 'used phraseology as bad as or worse than that common in the original southern states two or three generations later'.*

* In his *Colonization of American Negroes* (Oklahoma University Press, 1957), the historian Frederic Bancroft quotes an advertisement from the Boston *Continental*

The change of attitude among Northern whites, which later was to express itself in the abolitionist movement, can be attributed partly to economic forces. In contrast to the South, which needed unskilled labour to till the great plantations, the North depended on small, family farms and, increasingly, upon manufactures. Slaves were unnecessary, perhaps even inconvenient, for this more sophisticated labour. Most slaves in the North had worked as domestic servants and freedom brought little change in their economic condition. The threat of the sack and of starving was almost as frightening to the free blacks as the threat of the lash was to the slaves.

Another strong influence on the Northern whites towards the end of the eighteenth century was the spread of Evangelical fervour. Bible societies, Sunday School unions, missions and temperance leagues arose all over the Northern and central states. Men with an urge for 'benevolent' work championed orphans, stranded seamen, the urban poor or Jewish victims of persecution, while others, more stern, denounced drunkenness, dancing and breach of the Sabbath. American Evangelicals, like the Saints across the Atlantic, were the first whites to concern themselves with the plight of the poor blacks, and the first to advocate emigration, in this case to the settlement in West Africa which was ultimately to become Liberia.

The idea of emigration as a means of solving the free black problem was first mooted soon after the Revolution. A few suggested sending the blacks to the West Indies, Florida or Louisiana, which were then under the rule of European Powers, but most colonizationists favoured the English idea of forming a settlement in West Africa. One of these, a rich and rather flamboyant Quaker named William Thornton, had been to England and knew some leading Saints, whose ideas he wanted to transfer to America. 'In

---

Journal and Weekly Advertiser for January 4th, 1771: 'To be sold, An extraordinary likely Negro Wench, 17 years old, she can be warranted to be strong, healthy and good natured, has no notion of freedom, has been always used to a Farmer's kitchen and dairy, and is not known to have any failing, but being with child, which is the only cause of her being sold.' Doubtless the wench had been used to a Farmer's bed.

the winter of 1786-7,' he wrote, 'I was travelling in Rhode Island and Massachusetts. I found many free blacks and having been engaged in correspondence with some of the members of the Sierra Leone Society of London, among whom were some of my friends I was desirous of knowing what numbers of free Blacks in Mass & R.I. could be found desirous of joining in that settlement.' He claimed that hundreds of free blacks had assembled to listen to his suggestion, and that within two weeks, two thousand were ready to follow him to West Africa. He made his plan known to members of the Massachusetts Assembly, in the confidence that this body would furnish the settlers with transport, equipment and food. However, when Thornton explained that Africa was to be the free slaves' destination 'the members of the Legislature expressed an unwillingness to send them out of the limits of the U.S. and wished a settlement to be made in the most southern part of the back country between the Whites and Indians.'

Understandably, Thornton balked at this plan which would have dispatched the luckless blacks to death by arrow and tomahawk. He opposed any colonization *within* the United States, asking: 'Could they [the free blacks] ever be treated with an equality in a country where many of their colour were still held in Slavery?'

In Newport, Rhode Island, a Congregational clergyman named Samuel Hopkins was also interested in the fate of the free blacks. Even before the Revolution, Hopkins had planned to send Negro missionaries back to Africa and had trained a few men in theology. His enthusiasm being whetted by news of Sierra Leone he wrote to Granville Sharp in 1789:

> When I removed to this town, my attention was soon turned to the Slave Trade which had long been carried on here, and was still continuing ... I was, so far as I then knew, almost alone in my opposition to this trade and the slavery of the Africans, but have since read with great satisfaction your writings on that subject, some of which were published, I believe, before the time mentioned ... There were a number of religious Blacks, with whom I am acquainted, who wish to

be formed into a distinct church, or religious society; and to have a Black appointed to be their pastor and then to go, with all the Blacks who shall be willing to move with them, to Africa ... This plan I have had in view for some years, and have wished and attempted to promote it. But no way has yet been opened in America to carry it into execution, there being no means yet found to defray the charge of sending a vessel to Africa, with a number of blacks, to find out and procure the most convenient place for such a settlement. In the meantime, we have, to our great joy, been informed that such a plan has been projected and executed in England.

Transatlantic mail was slow in those days. By the time the letter from Hopkins reached Sharp, the news from Sierra Leone was most discouraging. In his reply, Sharp had to admit that most white settlers in Sierra Leone had left to join the slave trade but that any American Negroes were welcome to join his colony. Nothing came of Hopkins's plan. The Rhode Island Legislature, like that of Massachusetts, was not prepared to finance any foreign colonization; moreover, Hopkins had enemies among other divines, who regarded him as a crank and a utopian.

The mood of America at the time was hostile to foreign adventures. As war and revolution raged in Europe, the Americans were grateful for their distant isolation. It was too soon after 1776 for America to start founding colonies of her own. But as the number of free blacks grew during the early nineteenth century, more and more pious Americans nursed the vision of founding a settlement in West Africa. The end of the European wars in 1815, transformed this vision into a plausible plan. The Reverend Robert Finley of New Jersey, an Evangelical of energy and resource, adopted the colonization cause in 1816 and hired a younger clergyman, Samuel John Mills, to serve as itinerant fund-raiser. They spoke to mission and Bible societies, discussed the idea with the free blacks, asked advice from those who had been to Africa, and at last, in November 1816, were ready to launch the American Colonization Society. They also made the wise decision to transfer their headquarters from Princeton, New Jersey, to Washington, D.C., the seat of political power.

The British Saints who had founded Sierra Leone were sufficiently rich and powerful to finance their venture by private means, taking only occasional subsidies from the Treasury. The American colonizationists thought from the start that they would need financial support from the Government. They were hopeful of winning this support since by 1816 most politicians were just as concerned as the moralists about what to do with free blacks. In a mere forty years since the Declaration of Independence, the problems of race and slavery had become the most ominous facing the country.

Slavery, far from dying out with the end of the slave trade, was reinforced by a surprising boom in the price of cotton. The cotton exports of the United States rose from 130,000 lbs. in 1790 to 35 million tons in 1800. The cotton states like Georgia and South Carolina enjoyed a dramatic rise in the price of land and of slaves. In the other slave states such as Virginia and Kentucky, most slaves were used for domestic rather than plantation work; but politicians in these states tended to sympathize with their friends in the deep South.

Anti-slavery as a major crusade did not gain ground until the 1830s, but North and South were at issue over other matters as early as 1800. The manufacturers of the North favoured a tariff to guard their weak industries; while the Southerners, living off agricultural exports, wanted to keep the tariff down. The Northerners were inclined to favour authority, England, peace and sound finance; the Southerners favoured democracy, France and a boisterous foreign policy. These different attitudes and policies became tangled up in different beliefs on the morality of slavery, and came to a head in the question of the Missouri: should the new lands to the west of that river be slave or free? The resulting compromise only stitched up the wound that would later burst open in civil war.

The Evangelicals regarded the free blacks as a moral issue; the politicians regarded them as a social menace. The politicians,

94

exerting more power and possessing more money, were to become the driving force behind the colonization movement. Some of the greatest statesmen of the age helped to create Liberia.

Three Virginian presidents of the United States, with twenty-four years in the White House between them, were active supporters of African colonization. The noble Thomas Jefferson, the most pure and generous statesman in the history of his country, wrestled throughout his life with the problem of slavery. 'And can the liberties of a nation be thought secure', he asked in a much-quoted essay, 'when we have removed their only firm basis, a conviction in the minds of the people that these liberties are of the gift of God? That they are not to be violated but with his wrath? Indeed I tremble for my country when I reflect that God is just: that his justice cannot sleep for ever ... ' When he wrote these words, Jefferson owned 150 slaves—but he cannot be written off as a hypocrite. Although humane and even affectionate towards his personal slaves, he did not believe in the equality of the races. His writings on the Negro reveal the stock white prejudice of his age—and indeed of our own:

> They secrete less by the kidnies, and more by the glands of the skin, which gives them a very strong and disagreeable odour ... They seem to require less sleep ... They are more ardent after their female: but love seems with them to be more of an eager desire than a tender delicate mixture of sentiment and sensation. Their griefs are transient ... I advance it therefore as a suspicion only, that the blacks, whether originally a distinct race, or made distinct by time and circumstances, are inferior to the whites in the endowments both of body and mind.

These were not the views of some crass Southern red-neck but of the man who drafted the Declaration of Independence, a friend of the Revolution in France and the patron saint of the Left in American history.

Presidents Thomas Jefferson, James Monroe and James Madison all came from a slave state, Virginia, and owned slaves themselves, but felt uneasy about the institution of slavery. We learn from his biographers that Madison treated his slaves 'with a consideration bordering upon indulgence' and did not sell any until the end of his life, when he was badly short of money. Like many Americans after him, Madison grieved that the presence of slavery in the United States impaired the influence of her political example. Both Monroe and Jefferson favoured emigration by blacks to the European colonies. The solemn and raw-boned Monroe, known as 'the last of the Virginians', was perturbed by the possibility of a Negro revolt, such as that of Toussaint L'Ouverture in Haiti, which had sent a shudder of fear through white America. When Monroe was governor of Virginia in 1800 he discovered plans for a slaves' revolt, called out the militia and had the leading insurgents tried and executed—death was then the only penalty for revolt. Afterwards Monroe wrote asking Jefferson to purchase 'lands without the limit of the State, to which persons obnoxious to the laws or dangerous to the peace of society may be removed ... The idea of such an acquisition was suggested by motives of humanity... to provide an alternate mode of punishment for those ... doomed to suffer death.'

Not all the politicians who argued for colonization were Southerners or slave-holders. The famous orator Daniel Webster came from New Hampshire. Politically a conservative, he was opposed to Jefferson, Madison and Monroe, whom he thought addicted to heresy and reform. His chief contribution to the colonization cause was his outstanding skill as an orator, although some of his speeches, when read today, smack of Dickens's satire on the Americans: 'America, manfully springing from the torturing fangs of the British lion, now rises majestic in the pride of her sovereignty, and bids her eagle elevate his wings ... Oxford and Cambridge, those oriental stars of literature, shall now be lost, while the bright sun of American science displays his broad circumference in uneclipsed radiance.'

Webster's main rival in eloquence as in politics was the man who launched the movement to found Liberia. Swaggering Henry Clay, 'the Cock of Kentucky', 'the Hotspur of the West', 'Gallant

Henry of the West', sometimes 'the Judas of the West', was more than a state removed from the gentlemanliness and dignity of Jefferson's Virginia. Boastful and reckless, a windbag who seldom opened a book, Clay yet had verve and the brash high spirits that made him the darling of the frontiersmen. Kentucky was a slave state and Clay was a slave-owner versed in the casuistry of his class: 'My slaves', he used to say, 'are as well fed and clad, look as sleek and hearty, and are quite as civil and respectful in their demeanour and little disposed to wound the feelings of anyone as you are.' Clay's valet Charles was so loyal, a visitor said, that only animal force could have torn him away from his master. Strangely enough, some of these contented slaves actually tried to escape, and Clay had to send agents to recapture his property.

Whereas Webster, Jefferson, Madison and Monroe regarded the Negro with condescending benevolence, the crude Westerner Clay was unabashedly racist. He did not think the Indian 'worth preserving', and commonly spoke of the Negro with brutal disdain. He regarded colonization as tantamount to expulsion; as a means of removing a vicious, annoying minority.

Men such as these, who founded and stamped their character on Liberia, were far removed in thought from the British Saints. All were lawyers, accustomed to lusty and raucous polemics; men of the world without prissiness or cant. Webster was pious by repute, but all three Virginians were at best deists who dabbled in science and Jacobin thoughts; Clay got baptized at the unusual age of seventy. Patriotism, the West or the Constitution inspired them more than the Bible did; they feared adverse votes more than hell-fire; their private lives would have caused pursed lips at Clapham. In the boarding-houses where Washington Congressmen lived, decanters of brandy and whisky were produced without extra charge at all meals. Even the puritan Webster died partly of drink, having given his name to a punch of rum, brandy, champagne, arrack, maraschino, green tea, sugar and lemon juice. As a young Senator, Clay 'gambled much, read little and went out with the ladies almost every night'. When appearing in court he would pour out a glass of claret to treat the opposing counsel; he fought and survived two duels; he once lost and won back eight thousand dollars in one evening of cards.

Statesmen like these lent their fame and eloquence to the colonization movement. The actual work and organization was left to Evangelicals such as Finley and Mills. Throughout 1816, Finley had lobbied and made speeches and begged for funds. He was lucky to have an ally in Francis Scott Key, a politician turned pious, who is best remembered now for his authorship of 'The Star-Spangled Banner'. Through Key and other prominent citizens, Finley aroused the interest of the politicians and businessmen who could give the colonization movement the blessings of wealth and approval. On December 18th, when the time seemed ripe, an advertisement appeared in the *Washington Intelligencer*, inviting to a meeting all those gentlemen 'who are friendly to the promotion of a plan for colonizing the free blacks of the United States'. About twenty distinguished men attended the meeting, held in a small, smoky room of the Davis Hotel, which was Washington's leading tavern.

The meeting was chaired by Henry Clay, whose opening speech, as reported in the *Intelligencer*, was to prove the first, curious plea for the future state of Liberia:

> He understood the object of the present meeting, to be to consider of the propriety and practicability of colonizing the free blacks of colour in the United States, and of forming an Association in relation to that object. That class of the mixed population of our country, was peculiarly situated. They neither enjoyed the immunities of freemen, nor were they subject to the incapacities of slaves, but partook in some degree of the qualities of both. From their condition, and the unconquerable prejudice resulting from their colour, they never could amalgamate with the free whites of this country. It was desirable, therefore, both as it respected them, and the residue of the population of the country, to drain them off...
> We should derive much encouragement in the prosecution of the object which had assembled us together by the success

which had attended the colony of Sierra Leone. That establishment had commenced about 20 or 25 years ago under the
patronage of private individuals in Great Britain. The basis of
the population of the colony consisted of the fugitive slaves
from the southern states, during the Revolutionary war,
who had been first carried to Nova Scotia, and who afterwards, about the year 1792, upon their own application,
almost in mass, had been transported to the western coast of
Africa ... We have their experience before us; and can there
be a nobler cause than that which, while it proposed to rid
our own country of a useless and pernicious, if not dangerous
portion of its population, contemplates the spreading of the
arts of civilized life, and the possible redemption from ignorance and barbarism of a benighted quarter of the globe ... It
was not proposed to deliberate upon, or consider at all any
question of emancipation, or that was connected with the
abolition of slavery. It was upon that condition alone, he was
sure, that many gentlemen from the south and the west,
whom he saw present, had attended, or could be expected to
co-operate. It was upon that condition only that he had
himself attended.

A sceptical man in the audience might have asked how 'useless,
pernicious and dangerous' Negroes were going to redeem Africa
from its barbarism. The other speakers appear to have felt no
doubts. The Clerk of the Supreme Court, Elias Caldwell, stressed
the cruelty to free blacks of letting them get a relish for privileges
that would be for ever denied them. The acidulous John Randolph
—one of the men who later fought duels with Clay—called free
blacks 'promoters of mischief' and welcomed colonization as a
means of securing slavery.

This first meeting exposed the flaw that was later to split the
colonization movement. The American Colonization Society
tried to present itself in the Evangelical North as a means towards
abolition of slavery. In the South its agents presented it as a means
of safeguarding the same institution. This two-faced attitude was

observed at the time. Although the press on the whole was favourable to the society—the Georgetown *Messenger* said it would purge the land of 'inferior blood'—the free blacks were understandably cautious. A group of Richmond Negroes resolved that emigration might be beneficial but shied from the prospect of going to Africa, asking instead for a colony on the Missouri. Two Negro orators in Philadelphia said that they had no wish to separate from their present home and they prophesied, correctly, that emigration might become a condition of granting freedom. They feared that families would again be severed by the Atlantic and that those carried away would roam 'childless, widowed, and alone, over the burning plains of Guinea'.

Soon after the founding of the society, Finley left to take up a university post. His Evangelical colleagues, backed by their friends in politics and finance, continued to lobby and raise funds in the capital and the country. But the colony could not be founded until some representatives of the society went out to Africa, looked for a site, and purchased territory from the local kings.

Chapter Two

When I look at the prosperous condition of Freetown and
then cast my eye at Kissey-town, at Leicester Mountain and
Regents-town, at Cape Shilling, it causes my heart to pant for
the day that America shall have a foot-hold on the continent.
(Daniel Coker, a free black, who sailed with the first
emigrants to Africa. September 25th, 1820)

The Reverend Samuel J. Mills, who was chosen to go to Africa
and find a site for the colony, was typical of the earnest young men
who worked and died for Liberia. 'It was the privilege of this
beloved man to be the child of pious parents', exclaimed Mills's
equally pious biographer. These parents lived in Connecticut
which, like most of New England, was shaken by a religious revival
towards the end of the century. Young Samuel was so distressed
by a sense of his own wickedness that he would sometimes break
out in rebellion against his God. At the age of sixteen, during a
mournful talk with his mother, he 'raised his head and with eyes
streaming with tears, exclaimed "O that I had never been born!
For two years I have been sorry that God ever made me" ... "My
son", said she, "you are born, and you can never throw off your
existence, nor your everlasting accountability for all your conduct." This heavy thought was like a dagger to his soul.'

At Williams College, Massachusetts, religious anguish continued
to torture Mills, who wrote in his diary that 'it seems to me I have
never longed so much for the Sabbath as I do now.' But even at
college he cultivated his skill at making others sob for their sins.
After a prayer session, held for the Freshman Class, he noted with
satisfaction: 'A very good meeting. Many very solemn. K——
much cast down.'

From Williams he went on to Yale and to Andover Theological Seminary, where he took a special interest in missionary work. Afterwards he became a full-time fund-raiser for missionary and benevolent societies, and he twice toured the West, where the shortage of Bibles seemed to him a 'foul blot on our national character'. By 1816 he had grown concerned with the plight of the poor blacks and had offered his services, for the usual fee, to the new American Colonization Society. This society was delighted to get a man known as the best money-gatherer of his time.

There was no point in raising money to found an African colony unless the site, even a tentative one, had been chosen. The board of the society had already written asking for advice to Thomas Clarkson, the British anti-slavery agitator, whose brother John had served in Sierra Leone. He recommended starting a colony on the Island of Sherbro, eighty miles south of Freetown; it is now a part of Sierra Leone, but then it was ruled by independent kings.

The society suggested that Mills should take a companion on his journey—no doubt anxious lest he should die before coming home to report—and Mills chose Ebenezer Burgess, a mathematics professor from Vermont.

The two men went to Africa by way of England, and even this leg of the journey proved to be hazardous. The captain of the *Electra*, Mills recorded with pleasure, 'did not permit profane language, excessive drinking, nor any species of gambling on board the ship'. But when the *Electra* was wrecked in a storm and seemed on the point of sinking, the pious captain piled his family into the only lifeboat and abandoned his passengers and crew. However, the ship did not sink, and Mills and Burgess came safely to London, where they spent an instructive month meeting Wilberforce and other Evangelicals. They took another ship for West Africa and were thrilled by their stop at Sierra Leone. Even while still at sea, Mills gushed over the sight of the church on Leicester Mountain and gloated that pagan altars were falling before the 'temples of the living God, like the image of Dagon before the Ark'. On dry land, they were not disappointed. They praised the schools for recaptive children and said of Regents Town, where they rode to church, that 'the wilderness buds and blossoms like the rose'.

Had Mills and Burgess studied the early history of Sierra Leone, they might have avoided making the same mistakes as their predecessors when trying to buy land on Sherbro Island, where they put down on April 2nd, 1820. Eager and gullible, and quite unversed in African law and diplomacy, Mills and Burgess must have appeared to the kings as two rich fools to be milched. They were unfortunate in their choice of a friend on the island, a Negro trader, John Kizell, who had once been a slave in America. He was keen to please, very hospitable and very pious, so that soon Mills could write in his diary that 'no one can be more anxious for the temporal and spiritual welfare of Africans and descendants'. Kizell in turn, told the white men that their plan for colonization 'had its origin in heaven'. He was, in fact, a greedy and sanctimonious rogue. As a go-between and interpreter to the local chiefs in the long negotiations that followed, Kizell encouraged the white Americans in their course of diplomatic folly.

In their first palaver, at a tiny village called Samo, Mills and Burgess met Kings Samano and Safah, the latter 'dressed in a silver-laced coat, a superb three-cornered hat, a mantle around his neck, hanging nearly to the ground, blue bafta trousers, considerably the worse for wear; without stockings or shoes'. Although Mills wrote in a supercilious way of the kings, he was generous with the gifts which were all that the kings wanted.

Our present [he wrote in his diary on April 2nd] consisted of a piece of bafta, a keg of powder, a few bars of tobacco, and a small jar of rum. The last article Mr K[izell] was requested to obtain for us, as we were told they would in no case hold a palaver without it; and we have reason to believe our information correct. These people are only children of a larger growth and we would hope by a temporary conformity, gradually to wean them from their vicious customs. One jar only was first set before them; they contended that there were two Kings, and they must have two bottles; nor would they yield this point until a second was produced.

After two days of palaver, when the kings had a good haul of presents, they revealed that they were only junior chiefs and would have to consult with King Sherbro about a decision. King Sherbro, after taking his presents, told Mills and Burgess to see a King Couber, who in turn passed them on to a bevy of junior kings. On April 9th, Mills wrote, pathetically, in his diary: 'The Kings meet this morning for consultation. An additional present is necessary. Patience may almost have her perfect work in the disposition and hearts of those which wait on men so slothful in business and so eager to receive the tribute of strangers.'

King Couber sounds to have been a master of bush diplomacy. Why hadn't the settlers got a letter addressed to him in person? What if all the blacks in America wanted to come and settle in Sherbro? He would have to consult his people but this was the busy season of the year: rains were coming on; the people were clearing their plantations and sowing their rice; the kings were poor and must work as well as the people... If only the Americans had more goods to buy land...

At last even Mills despaired of getting a treaty, and made preparations to leave for another part of the coast. But the Sherbro Kings would not say goodbye to their visitors without a last appeal for a present. 'They said it was a custom of their country', Mills wrote in his diary, '... to pour a little wine on the graves of their fathers, and say "good strangers have come to us, O bless good strangers", and they wanted a little wine to pour at the root of the tree, once fallen, now standing erect.' Mills missed the erotic symbolism of the tree, but was otherwise not so naive as when he first came to the coast. 'Having taken an affectionate leave of them, we returned on board, and sent them a bottle of wine, rather to bedew their royal lips, than to sprinkle the ashes of their fathers, or irrigate the marvellous tree.'

After a month on Sherbro Island, where every day they regaled the natives by singing 'Salvation, oh the joyful sound', Mills and

104

Burgess made their slow way back to Freetown, where Governor MacCarthy gave them a friendly reception. Indeed, Mills wrote that the governor was justly esteemed as father and patron of the colony. From Sierra Leone the two men took ship for America. Already they had decided that Sherbro Island should be the site of the colony. They believed that the soil was fertile, the water good, the climate salubrious and the natives friendly—all of which conclusions were later to prove false. The English, as well as the native kings, had tricked these greenhorns on the coast, for MacCarthy did not intend to permit a rival colony near his own and had written to London for leave to take over Sherbro.

Mills did not live to see the result of his unwise recommendation. Because of the long-drawn-out palavers, the two men had stayed on the coast into the feverish period of the rains. In June the lugubrious Mills was struck down. 'Death had no terrors,' said his biographer, for Mills 'seemed to be looking forward to the immediate presence and enjoyment of God in heaven. Between 2 and 3 p.m. [on June 16th, 1818] his hiccup ceased. He gently closed his hands on his breast, as if to engage in some act of devotion—and, while a celestial smile settled upon his countenance, and every feature expressed the serenity and meekness of his soul, he ceased to breathe.'

Joyous death ended a sombre life. But Mills must have been a man of considerable charm for the crew of the ship joined Burgess in tears when the corpse was dropped into the ocean. Mills's life, and still more his death, became a favourite text for Evangelical sermons.

While Mills and Burgess were away, the American Colonization Society had sponsored more lecture tours, raised more funds and lobbied Congress and government for support. The future of the colony seemed to depend on the news from Africa and when Burgess returned, bearing the news of Mills's death, the society for a time could only bewail his martyrdom. But grief soon gave way to joy over the document that Mills and Burgess had written. The committee of the society read of the great prospects of rice, cane, livestock and spices, the exquisite native goods one could buy for a few leaves of tobacco, the honest commerce that must assuredly flow as soon as the slave trade was broken and when, in a flight of fantasy, a line of American colonies were to stretch down the African coast.

Washington at this time was ripe for colonial fantasies. Congress was about to pass a bill to set up an agency in West Africa, very similar to the British one in Sierra Leone, for receiving cargoes of freed slaves intercepted by U.S. naval vessels. The American Colonization Society wanted to merge this government agency with their own future settlement of free blacks, but certain groups in Congress, who were opposed on constitutional grounds to any form of colonies, managed to block this plan in law. Whereupon President Monroe hit on an ingenious compromise. He arranged that the two government agents in charge of recaptured slaves should at the same time serve as agents of the American Colonization Society, while the labourers and mechanics required for the recaptive station should be those free blacks wishing to start a colony.

The man chosen to act as agent both for the government and the society, was Samuel Bacon, aged thirty-eight, and an episcopal clergyman. Like Mills before him and others that followed him, Bacon regarded life as a sombre pilgrimage. He too had a pious biographer, Yehudi Ashmun, who later played a major part in the founding of Liberia.

A New Englander of the middle class, like most of these clerical colonists, Bacon had dabbled in several careers before entering the ministry. He had worked as a schoolmaster, served as a captain in the United States Marines, taken part in the war of 1812, and fought a duel. About 1816, when he was thirty-four-years-old, he developed the usual symptoms of a revivalist hysteria, and his biographer reports with apparent approval how Bacon was driven almost mad with guilt when riding a horse on the Sabbath. He first became interested in the colonization plan at free state Sunday Schools, where he specialized in a kind of morbid arithmetic. 'If a miserable soul could come from Hell and tell you of the unheard of and unexpected torment, it found there, you would all fall upon your trembling knees ... So many are dying in the world that learned people say, sixty persons die every minute. They are dying as fast as you can say dead, dead, dead, dead. Four persons are supposed to have died, while I was saying those words...' Bacon helped to establish twenty-six Sunday Schools. He became an Episcopal clergyman and was sent on missionary work for a Bible society. His energy, and perhaps his military background, convinced the American Colonization Society of his fitness to serve in Africa.

According to his biographer, Bacon's 'breast seemed to be a sanctuary hallowed by the constant residence of the most devout and sublimated affections', while 'the most natural employment of his thoughts was prayer, and their most delightful exercise, praise.' He was also irascible (even Ashmun admits that), practical, hard-working and rather neurotic. He was tall, energetic and strong—at least until he went to the West Coast of Africa.

Samuel Bacon with two other white agents and eighty-nine free black emigrants left New York on the *Elizabeth* on January 31st, 1820. The sailing of the *Mayflower* in reverse had provided a local sensation. When five or six thousand New York Negroes thronged the bank of the North River, Bacon feared that the crowd would plunge into the water, and had to create a diversion by holding a prayer meeting near by. All we know of the voyage comes from the journal of Daniel Coker, a Negro from Baltimore, who was chaplain to the Methodists among the settlers. As unofficial second-in-command, Coker shared the anxieties about life in unknown Africa. 'Mr Samuel Bacon and I sat up late last night', he reported on February 19th, 'poring over our plan of a town.' The only mishap of the voyage occurred the following week when a dog owned by a Negro emigrant fought with the captain's dog to the wrath of both owners. The settlers grew angry, the captain called for his pistols, and Mills had to intervene before the captain was pacified and the settlers went below deck. Afterwards, a weeping Bacon cried, 'Brother Coker, this is an awful judgment come upon us; come let us go below and have religious worship. Bacon later told Coker how lucky the expedition was to have him

(Coker) as middle link between the white and coloured people, to which Coker replied, politely enough, that Bacon only wanted 'a sable skin to make him an African'. At Freetown, Bacon admired the native Africans: 'The sickly and depressed countenance of a Philadelphia coloured man is not to be seen amongst them,' he wrote, and licked his lips at the missionary prospects— 'Oh what a field of evangelical labour!'

The American government had intended to send a naval vessel to visit Sherbro before the settlers and to buy some suitable land for their arrival. Unhappily the chosen vessel was meanwhile diverted to some other task on the coast, so that the settlers on the *Elizabeth*, like the pioneers at Sierra Leone, were faced with the need to buy land before they could build. To make matters worse, they were greeted and deluded by the rascally John Kizell who explained, with oily professions of welcome, that he had bought land at Campelar and built huts for their shelter.

Bacon was taken in by Kizell's apparent sincerity and agreed with gratitude that the party should stay at the huts until they had purchased land of their own. 'I was received with joy by Mr Kizell and his people,' Bacon wrote in his diary. 'He wept as we walked together to his house. I dined with him on fish and rice, dressed with palm oil ... Mr Kizell is a pious man.'

After disembarking their goods the settlers found that Campelar was marshy, fetid and dense with mangrove swamps. While Kizell imported his drinking water from the mainland, the settlers had to drink from the stagnant marshes. The huts were poor and there was no fresh food.

The *Elizabeth* was too big to approach the island, so that supplies had to be ferried to and fro in a schooner. This took a further exhausting two weeks. Meanwhile, Samuel Crozer, another representative of the American Colonization Society, resumed the abandoned work of bargaining with the chiefs. He met no success. The chiefs were eager for presents, but did not want the settlers on their own ancestral land. Moreover, Kizell, who acted throughout as interpreter, had equally cogent reasons for keeping the settlers at Campelar.

Like the early settlers in Sierra Leone, the colonists on the *Elizabeth* had arrived at the wrong time of year. What with arguments over the purchase of land, and the long delays for unloading, they were still without proper protection when the rains began. By early in April, fifteen people were ill. On the 6th of the month, Bacon wrote:

> We now have twenty-one sick of a fever ... I have heard the complaints of the people today, because there is no good water to be had on the island—because they were brought to this place—because I did not take possession of the land by force—because the people are visited with sickness—because there is not fresh meat, sugar, molasses, flour ... because I have not shoes and clothing for them, because I cannot give them better tobacco—because the palaver is not over ...

and so on.

As more men got sick, more work devolved on to Bacon: prescribing medicines, building houses, unloading the schooner, rowing a boat and hauling the goods inshore. Without stockings, sometimes barefoot, often without either hat or coat, he worked from dawn till late at night, on a diet of ship's bread, salt meat and water. 'And yet, blessed be God, I continue in health,' he wrote. But he did not continue so for long.

By April 13th, only six men were still healthy. On the 15th Crozer died, and on the 17th there were only two fit men, who both had to be employed in the maddening, vain palavers with the chiefs. But the chiefs and the jackal Kizell bided their time until the settlement was destroyed by disease and the stores would be theirs for the picking.

On April 8th, 1820, scarcely two months since he had left New York, Bacon wrote in his notebook: 'As regards myself, I counted the cost of engaging in this service before I left America. I came to these shores to die, and anything better than death is better than I expected.' On the 16th, he felt ill, took an emetic and prepared himself for the fever which soon followed.

Lying delirious on his sick-bed, Bacon heard that a ship had arrived from Sierra Leone with a doctor among the company. The settlers begged in vain for the doctor to come ashore and treat their sick, but the captain agreed to take Bacon away next morning. The incident that follows sounds like the nightmare of a feverish man.

The next morning, Bacon was carried into a small boat and rowed out to meet the ship. The time was an hour before that agreed for a rendezvous. But on the approach of Bacon's boat, the ship drew up her anchor, and set sail for Sierra Leone. Bacon ordered the men at the oars to overtake her, and thanks to the lightness of the wind, they managed at first to keep up speed. 'A press of sail was, however, set; and though followed at a moderate distance for several hours, the vessel at length ran so far ahead as to set the exertions of the boatman at defiance.' The fevered Bacon had spent six hours in the scorching sun, with no more covering than a light umbrella, and the boat was now miles from home. They sheltered the night on the Plantain Islands and rowed all next day, again without shelter, until they came to Cape Shilling. Here an English family treated Bacon with kindness, but fever, aggravated by two days out in an open boat, had sentenced him to death. Since there were no fellow divines at Bacon's side, we lack the usual uplifting account of his last pious words and comportment. The date, however, was May 2nd. He had gone to those shores to die, and received no better than he expected.

There was little hope of survival for those who were left at Campelar. With the white Americans dead or escaped, the leadership of the settlement went to Daniel Coker, who fought hard to maintain its discipline and morale. He harangued the settlers and gave religious instruction to the natives. But the former had lost all heart for a life on that sickly and wretched island, while the latter had grown so mercenary that they demanded fees for having attended Sunday School. An American naval officer who called at the island on October 18th, 1820, wrote that Coker, whom he esteemed, was in a state of despondency and was shortly to quit the settlement. And indeed, soon afterwards, Coker and most of the rest returned to Fourah Bay in Sierra Leone, where the British had offered them a refuge.*

The first settlement in Sierra Leone, made in 1789, had lasted only two years. The first settlement of the American Colonization Society had lasted less than two months. The Americans had learned nothing from the Sierra Leone experience. They made almost all the same mistakes. They had come to bad land, at the wrong time of year, and without getting agreement from the chiefs. Men like Mills, Burgess and Bacon had no knowledge of Africa, and were too obtuse and bigoted to learn.

At their next attempt at colonization, farther down the coast, the Americans made fewer mistakes, and perhaps more important they found as their agent a man with a genius for the work— Jehudi Ashmun.

* Some of the refugees from the Sherbro Island settlement were to accompany the expedition next year to what was to become Liberia. The admirable Coker stayed on in Sierra Leone. In his huge *Political and Legislative History of Liberia* (New York, 1947), vol. I, p. 137, Charles Henry Huberich called it 'a signal mistake on the part of the American Colonization Society not to appoint Coker to some position of honour and trust in the new settlement, and thus secure a continuance of the services of one of the most loyal, intelligent and capable of the early settlers. It was but the first instance of the uniform policy of the Society not to entrust power to men of colour . . .'

Chapter Three

There has never been an hour or a minute, no, not even when the balls were flying round my head, when I could wish myself again in America.

(The Reverend Lott Carey, one of the black pioneers in Liberia)

The surviving American settlers, late in 1821, were still living as refugees in Sierra Leone. Nearly two years had passed since the *Elizabeth* sailed from New York, yet the American Colonization Society still had no colony and the United States Government still had no station for the recaptured slaves. The members of the society board were not dismayed by these setbacks; indeed, the fact that so many lives had been lost in the opening, blundering venture only made them more resolute to succeed. Nor had President Monroe forgotten his project for the recaptured slaves. Late in 1821 he sent four white agents and thirty-three blacks to set up another West African colony, instructing them to choose anywhere but on Sherbro Island. The new mission went first to Sierra Leone where, predictably, two of the white agents died and a third fled in terror of dying. The job of chief agent to the government and the society was given to Dr Eli Ayres, a surgeon from Baltimore, who was joined by a naval lieutenant, Robert Stockton. Impatient and stubborn, these men resolved to buy land for Liberia at Cape Mesurado on the Grain Coast, 225 miles southeast of Sierra Leone.

Cape Mesurado, which was to become Monrovia, is the end of a peninsula between the river of that name and the ocean. In shape it is similar to the Sierra Leone settlement and the settlers, in both cases, sited their town on the north, or inland side of the cape.

When Ayres and Stockton landed on December 12th, 1821, the cape was 'covered with a lofty and dense forest, entangled with vines and brushwood; the haunt of savage beasts, and through which the Barbarians were accustomed to cut their narrow and winding pathway to the coast'.

These 'Barbarians' were well accustomed to white men. The Normans are said to have come here in the fourteenth century and the Portuguese brought a prisoner from this coast to show off to their king in 1461. The Portuguese gave the coast some of its names, such as Mesurado, and introduced oranges, coconut palms, pineapples and the tobacco plant. Then came the English and the Dutch, who sweated in thick northern clothes but were amused that the natives constantly washed their bodies with water and soap. The Europeans wanted gold, ivory, slaves and Malagueta peppers, the 'grains of Paradise' that have given the coast its name. The Grain Coast was also well known for the Kru tribesmen or Kru-boys, the sharp-witted, adventurous sailors who still provide the deck hands for the cargo ships of West Africa.

The two principal tribes around Cape Mesurado were the Mamba and the De.* In dealing with them, the Dutch and English normally went armed and took hostages, but the French Chevalier des Marchais thought this was quite unnecessary. After a visit in 1723 he was full of praise for the natives:

> They are intelligent, shrewd, true-speaking, know perfectly their own interests, and like their old friends the Normans, comport themselves with address and even politeness. Their lands are carefully cultivated, they do everything with order and regularity, and they labour vigorously when they choose, which, unfortunately, is not as often as could be wished. As these people deal no further in slaves than by selling their convicted criminals to the Europeans, the country is not depopulated like those in which the princes continually traffic in their subjects.

* In writing the names of tribes I use the normal modern spelling, e.g. De, Vai, Mende, Temne, etc. In quoting other authors I have left their spelling unchanged.

Nearly one hundred years after des Marchais's visit, the Dei and the Mamba encountered a new breed of white man. Early in 1821 the agents of the United States Government and the American Colonization Society had asked the Mesurado chiefs for permission to settle. King Peter, the principal chief, had given a definite though courteous refusal. Now Ayres and Stockton returned for a new palaver, convinced by their British friends in Sierra Leone that Cape Mesurado was just the place for a colony. On December 12th, 1821, they landed, asked for King Peter and while they waited for him gave an impromptu lecture on civilization. King Peter at last arrived, accepted presents of rum and tobacco, but stated that he could not sell the Cape as 'his women would cry aplenty'. However, he consented to talk again with his visitors on the following day.

The Americans waited two days in neglect. On the third day, Stockton grew angry and persuaded Ayres that they should beard the unmannerly king in his own village six miles away. After cutting a path through the jungle and wading through several marshes and streams, the two Americans reached the village to find an enraged King Peter. 'What do you want that land for?' said the king, who clearly had not believed in the American Colonization Society. Other villagers accused the white men of wanting to stir up wars, of kidnapping and trying to stop the slave trade. Angry and bitterly disappointed, the Americans had resource to unconventional business methods. Lieutenant Stockton pulled out a pistol, cocked it and gave it to Ayres with instructions to shoot if necessary. He then aimed another pistol at King Peter's head. Having thus ensured an attentive audience, he lectured the company on the advantages of a settlement. He lifted his arm in an oratorical flourish and just at that moment, the sun broke through the clouds. This *coup de theâtre* may not have impressed the Africans—who no doubt kept their eyes on the guns—but it did impress a generation of pamphleteers, parsons and lecturers for the American Colonization Society.

The Stockton approach achieved success of a kind. On December 15th, King Peter and five chiefs sold Cape Mesurado by deed, in return for guns, powder, beds, clothes, mirrors, food, rum and tobacco, all worth less than three hundred dollars. The two Americans were inordinately pleased with themselves but the deed was, in fact, quite valueless. King Peter did not want the settlers; he hoped, and later almost managed, to see them off by force; the deal had been made quite literally at pistol point. It is odd that these pious Christians of the American Colonization Society, so ready to mouth their concern for the plight of the Negro race, should have behaved towards this African king with such brutal and ignorant arrogance.

The American Colonization Society named its colony Liberia, after liberty, and its capital, yet unbuilt, was christened Monrovia, after the President. But Monroe, though the colony's godfather, had no right to give it subsidies or offer protection on behalf of the United States. The government of Liberia consisted of a group of private citizens in the Washington offices of the American Colonization Society. They drew up its constitution and framed its laws, which were based on the United States' laws with such modifications as the banning of 'spirituous liquor'. Even the grand town plan of Monrovia was drawn up by a Washington architect.

The new settlers and some survivors from Sherbro Island were ferried from Sierra Leone in a series of trips on two small schooners. While land was being cleared on the cape itself, the first Liberians sheltered on Perseverance Island, a mere patch of rock off the shore. The first clash with the natives came when the settlers were still on Perseverance Island. A British naval vessel carrying recaptured slaves for Sierra Leone was wrecked on the coast opposite Cape Mesurado, whereupon, following West Coast custom, the local Dei rushed in to loot or 'salvage' the cargo. These African wreckers seldom harmed seamen and there is no proof that the crew of the ship was in danger of their lives, but the settlers, not knowing African custom, decided to intervene. From Mesurado Island they fired a charge of shot into the natives, killing and wounding seven men. Moreover, the flame from the cannon's fuse set fire to the settlers' storehouse, destroying arms, ammunition, trade goods and food to the value of three thousand dollars.

This one rash shot had infuriated the natives and wiped out half of the colony's own supplies.

The settlers moved onto the cape itself on April 28th, 1822, and cheered up their spirits by holding a solemn ceremony. They worked quickly, but not quite quickly enough, to build a proper settlement before the rains, and morale declined again when the rains started a few days later. Few of Monrovia's thirty houses possessed an adequate roof; the fever broke out with the rains and, worst of all, the settlers were menaced by hundreds of angry natives. Even the agent, Dr Ayres, thought it prudent to leave for Sierra Leone and timid settlers asked to accompany him. There was much hesitation even among the more brave. Then Elijah Johnson, one of the most respected Negroes, who had survived the disastrous settlement on the Sherbro, rallied the waverers with a brief, fine speech: 'Two years long have I sought a home; here I have found one, here I remain.' His hope and courage were justified when, on August 8th, the brig *Strong* arrived off Monrovia with thirty-five settlers, fresh supplies and Jehudi Ashmun, the strange young trader who was to create a nation. For the next six years he was to be the Liberian general, governor, arbitrator, economist and chronicler. Pale and delicate, he survived war, fever and despair on that daunting coast where much stronger men died or gave up in a month. In piety and fanaticism he resembled those other Americans, Mills and Bacon, but Ashmun had some extra quality that distinguishes the great from the worthy. He was restless, frustrated, vainglorious and imaginative; above all, was a leader, and he had good luck and knew how to exploit it. If Liberia were now a big and important state, Ashmun would rank in the African history books as one of the great pioneers.

What we know of him comes from his own copious books, tracts, articles and dispatches, and from the biography by his friend Ralph Gurley, the secretary of the society. Ashmun was born in Champlain, New York, in 1794. Of a scholarly bent, he specialized in the classics, and by 1815 had gained a job teaching Latin and Greek at a missionary seminary. 'My genius and habits, much of the time,' Ashmun later wrote of this period, 'were decidedly of the ascetick cast. I determined not only to forsake the gay, but the civilized world; and spend my life among distant savages.' This doleful self-mortification was fashionable at the time but hints remain that Ashmun's habits were not quite as 'ascetick' as he pretended.

In 1815 he met his future wife, then promptly abandoned her for another girl—'a vision of singular brightness ... an image of unrivalled loveliness. The chain that had been worn uneasily, was exchanged for the golden links of enchantment; but alas! Honour and religion bade him sever the bond which he wished to be eternal.' In October 1818 Ashmun married the first girl who had been waiting in New York. We shall probably never know what went on between the passionate Ashmun and his 'image of un-rivalled loveliness', but it certainly outraged the seminary. When Ashmun returned from New York (his wife had gone down to Virginia), lewd rumours were rife and the students boycotted his lectures. 'I have blotted my character as a Christian,' he wrote in his lachrymose journal. 'The Foreign Missionary Society, I am certain, would not at present admit me into their service.' Disgraced and in debt, he left to join his wife in the South.

His journal reveals good earthly worries as well as the usual religious breast-beating:

> I am now twenty-five years of age; almost three from college; have no profession; and my employment has been such since I left college, as to force me to habits unfavourable to the acquisition of one. I am involved in debt, possess neither book nor money, and have a delicate and beloved wife to provide for ... My soul is full of carnal desires and worldly attachments ... Suffer me not to be reduced to poverty and want, lest I be diverted from my great object. I desire not wealth without an increase of grace.

Wealth, if not grace, eluded Ashmun during the next three restless years. He first got a job as a tutor to young ladies; then as a journalist for an Episcopalian magazine. He studied medicine for a few months, abandoned it and took up law. In 1820 he started

117

to write for the *African Intelligencer* which purported to be a general magazine but was in fact a propaganda sheet for the American Colonization Society. As a journalist, Ashmun wrote many articles on the life and death of Bacon, and later, making a blunder all too common with journalists, he decided to turn the articles into a book. His friends advised against the project, but Ashmun convinced himself that the book would enjoy good sales and help to pay off his debts. Ashmun was so convinced of this, and the publishers so unconvinced, that he borrowed more money to meet the printing costs, and ended by making a loss on the book.

Humiliated by failure and persecuted by duns, Ashmun resolved to make a journey to Africa. He knew, from Bacon's fate, of the dangers of West Africa, but there is no suggestion that Ashmun hankered after a martyr's death. Indeed, his ambitions were largely commercial. He would earn his fare and a fee by taking a party of emigrants for the American Colonization Society, but once in Africa he would act for a Baltimore trading house. In a mood of what he called 'mercantile mania' Ashmun hoped that the society would grant him monopoly privileges on Liberia's imports and exports, perhaps even providing a packet line to transport the goods. Since Ashmun did not intend to stay in West Africa any longer than necessary, he agreed, with reluctance, to bring his wife on the trip although he feared for her health. They left in the *Strong* in May 1822, with a party of freed slaves from Georgia.

When Ashmun arrived in the middle of August he found that both white agents had left, that Monrovia was simply a forest clearing, that there were no provisions to spare for the new settlers and no shelter in the height of the rainy season. As if these worries were not sufficient, the settlement was menaced by many hundreds of angry Africans, armed with muskets, who had made known their intention to attack. 'Of the native Americans,' Ashmun later recalled, 'twenty-seven, when not sick, were able to bear arms; but they were wholly untrained to their use; and capable, in their present undisciplined state of making but a very feeble defence indeed.'

From the day he set foot in the settlement, Ashmun abandoned his hope of a trading venture because the natives of the interior, from whom he must buy his goods, were bent on war rather than business. If he wished to stay in Liberia, all his time and energies would have to be spent on fortifying the settlement. Ashmun had no obligation to stay. He was not yet a paid agent of the society. Nobody instructed him to take on the job of Ayres, the departed agent. To stay meant risking the lives of his wife and himself. But stay he did, and the settlers appear to have welcomed him as a leader.

In spite of his frail appearance and his scholarly, even retiring past, Ashmun quickly proved himself as a man of action. His overriding concern during the first few months in Liberia was the military threat from the natives. He first tried to counter this by diplomatic missions to some of the principal kings, but he found them cool and suspicious. The kings had never wanted the settlement; they had signed a treaty under duress; and they could not understand the Liberians—these eccentric persons—enthusiastic, thin, fever-stricken white men, who loathed drink, debauchery and the slave trade, and English-speaking Christian Negroes dressed in European fashion.

Ashmun guessed that the kings were planning a war and he urged on the settlers to prepare defences. The first necessity was to clear the bush on the three land sides of the settlement, so that the enemy could not sneak up close for a charge. While most of the settlers were employed on this work, another squad built a martello tower, to serve as the main fort and arsenal. In the intervals from this work, the settlers were drilled by Ashmun who also conscripted and trained troops from among the friendliest natives.

Within a month, Ashmun had finished the basic fortifications. His plan of defence 'was to station five heavy guns at the different angles of a triangle which should circumscribe the whole settlement—each of the angles resting on a point of ground sufficiently commanding to enfilade two sides of the triangle and sweep a considerable extent of ground behind the lines'. The one brass cannon, mounted on rails, was placed by the martello tower which was fortified by a barricade of stakes. It was a good plan of defence as was proved in the subsequent battle, and Ashmun took care to explain it thoroughly to the settlers, in case he was killed or laid low.

In his history of these early days, Ashmun acknowledged his gratitude to God for sparing him from disease long enough to build the basic defences. A scientist would observe that he was spared during the incubation period of his first bout of malaria. He came down with this disease* in the middle of September, just over two weeks after his arrival. Three days after this, his wife became ill with a far more serious fever. She was always a delicate woman—so delicate that she should not have gone to the coast—and her sick-bed was 'a couch literally dripping with water, which a roof of thatch was unable to exclude'.

The wretched Ashmun, exhausted by heat and work, himself shaking with fever and racked by malarial pains, kept watch four nights by the bedside of his wife. Theirs had not been a love match, but Ashmun was fond of his wife, and felt remorse for having brought her to Africa. By the day of her death—September 15th, 1822—Ashmun was himself completely delirious with the fever. From then until the first week in November, he was 'so entirely debilitated in body and mind, as to be nearly incapable of motion, and insensible to everything except the consciousness of suffering'. He could not walk without support. Moreover, he was so depressed by his wife's death and by fears of his own that he could not help in the work of administration. The leadership of Liberia devolved on to those Negro elders who had not themselves come down with the fever.

When Ashmun shook off his illness during the first week of November, he learned that the native attack was expected any day. The chiefs Bromley, Todo, Governor, Konko, Jimmy, Gray, Long, Peter, George and Willy had added their warriors to King Peter's army which had assembled on Bushrod Island about four miles from Monrovia, and also at camps in the St Paul's river. The natives numbered about eight hundred men, armed with muskets, spears and swords. Against them, Ashmun could match hardly a score of settler troops with a few unreliable mercenaries.

* Or possibly yellow fever. See Part III.

Whether trusting in his defences or merely trying a bluff, Ashmun sent a messenger to the enemy camp to say: 'He was perfectly apprised of their hostile deliberations, notwithstanding their pains to conceal them; and that, if they proceeded to bring war upon the Americans, without even asking to settle their differences in a friendly manner, they would dearly learn what it was to fight white men.'*

Ashmun had little hope that the threats would prove effective and he did not relax his vigilance. The settlers were obliged to man guard pickets throughout the night, as well as to do fatigues by day. On Saturday and Sunday nights, November 10th, 11th and 12th, the exhausted men had to go without sleep, because Ashmun's native spies brought news of impending attack. The spies were correct and the vigilance had been justified. At dawn on November 11th, a group of the enemy emerged from the forest sixty yards away, fired their muskets and rushed forward, waving their spears. They attacked and seized the westernmost of the three forts that Ashmun had built to cover his flank. The settlers fell back before they could fire their cannon and then ran in panic to the martello tower.

Had the natives charged the martello tower they could have destroyed the settlement; but their warriors stopped to plunder the settlers' huts they had overrun in their charge. During these minutes, Ashmun and the Reverend Lott Carey, his Negro lieutenant, rallied the settlers' courage and fired a charge of ball and grapeshot into the enemy rank.

The natives first recoiled, then paused to pick up their dead and wounded.

The Americans, perceiving their advantage [wrote Ashmun in a blood-curdling passage], now regained possession of the western post, and instantly brought the long nine to the whole line of the enemy. Imagination can scarcely figure to itself a throng of human beings in a more capital state of exposure to the destructive power of the machinery of modern

* The Africans used the phrase 'white men' for civilized people of any colour.

warfare! Eight hundred men were here pressed shoulder to shoulder, in so compact a form that a child might easily walk upon their heads from one end of the mass to the other, presenting in their rear a breadth of rank equal to twenty or thirty men, and all exposed to a gun of great power raised on a platform, at only thirty to sixty yards distance! Every shot literally spent its force in a solid mass of living human flesh! Their fire suddenly terminated. A savage yell was raised which filled the dismal forest with a momentary horror. It gradually died away; and the whole host disappeared.

According to Ashmun, the settlers had routed their enemy with a fighting force of only thirty-five men, of whom six were 'native youths not 16 years of age' and half did not take part in the battle. Their casualties, mostly non-combatants, amounted to four dead, four wounded and seven children missing. The casualties of the enemy were too huge for a proper estimate, but Ashmun reports that a large canoe needed ten to twelve trips to ferry their dead and wounded across the Mesurado River.

Once more Ashmun tried to treat with the natives, who again complained that the Americans had no right to the land they had seized. King Peter's army then launched a second attack on the colony on December 1st, making repeated charges against the martello tower. But Ashmun had laid strong fortifications. 'In this conflict of scarcely an hour and a half, the quantity of shot lodged in the paling, and actually thrown within the lines, is altogether incredible; and that it took effect in so few cases can only be regarded as the effect of the special guardianship of Divine Providence.' One settler only was killed in this second attack, and two seriously wounded. Ashmun himself was unhurt, although three bits of shot passed through his clothing; he must have been doubly grateful for his escape after seeing what went on in the hospital:

There was at this time little surgical knowledge, less skill, and absolutely no instruments—not a lancet or a probe in the settlement! Its little dispensary had no lack of James's powders, and stores of febrifuges—but for medicating broken bones, and extracting fragments of pot-metal and copper ship-bolts from the shattered limbs of the Colonists, there had been no provision whatever. A dull penknife and common razor were substituted in the place of the first, and a pinning wire made to answer the purpose of the last.

These two victories over the natives gave the settlers confidence at last that they belonged and would stay in Liberia. 'Such had been their hardships and distressing suspense for the last twenty days,' wrote Ashmun of the second battle, 'that the first volley of the enemy's fire brought sensible relief to every breast; for it gave assurance that the time had arrived which was to put a period to their anxieties.'

The settlers had been fighting for their existence and Ashmun said of them that 'not the most veteran troops could have behaved with more coolness or shown greater firmness'. These fighting forefathers are still regarded with reverence in Liberia. December 1st is Matilda Newport Day after the settler lady who fired a cannon at the foe by dropping a coal from her pipe into the powder. Or so the legend runs. The only witness who left a written account, Ashmun, did not mention Matilda Newport, but singled out for especial praise the Reverend Lott Carey. It was he who rallied the frightened forces during the first assault and who tried his primitive surgery on the wounded. Born a slave in Richmond, Virginia, Carey had ransomed himself and family with the money he earned as manager of a warehouse. Even as a slave he studied hard—reading Smith's *Wealth of Nations* at work—and afterwards got ordained as a minister. His reasons for going to Africa were simple: 'I am an African, and I wish to go to a country where I shall be estimated by my merits, not by my complexion.'

In a letter to the United States, Carey compared these first Liberians to those ancient Jews who, rebuilding their city, 'grasped a weapon in one hand while they laboured with the other'. The same comparison could be made with the modern Jews who, building Israel, launched two punitive raids on the Arabs. The

123

Liberians, like the Israelis, had no real right to the territory they had occupied, but justified their presence by their persecution abroad and by their claim to superior civilization. Skill, firepower and the will to survive were on the side of Liberia—and of Israel; few spared any sympathy for the Vei or the Palestinian Arabs.

Chapter Four

We have preaching every Sunday, and prayer meetings every night through the week. Many of the recaptured Africans come to be baptized and we expect more shortly; they appear to be more diligent than the Americans.

    (A settler in Liberia writing to his former owner in the United States)

Liberia, by February 1823, was a confident little country. King Peter and his allies had retreated into their villages after two colossal defeats, and the settlement could at last relax its vigilance. The wounded settlers were not yet back at work but could at least get around with their slings and crutches. Most of the children who had been kidnapped in November were given back to the settlers early in the New Year. Although Ashmun had predicted a dreadful fate for them, the children in fact had been so well treated, indeed even spoilt, by the natives, that they did not want to return to their more puritanical parents. The settlers now had fifty houses of their own as well as some well-thatched huts to shelter the next batch of immigrants who were expected in the summer. There was little food left in the store but a good supply of tobacco, to trade in the interior for goats, bullocks, chickens and vegetables.

Ashmun, whose valour had helped to preserve Liberia, was one of those men who feel at their best in times of danger and difficulty, but who fret when things go well. His journals and letters in 1822 had been full of excitement, energy, even flashes of humour, but in 1823 a whining note reappeared. 'It is not my nature to complain with too much facility,' he wrote on March 23rd, and then went on to complain with great facility for a page ... 'But think you see a young man formed for society, separated almost entirely from the civilized and Christian world; his constitution broken with a fever of six months; his only earthly comforter snatched away.' It is easy for us to sympathize with his misery but one should remark that Ashmun, Bacon, Mills and countless others both in Liberia and Sierra Leone had known exactly what to expect in West Africa. Bacon had gone there expecting to die; Ashmun, Bacon's biographer, had wanted to 'forsake the civilized world' and spend his life among savages. If they did not like it, they had only themselves to blame.

However, Ashmun's moods of self-pity were rare and sometimes, at least, fully justified. On May 23rd, 1823, Dr Ayres, the official agent, returned to resume his command. We know that Ashman had a poor opinion of Ayres, who had fled from Liberia one year before and had tried to persuade the settlers to go with him. It was Ayres who had obtained the botched and useless treaty with King Peter, which had been the origin of the war. Now Ayres came back after the fighting was finished, prepared to take up his post once more. These reflections alone gave Ashmun good reason for chagrin. Still worse news came in letters from the American Colonization Society. While the government and the society thanked Ashmun for his services, they declined to give him any official appointment; they did not fix any sum to compensate him for the services he had rendered, and they declined to pay for the goods he had ordered on their behalf.

The managers of the society had never approved of Ashmun, and they asked Ayres to strip him of all authority in the settlement. Most men with Ashmun's grounds for grievance would have left Liberia in a huff. However, Ashmun still dreamed of making a fortune by trade; he still hoped for compensation by the society. Perhaps he guessed that when things got difficult, Dr Ayres would once again flee from this dangerous colony, leaving him as its ruler.

Deprived of official duties, Ashmun threw his energies into trade. Like Zachary Macaulay in Sierra Leone, he was tempted by avarice. Unlike Macauley, he recognized this fault and hypocrisy in himself:

> The pursuit of gain has presented attractions which I never discovered before. This is the perversion of a purpose, originally good. I have debts to pay; and money must be raised. But once given up to the pursuit, my thoughts directly extended themselves to other views of personal aggrandisement and slothful self-indulgence... And where money is the main drift of existence, how does the vile passion stifle in its birth every noble sentiment of the soul.

One might imagine from this complaint that Ashmun's life was entirely devoted to trade and to enjoyment. Yet he wrote essays, articles and a series of rules of conduct, such as: 'To eat meat, fish or fowl but at one meal in twenty-four hours', and 'To despise all wit but the pure attick', and 'To prefer the society of dead authors of eminence, to that of living actors of simple mediocrity'—an easy rule to obey in Monrovia where there were no actors, good or bad. His industry was prodigious. Every day he devoted four hours to the study of Blackstone's *Commentaries*. Anyone who has lived on the West Coast knows how hard it is to devote four hours to a simple detective story, let alone Blackstone, especially after a long day of trading, writing journals, and reading philosophical and religious books. Yet Ashmun could write, in April 1823: 'I am burdened with my own sloth and stupidity in my Heavenly Master's work. Alas! Alas! my sincerity in prayer, in reading God's word, in religious conversation.'

Ashmun did not remain long out of office. The bad-tempered and tactless Dr Ayres offended the colonists almost at once by imposing the town plan drawn up in Washington. Those settlers, who had built and fought for their own houses, understandably did not want to move. They resented the new group of settlers from America who were given equal food and supplies. The discontent was serious by the time of the first rains, when Ayres caught fever and once more fled—this time not to return to Africa. Ashmun once more became agent by default.

In 1822, when they were fighting for survival, the settlers had proved disciplined and hard working. In 1823, their mood was tired, carping and indolent, making them disinclined to till the land, or to do public works, or to justify their rations of food from the stores of the society. Ashmun was eager to please the society, and therefore persisted with Ayres's stern policy. He went ahead with re-allocations of land. He insisted that men spend two days a week in public works, and threatened to stop the rations of any defaulter. Discontent grew into riot when settlers raided the storehouse and wrote letters to the society accusing Ashmun of graft.

Isolated and angry, Ashmun scolded the rebels for their recklessness. 'You have nothing growing in your fields—not a week's supply of vegetation in prospect. You feel the pinching hand of want today. It will be worse tomorrow. Continue to neglect your duty, and it will either disperse you up and down the coast or destroy you by starvation.'

The leader of the malcontents was the same Lott Carey who had come out to Africa with Ashmun, fought so gallantly by his side and behaved as a model of loyalty for the settlement. Ashmun reported his difficulties to the board of the American Colonization Society, who in turn demanded a stern hand for the settlers. They revoked Lott Carey's licence to preach, criticized Ashmun for excessive leniency and told him in future to punish any insolence with summary fines or imprisonment. If the need arose he should call in support from ships of the United States Navy.

By the time these instructions arrived, Ashmun had been forced out of Monrovia. The majority of the settlers were by now viciously hostile, and rose in armed revolt in March 1824 after Ashmun had rationed the colony's food supply. Helpless in the face of this popular agitation, he decided to leave for the Cape Verde Islands, which are kinder in climate but not too far from the coast to prevent continuing trade. Before leaving Liberia, Ashmun drew up a bitter testament to defend himself against all accusers. 'Whoever says, after my absence, that for all my sacrifices, labour and suffering in this Cape, I have received one farthing of emolument, excepting only a valuable present of clothing by the

128

Oswego, asserts a falsehood which will one day cover him with shame.' The food served at the agent's house had never 'made the dinner of a colonist a cabbage-leaf the less'. The testament once or twice breaks out into shrill insults against individual colonists such as 'B.J., a man without principles who, Devil-like, dared to belch his scandal into my face'.

Ashmun's departure from Liberia on April 1st, 1824, was a melancholy occasion. A few days before, while trying to extract a poisoned tooth, he had ruptured an artery in his mouth and could not stop the bleeding. While he was in this wretched state, thieves broke into his stores and robbed him of property worth $175.

The society and the United States Government were so vexed by the news of the insurrection that they sent a representative to Liberia on a naval vessel. The man they chose was Ralph R. Gurley, then twenty-six, who had recently joined the society as a fundraiser. A serene, gentle man, with a tolerance rare among puritans, he was to devote his long life to Liberia and the society.

When Gurley embarked on the U.S.S. *Porpoise*, he seems to have shared the general doubts about Ashmun's competence. The complaints of the settlers had been given currency by officers of the United States Navy who had touched at Mesurado, soon after Ashmun's departure, and heard 'the rumors of the weak and the calumnies of the wicked'. However, Gurley was anxious to hear both sides of the story and sailed first of all to the Cape Verde Islands for an interview with Ashmun. The two men formed an instant respect and liking for one another. In his biography of Ashmun, Gurley wrote twelve years later that he recalled his first impressions of a 'storm-shaken but self-contained spirit ... towering like an eagle against the storm and thundercloud, and already catching glimpses of the purity and brightness of the Heavens'. Less lyrically but more to the point, Gurley said that his 'favourable impressions of Mr Ashmun's character, received at our first interview, were sharpened by each successive conversation ... not a shadow of evidence existed to substantiate the charges that had been urged against him.'

After three weeks at Porto Prayo, Gurley decided to reappoint Ashmun as the agent of the society, although knowing well that this would not please the managers. Then both men took ship for Liberia where Gurley spent one week and Ashmun stayed on in office. Although Ashmun was still annoyed with the settlers because of their nasty behaviour a few months back, Gurley favoured a policy of conciliation. He took no legal proceedings against the insurgents, he set up a council of settlers to advise on government; he encouraged colonists to take office under the agent, at the same time lecturing them on their duty as citizens in this new republican commonwealth. The managers of the American Colonization Society did not agree with Gurley's policy and would not ratify his reforms, calling instead for punishment of the rebel leaders. But because of the long delays in the transatlantic mails, these instructions did not reach Liberia until they were patently obsolete. By that time Gurley's reforms, carried out by Ashmun his agent, had transformed the volatile settlement into a genial, prosperous community.

The change of sentiment must have begun during the five months of Ashmun's absence. The settlers, under Lott Carey's rule, came to regret their hostility to the agent, not least because they were now deprived of provisions from America. 'The welcome given to Mr Gurley and myself,' wrote Ashmun after returning, 'I at first treated as insincere; but however extravagant in expression, I am now convinced that it was dictated by the heart. Since the 24th of August, I know not that your agent has, in a single instance been treated with disrespect, but every day witnesses some expression of affection and deference.' Many settlers gave up the rations they had been receiving from the society and promised in future to live off their own labours. Most former dissidents expressed their regrets to Ashmun. This change of heart was most noticeable in Lott Carey himself, who had conquered his former 'revolting and unfeeling churlishness' and now bore 'an inimitable air of sweet and profound humility'.

Ashmun exploited the changed mood of the settlers to put through a programme of public works. Within months of his return he had supervised the construction of a stone pier, the improvement of fortifications and the extension of farming land. His copious letters to Washington described the spiritual changes wrought on the settlers, their piety and their 'good character'. The managers of the society were at last convinced, and early in 1825 they appointed Ashmun as permanent agent for the colony, at the same time thanking him for his 'prudence and propriety'.

Ralph Gurley too had been proved right in supporting Ashmun and in taking a lenient policy to the settlers. In 1825, he was voted secretary of the society with a salary of $1,250 a year. Together with Ashmun, he could now work to strengthen, improve and expand the little colony. Reading the history of Liberia, as of Sierra Leone, one is often surprised by the abrupt changes of fortune. Early in 1823, it was happy, united and confident. Early in 1824, it was bitter, rebellious and gloomy. Early in 1825, with the same settlers, under the same agent, it was once again happy, united and confident. Fear, in the West Coast, can spring up as fast as the foliage after the rains, while hope can return as suddenly as blue skies. A clever leader of men, as Ashmun undoubtedly was, understood how to suppress the fears and to nourish the hopes. His next three years of government were an almost complete success.

His position as agent of the society gave Ashmun power over the colony. His second position as United States Government agent for recaptured Africans gave him a large and most welcome revenue from the funds set aside by the Slave Trade Act of 1819. Much of this money was spent on fortifications. Fort Stockton, which had withstood the native assault in 1822, was replaced by the Central Fort, a stout triangular battery. Ashmun placed four twelve-pounder guns in a second battery near the top of Cape Mesurado and a fort with eight gun mounts on Crown Hill. Having protected the colony against natives, pirates and slavers, Ashmun then constructed a camp for the recaptured slaves brought in by the United States Navy. Soon building was extended to other projects not strictly relevant to the Slave Trade Act. The United States Government paid for two warehouses, a grain storehouse, a stone magazine, a schooner and Ashmun's own Agency House, a frame building of yellow pine brought from America and valued at $7,500. The richer among the settlers were obliged to pay a tax for municipal buildings, which soon included two big chapels, five schools and a small colonial library.

Relations with the neighbouring tribes were so improved that Ashmun could invite fifty natives to dine on a bullock and 'very little rum'. But just to be safe, he raised four companies of militia, of which the first in line were 'Captain Barbour's Light Infantry, composed of select young men, completely armed and equipped, highly disciplined (relatively) and consisting of about forty men. Uniform, light blue, faced with white.'

The size of the colony grew with each arrival of settlers from America: 66 in 1825; 182 in 1826; 222 in 1827; 163 in 1828. As the colony progressed, there was proper shelter and food for the new arrivals so that few died from 'initiation fever'. Moreover, Lott Carey had progressed in his medical studies to become a good amateur doctor and surgeon.

Like many governors of Liberia and Sierra Leone, Ashmun berated the settlers for living by trade rather than agriculture. This annoyance was strange since, like Macauley in Sierra Leone, Ashmun was himself a trader by choice and a most unsuccessful farmer. However, as agent of the American Colonization Society he felt in duty bound to promote their plans for plantations of sugar, coffee and cotton. He wrote and published a manual of tropical farming; he gave free advice to farmers on how to improve their crops and he constantly warned of the risks of neglecting agriculture. If the settlers had to rely for their food on the natives of the interior, the price would be bumped up four- or five-fold.

These arguments could not prevail over economic reality. The soil was poor and thin near Monrovia; there were no draught animals in the colony; the rains and the strange pests often destroyed the results of work done painfully under a roasting sun. Moreover, the settlers simply did not enjoy the local cassava, plantains and yams, preferring to pay for expensive imported foods. They kept pigs, goats, chicken and ducks for the home, but were less eager to farm full-time for the market. When an artisan could earn two dollars a day working for someone else, he was not tempted to risk his savings and time on the uncertain fortunes of farming.

Most settlers who could afford to went into trade. They bought goods such as cloth, rum and tobacco from America, and sold them to the interior for African goods. The range of trade can be seen from this advertisement in the first *Liberian Herald* published in 1826:

> Wanted immediately—the following articles, viz., boards, plank, shingle, window glass, nails, crockery, all kinds of hardware, household furniture, cutlery, tobacco, pipes, pound beads, American cottons, ginghams, calicoes, shoes, hose, cambrics, muslins, linens, buttons, thread, combs, butter, lamb and hams. In exchange for which, may be had—camwood, ivory, turtle shell, gold dust, deer, leopard and tiger skins; rice, fowl, fish, goats, sheep and fruits.

This list of goods does not mention alcohol, which suggests that the trader may be the same man who warned the public in the same newspaper that 'any traffic in human blood or spirituous liquors with the natives is a violation of the Constitution'.

Violation was very frequent. As Ashmun explained to the managers, liquor was bound to be smuggled in as long as it proved effective in trade, and he therefore proposed that it should be sold by licensed retailers. The wholesaler of rum and whisky was given a total monopoly and exacted a profit of 300 per cent. Ashmun himself was the wholesaler.

Except for Ashmun there were no white traders, but blacks took to commerce with eagerness. One colonist was amazed to see 'what little time is necessary to qualify, even the youngest, to drive as hard a bargain as any roving merchant from the land of steady habits, with his assortment of tin ware, nutmegs, books or dry goods'. Even the clergy rushed into trade; the good Lott Carey became the representative of a Richmond trading house to whom he sent six thousand pounds of home-grown 'Liberian'

133

coffee. The American buyers were much impressed until it was later revealed that Carey had bought the beans from a visiting merchant ship.

Some of the settlers made very considerable fortunes. One Francis Devaney started in 1823 with $200 as capital which he turned in seven years to assets of $20,000. The Reverend Colson M. Waring developed a business that grossed $70,000. Black capitalism—so frail in the modern United States—flourished in Africa in the 1820s.

Prosperity inspired the decision to widen Liberia's borders. Ashmun acquired Bushrod Island in 1825, by a treaty with King Peter, then a site twenty miles up the St Paul's River, and a station near Stockton Creek to serve as depot for the recaptured slaves. But Ashmun's ambition was not confined to the patch of coast near Liberia. He talked and wrote of a great American empire, devoted to God and freedom, stretching far into West Africa. He justified these imperial dreams by the wickedness of the slave trade, which was carried on within sight of Monrovia. He claimed, with justification, that slavers used kidnapping and piracy to increase their commerce. But Ashmun's work against the slavers was partly inspired by commercial jealousy. 'The purchase money of two hundred slaves has, during this week, been landed in our waters,' he wrote on July 18th, 1825, 'to the incalculable detriment of the colony.' Not only did the sale of slaves increase the price of other native produce, but the slavers paid for their purchases with that unfair currency, rum.

In August of the same year, Ashmun launched an attack against a depot of Spanish slavers whom he regarded as guilty of piracy. On their march down the coast, Ashman and his troops passed another slave factory, from which came the sound of groans and clanking fetters, but they felt unable to interfere because no piracy had been committed there. Their assault on, and destruction of the offending factory, proved a military and moral triumph: 'Not one instance of disorderly conduct was witnessed among the fifty-four men, who composed the force on the occasion ... Not a fowl nor a plantain was taken.'

In 1826, Ashmun mounted a more ambitious attack on the infamous Trade Town in the Young Sesters territory. Charging ashore with marines from three U.S. naval vessels, Ashmun was dashed against a rock and injured. But pain did not diminish his pleasure at seeing the Trade Town set alight and destroyed by the blast of two hundred and fifty flasks of gunpowder. 'A sense of terrific grandeur was displayed,' wrote Ashmun, who relished the noise of battle.

These small engagements stirred Ashmun into a mood of restless belligerence. 'We don't want to fight, but, by Jingo, if we do' is the message of his report to Washington on November 28th 1828, referring to recent disputes with slave-trading Bassa tribes: 'May Heaven avert the necessity of bloodshed! But our little armed force is fitting for sea—and if the Board of Managers intend that arms shall not be used—and the calamity of war be forever and entirely avoided by their colony, I see not but that their present agent must be recalled, and a much wiser (I will not say more pacific) substituted in his place.' Ashmun knew very well that his warlike policies were popular with the society. American colonizationists at this time talked of 'reversing the tide of empire' from west to east and of building a new America to include the present countries of Senegal, Gambia, Guinea, Sierra Leone and Liberia.

By 1828 and for several years to follow, the colonizationists in America felt pleased with, and proud of, Liberia. Most reports from the settlements justified every hope of a better life in Africa for free blacks. Outsiders added their praise for Liberians. A British naval officer wrote in 1832 that:

> Their houses are well built, ornamented with gardens and other pleasing decorations, and in the inside are remarkably clean—the walls well white-washed and the rooms neatly furnished. They are very hospitable to strangers and many English naval officers in the station have been invited to dine with them, and joined in their meals, which were wholesome and good ... They all speak good English without any defect

of pronunciation. They are well supplied with books, particularly Bibles and liturgies.

The English writer, Harrison Rankin, compared Liberia favourably with Sierra Leone where he had spent a few months and singled out for praise Monrovia's journalism.

Many Liberians wrote to America giving good accounts of the colony and their new life. Sometimes former slaves wrote to the owners who had released them. A Mrs Hatter wrote to her old mistress:

> Our house has one front room, a shed room, and one above stairs. Our lot is in a very pretty part of the town and I have a great many very pretty trees growing in it. I send you, by Mr Hatter, some tortoise shell and a little ivory tooth; and some shells to Miss — — and Miss — —. Give my love to them, and tell them I wish they had such a sweet beach to take their morning and evening walks as we have here. My dear Mistress, you do not know how thankful I am to you for buying my husband.

Another Liberian, pleased with the sermons on Sundays and with the prayer meetings every night, wrote: 'I would not give the enjoyment I had had since I have been in Africa for all I have seen in America.'

Letters like this, so flattering to the white colonizationists, were used as propaganda by the society, but there is no reason to doubt their sincerity.

For years, Ashmun had been the only white man on the colony and he looked on his black fellow citizens as equals. Nothing in his journals suggests either disdain or condescension; he seems to have been immune from the racial prejudice of his countrymen. There were blacks whom he disliked for their laziness or spite, but he did not generalize from the person to the race. His black friends, too, he valued as individuals and not as fanciful symbols of Negro piety.

In March 1828, Ashmun fell ill once again and decided to try to recuperate in the West Indies. When he left Liberia on the 26th—to quote Lott Carey's account—'Nearly the whole (at least two-thirds) of the inhabitants of Monrovia, men, women and children, were out on this occasion, and nearly all parted from him with tears, and in my opinion, the hope of his return in a few months, alone enabled them to give him up.' But Ashmun's illness grew worse on board ship and after he had arrived at St Bartholomew's in the West Indies. Even here, in his last illness, Ashmun had the energy to write numerous tracts, prayers and exhortations—'O keep my heart like fresh tilled soil, forever, that it may drink freely the gentle dews of heaven.' He was taken, dying, to New Haven in Connecticut where his friend and biographer, Gurley, saw him and comforted him. During the evening of his departure, 'he conversed with several gentlemen who visited him, gave instructions concerning an African lad rescued by him from pirates, and who had accompanied him on his voyage ... Just before twelve, he sat up, made one or two requests and when reclined again upon his pillow, almost instantly slept in his Saviour.' It was August 25th, 1828, almost six years to the day since Ashmun had landed in Africa.

The news of Ashmun's death had not yet reached Liberia when Lott Carey, the acting agent, was killed in a gunpowder accident. The deaths of the two men, white and black, who had done most to build and defend Liberia, inspired some awed reflections among the colonizationists. 'How unexpected, how interesting, how affecting,' said the *African Repository*, 'the meeting of these two individuals, so long united in Christian fellowship, in benevolent and arduous labours, in that world of glory and immortality!'

Chapter Five

O God, we pray that that seven-headed, ten-horned monster, the Colonization Society, may be smitten through and through with the fiery darts of truth, and tormented as the whale between the sword-fish and the thrasher.

(Father Snowden, a Negro preacher, whose congregation was mostly from Boston's whaling fleet)

Ashmun's dream of an African empire did not long survive him. Although Liberia pushed its boundaries down the coast, it is still one of the smallest states in West Africa. A century and a half have passed since the Yankee Evangelists led the crusade to spread Christ's word through Africa—yet nine-tenths of the continent is still Muslim or pagan. This failure should be blamed not on the black American settlers, who indeed never wanted to build an empire, but on the white politicians of the United States. In the late 1820s and early thirties, just when Liberia was most prosperous, the American Colonization Society became involved in a damaging, even disastrous wrangle.

The nation at this time was slowly being pulled apart over the issues of States' Rights and slavery. This argument, which went back to the first years after independence, was closely involved with economic differences. The northern, manufacturing states favoured high tariffs to guard their industries. The exporting, agricultural states of the South wanted low tariffs and cheap imports. Inevitably this dispute became involved with slavery. The Northerners, who did not need slaves for their factories, grew critical of the Southerners, who wanted cheap slave labour for their plantations. The hostility between North and South grew more acute as both sides tried to claim for their principles territories of the West. The Missouri Compromise on the new lands west of the Mississippi did not resolve this hostility.

One of the minor casualties of this dispute was the American Colonization Society. Only federal grants could provide enough goods, ships and settlers to turn Liberia into a flourishing state. The Southerners on principle were opposed to federal aid, and the society was to suffer from its links with Henry Clay, who was for years a presidential aspirant. The Southern diehards complained that Clay was using the society as a means of getting popular in the North, and they argued that the United States had no constitutional right to found an overseas colony. 'Of all the extravagant schemes that have yet been devised in this country, I know of none more wild, impracticable or mischievous than this of colonization,' shouted an anti-Clay Senator, who also railed at Ashmun for having 'made war upon the Spaniards and the French, as well as on the natives'. When Andrew Jackson, the Southerner, beat Clay in the presidential election of 1832, one of his first acts was to veto a bill for large-scale expansion in Liberia. From then on, Liberia had to depend for support on private charity and on public goodwill. But here too the society suffered a set-back.

When Southern politicians attacked the colonizationists they often accused them of trying to abolish slavery. Southern legislators and newspaper editorials described the society as 'a repository of all the fanatical spirits in the country' and its views as 'phials of wrath'. A less wild but far more deadly attack came from Thomas R. Dew, a historian. He predicted that the removal of blacks to Africa would merely put up the price of slaves, encourage the breeding of slaves and ultimately increase the black population. His arguments were made all the more powerful by a rise in the price of slaves at the time, caused by a rise in the price of cotton.

The society protested that it was not opposed to slavery, and was merely concerned with the free blacks. 'This Society promulgates no new and dangerous doctrine,' said Ralph Gurley, its secretary. 'Their only aim was to get rid of a people which are injurious and dangerous to our social interests, as they are ignorant, vicious and

139

unhappy.' In order to carry their point, the colonizationists harped on the wickedness and the fecklessness of the free blacks. 'In 1826,' wrote one of their pamphleteers, 'of 296 persons convicted and brought to the Philadelphia prison, 117 are coloured, being nearly in the ratio of 3 to 7. Had the number of coloured convicts been proportioned to the coloured population of the state, there would have been but 6 instead of 117.' He went on to claim an equally high proportion of coloured paupers, and warned that in sixty years' time (1898) there might be eight million negroes in the United States—'a nation of 8,000,000 of degraded, despised, oppressed beings!' Statistically, at any rate, his forecast was correct.

Such anti-Negro arguments may have blunted the enmity of the slavers but they much offended free blacks. In Philadelphia, whose prison and workhouse were so overcrowded with Negroes, the agent of the society complained that among the free blacks 'not a man will listen to the scheme, much less emigrate'. A convention of free blacks in New York resolved that: 'This is our home, and this our country. Beneath its sod lie the bones of our fathers: for it some of them fought, bled and died. Here we were born, and there we will die.' The free blacks complained that the emigrants sent to Liberia were either the riff-raff of their community, or unwanted slaves who had been freed only provided they went to Africa. By and large this accusation was true. Of the 11,909 emigrants sent to Liberia up till 1866, 4,541 were born free, 344 purchased freedom and 5,957 were set free for the express purpose of emigration. Although many of this largest group were no doubt content, they had not emigrated, but been expelled.

The society had compromised with its principles in the hope of appeasing the slave-holders. By doing so it invited attack from the fierce and growing forces of abolition. This attack was to open, with shattering force, from the pen of William Lloyd Garrison.

The anti-slavery movement would have grown up without this man, but Garrison set it ablaze with his rhetoric. Like Luther, Rousseau and Paine, like Marx and Hitler and Mao Tse-tung, he was able to express the fury and hope of a revolutionary movement. A white man who gave his life to the blacks, a Christian with the

Devil's rage, and a pacifist who prodded a nation to war, his views were ill-digested and paradoxical; but right or wrong, Garrison wrote with wrath and genius. He is remembered now for his great crusades against slavery, but for many years his main hatred was turned on the American Colonization Society, which never entirely recovered from its shock.

His very upbringing was calculated to make a rebel. His drunken father deserted him; his nagging mother neglected him; and his schoolteachers rapped his knuckles to stop him writing left-handed. Apprenticed to a printer, he soon discovered his talent for journalism and bought his first newspaper when he was twenty-one. At twenty-three he moved to a temperance sheet where he flayed the evils not only of booze, but of theatre, dancing, gambling, swearing, prostitution, breach of the Sabbath, duelling and the imprisonment of debtors. This last was particularly close to his heart for he had to start his newspapers on credit.

Garrison, at twenty-three, was well disposed to the colonization movement and not deeply concerned about slavery. Then, in prison for libel, he met some runaway slaves who were waiting to be reclaimed by their masters. This cruelty so appalled him that he decided to give his life towards the abolition of slavery, and to that end founded the *Liberator*, which first appeared on New Year's Day, 1831. He raised subscriptions beforehand from interested whites, free blacks and various friendly ministers; but the triumph of the newspaper was due to Garrison's style. Already at twenty-five he was a veteran of polemics. The front page of the first issue carried an editorial trumpet blast that echoed across the country and is quoted in every history book on the period:

I am aware that many object to the severity of my language; but is there not just cause for severity? I *will be* as harsh as truth, and as uncompromising as justice. On this subject I do not wish to think, or speak, or write with moderation. No! no! Tell a man whose house is on fire, to give a moderate alarm; tell him to moderately rescue his wife from the hands of the ravisher; tell the mother to gradually extricate her babe from the fire into which it has fallen; but urge me not to use moderation in a cause like the present. I am in earnest—I will not equivocate—I will not excuse—I will not retreat a single inch—AND I WILL BE HEARD.

The readership of the *Liberator* was small for the first few months and confined almost wholly to free blacks. Later in 1831, after Garrison had backed up his editorial blasts with a series of lectures in New England, more whites as well as blacks became convinced by his arguments. By the end of the year, he had gathered enough support to found the New England Anti-Slavery Society. Garrison's final aim was the abolition of slavery, but his first aim was to crush the colonization movement. The *Liberator* gave ten times as much space to attacking colonization as it gave to attacking slavery itself. Garrison swore to his audiences of Negroes that he would lead a crusade 'against these promulgators of unrighteousness'.

The colonizationists did not at first understand the danger of Garrison's enmity. In April 1831, Gurley referred in the *African Repository* to a 'rash and deluded youth, who is scattering firebrands from Boston' and later reproved the still unnamed man 'who professing to condemn war, is doing all in his power to kindle hostile feeling, and the fiercest passions'. The society's New England agent, Joshua Danforth, warned Washington of the peril, but the board of directors would not take alarm. Like the Girondins and the Russian socialists, these gentle reformers failed to grasp that, in a revolutionary epoch, the most fearsome enemy stands to the Left.

In the summer of 1832, Garrison opened the full arsenal of his wrath to smite the colonizationists. He had long been collecting and analysing numbers of the *African Repository* and he now used this organ of the society as evidence of its wickedness. His book, *Thoughts on African Colonization*, written in 1832, was intended to damn his opponents by the evidence from their own mouths. He cited chapter and verse to prove that colonization encouraged the slave trade, degraded the Negro, was harmful to Africa, and

142

helpful only to Southern plantation owners. 'I perused page after page,' he wrote of the *African Repository*, 'first with perplexity, then with astonishment, and finally with indignation.'

Garrison argued in *Thoughts on African Colonization*, and it must be admitted he argued well, that colonization could never remove the system of slavery in America. According to a circular published by the society, there were about 2,000,000 slaves and 500,000 free blacks in the country, and both groups were rapidly increasing. The receipts of the Colonization Society during the last ten years had been $112,841.89, and the expenditure $106,457.72. During that period, 1,857 people were transported to Africa. How much time and how much money would it then take to transport the entire Negro community?

In pages spattered with exclamation marks, Garrison lambasted the colonizationists' argument that Negroes, although too depraved for America, could bring enlightenment to the Africans. 'All that is abhorrent to our moral sense, or dangerous to our quietude, or villainous in human nature, we benevolently disgorge upon Africa, for her temporal and eternal welfare.' After quoting colonizationists who had called free blacks 'notoriously ignorant, degraded and miserable' Garrison's anger rose to a howl: 'My bowels, my bowels! I am pained at my very heart; my heart maketh a noise in me.'

Nothing so angered Garrison as Ashmun's account of victories over the hostile native troops:

> Their 'dread of the great guns of the islanders' (to adopt the language of Mr Ashmun), must from the beginning have made a deep and salutory impression upon their minds, and when, not long afterwards, 'every shot' from these guns *'spent its force in a solid mass of living human flesh'* —their own flesh— they must have experienced an entire regeneration! ... How eminently calculated to inspire the confidence, exact the gratitude and accelerate the conversion of the Africans.

Every article in the *African Repository* was treated by Garrison as the official policy of the American Colonization Society. He took sentences out of context; he ignored the many successes of Liberia; he distorted the motives and methods of its creators; in short, his book was unfair. But Garrison had set out to do something more than simply question the merits of colonization. He had started a moral crusade. The question was not

> whether the climate of Africa is salubrious, nor whether the colony is in a prosperous condition, nor whether the transportation of our whole coloured population can be effected in thirty years or three centuries; nor whether any slaves have been emancipated on condition of banishment; but whether the doctrines and principles of the Society accord with the doctrines and principles of the Gospel, whether slaveholders are the just proprietors of their slaves, whether it is not the sacred duty of the nation to abolish the system of slavery now and to recognize the people of color as breathren and countrymen who have been unjustly treated and covered with unmerited shame.

The colonizationists wanted reform. The abolitionists wanted a revolution. And Garrison, with a true revolutionary's instinct, knew that he first had to crush the reformists. 'I look upon the overthrow of the Colonization Society', he said at this time, 'as the overthrow of slavery itself. They must both stand or fall together.' The *Thoughts* did not smash slavery but they dealt a serious blow to the colonizationists' cause. Representatives of the society in New England, New York and as far away as Ohio reported massive defections to the anti-slavery camp. The gentle Gurley was not the man to resist so virulent an attack. He answered Garrison's abuse with a mild appeal for benevolence; he warned of the dangers that stem from too rash a demand for the rights of man; he complained, rather dolefully, that the abolitionists had gained adherents only by the sheer quantity of their tracts. 'They print, I have not a doubt, ten times as much as the Colonization Society, and send their publications gratuitously to all the clergy, and to a large portion of all respectable men in the Union.' The style of Gurley's replies to Garrison reflected the uncertainty of his own feelings. He personally hoped for complete emancipation and knew that the question 'cannot fail to come more and more into discussion as we advance'. His advice was 'to move as fast as we can, and carry public sentiment with us, yet not so fast as to produce reaction at the South'. Gurley had failed to see what Garrison saw with great clarity—that the argument over slavery could no longer be settled by compromise and good will. The South wanted to keep slaves; the North, increasingly, wanted to set them free. The colonizationists wanted to please both sides—and therefore appeared to both sides as hypocrites.

The disagreement among the colonizationists came into the open during their annual meeting in January 1833. The 'Northern' faction, led by Gurley himself, attempted to depose five of the board of managers who were either themselves Southern slaveholders or friendly to slave-holding interests. The delegates, after a boisterous meeting, turned down Gurley's plan and reinstated the 'Southerners'. Although Gurley's new-found hardness embittered the Southern colonizationists, it did not win him respite from the abolitionist baiting. New voices, just as harsh as Garrison's, joined in abuse of Gurley and his society.

A Westchester judge, William Jay, wrote of the free black girl who had been turned away from a boarding-school in Canterbury, Connecticut. When she claimed her rights as a free United States citzen, the magistrates of the town imposed a fine, in default of payment of which 'she was TO BE WHIPPED ON THE NAKED BODY NOT EXCEEDING TEN STRIPES' (Jay's capitals).* This scandalous behaviour, which was laid at the charge of the colonizationists, helped to inflame abolitionist sentiment. In the spring of 1833, Arthur Tappen, a merchant, deserted the colonization cause, bringing a wealth of damaging secrets to help the other side.

> The first thing that shook my confidence in the Society (he revealed to Garrison's delight), was the fact that ardent spirits were allowed to be sold at the Colony, and, as the agents

* The abolitionist pamphleteers, like less high-minded authors, understood that details like this were likely to bump up sales.

wrote me from Liberia, in giving me the assortment suitable to make up an invoice, were considered 'indispensable'. I used the little influence I had with the Society to obtain a prohibition to the admission of ardent spirits into the Colony, with what success may be seen in the fact that no less than FOURTEEN HUNDRED BARRELS of the liquid poison have been sold there within a year.

In vain the colonizationists explained that rum was indispensable for the commerce of Liberia. In vain they reported that a Liberian temperance society included one-fifth of the colony's population; in vain they quoted the testimony of a U.S. naval officer who had spent some time in Liberia: 'I saw but one man the worse for liquor while I was at Monrovia, that is, among the Americans, but before I arrived, I expected to see them lying about the streets as we do in the States.' It was no use. The damage was done. The defection of Tappen had swung the teetotal faction.

The colonizationists, losing at home, attempted to rally their friends in Britain, the country that had pioneered both the anti-slavery crusade and the colonization of Africa. A rich Quaker, Elliott Cresson, went to England in 1831 to canvass contributions for the society and to preach the success of Liberia. He soon found that Garrison's propaganda had made its impact in Britain too. The prominent anti-slavery agitator, Charles Stuart, described the colonizationists as the 'Ministers of Hell' and went on to advocate mixed racial marriages. Old Zachary Macaulay, whose temper had not mellowed with age, refused Cresson a hearing in the *Anti-Slavery Reporter*. In Liverpool, a total stranger accosted Cresson on the street and accused him of anti-Negro sentiments.

By spring 1833, Cresson had written off the British Anti-Slavery Society and had launched a rival colonization group, under the patronage of the Duke of Sussex. The officers of this new society included several leading peers and the Archbishop of Dublin, but they did not include the radicals and dissenters. In Britain now, as in the United States, the leadership of the colonization movement had passed out of the hands of the idealists, whose main concern

146

was the Negro, and had been assumed by men with political motives. Cresson urged the advantages of acquiring more British territory in West Africa and he talked of merging Sierra Leone into a greater 'Empire of Liberia'.

In a moment of petulance, Cresson called Stuart a 'second Garrison'. To make things worse for the colonizationists, the real William Lloyd Garrison sailed to England from the United States in the summer of 1833. His stated aim was to raise funds for a Negro school in America, but he did not miss a chance to badger the colonizationists. He urged Britain to storm 'that great Bastille of Oppression, the American Colonization Society... Let the British nation assail it with the battle-axe of justice; let their artillery of truth, charged to the muzzle, blaze against it.'* Deriding Cresson as an 'impostor', Garrison challenged him to an open debate. When Cresson refused, Garrison prodded him with personal jibes: 'I cannot boast, like Mr Cresson, of defraying my own expenses; for he is opulent and I am poor.' 'I affirm', he wrote in an open letter to Cresson, 'that the American Colonization Society, of which you are an agent, is utterly corrupt and prescriptive in its principles.'

The earnest Englishmen of that age relished nothing more than a stand-up metaphysical prize-fight. Their sympathies fell heavily on the younger contender's side. Garrison's triumph came when eleven British philanthropists, including the legendary Wilberforce, signed a condemnatory 'Protest' against the American Colonization Society. When Wilberforce died a few days later, this 'Protest' came to be seen as his intellectual testament.

Other luminaries of the British anti-slavery movement gave their support to Garrison. The philanthropist William Allen, wrote to him:

Having heard the exposition of the origin and main object of the American Colonization Society, at the meeting on the 13th instant at Exeter Hall, and *having read their own printed documents*, I scarcely know how adequately to express my

* Like many pacifists, Garrisonl oved military metaphors.

surprise and indignation, that my correspondents in North America should not have informed me of the real principles of the said Society; and also that Elliott Cresson, knowing, as he must have known, the abominable sentiments it has printed and published, should have condescended to become its agent.

This rebuke was all the more sharp since Allen and Cresson were fellow Quakers.

Thomas Buxton, the successor to Wilberforce as the leading anti-slavery voice in the House of Commons, told Garrison: 'My views of the Colonization Society you are aware of. They do not fall far short of those expressed by my friend Mr (James) Cropper, when he termed its objects *diabolical*.'

The unlucky Cresson had come to London with great hopes of support from Zachary Macaulay, the man who had worked so hard for Sierra Leone. When Macaulay had turned out cool, Cresson wrote him off privately as a 'great boor', 'who envied the progress of Liberia'. He cannot have thought that the 'old Turk', as he also called Macaulay, would give open support to Garrison, in a letter in 1833:

> I can have no objection, indeed, to the plan of colonizing in Africa, with a view to its civilization, and to the extension of Christianity in that deeply injured quarter of the globe ... But the Colonization Society appears to me to adopt, as the basis of its schemes, not the love but the hatred and contempt of the negro race, and to regard everyone tinged with their blood as an object not of kindness and brotherhood, but of abhorrence ...

By the start of 1834, the American Colonization Society had come to a serious pass. Under constant attack at home, and roundly trounced by British public opinion, it had also become hampered by debt. The board of managers discharged some of the staff, cut down on the print of the *African Repository* and published a frank analysis of accounts, which revealed, to the vicious glee of their enemies, that 1,857 gallons of whisky, brandy and rum had been sold in Liberia by the colonial agent. On a fund-raising tour through the United States, Gurley discovered a general gloom among former colonizationists. He was now fully aware of the threat from the abolitionists, whose cause, he prophesied, would bring catastrophe to the country. He warned that their agitators were stirring up the 'deepest and most terrible elements of society —elements which once wrought into fury, will shake the land if not cover it with blood.'

Branches of the American Colonization Society started to break away from the Washington organization. The New York and Philadelphia branches came out on the side of emancipation and wanted to cut all ties with the South. Meanwhile, Maryland had founded its own little colony at Cape Palmas, down the coast from Monrovia. Maryland in Liberia, as it was called at first, experienced all the troubles once suffered by earlier settlers in Monrovia and Sierra Leone, only, being smaller and under the care of an even smaller society, it was even more short of supplies and cash.

In 1838, the American Colonization Society adopted a new constitution that gave more control to the branches in different states. The new board of directors appointed a president with executive powers, so that Gurley was now almost unemployed. In 1840 he went on a visit to England to try to revive the society's wan prestige. His speeches there and his tone of aggrieved disappointment reveal the slow decay of the colonization ideal. In speaking to English audiences, he found himself tending, not just to refute abolitionists, but to defend the very institution of slavery:

'Generally (and I speak from personal observation in nearly all the southern states of the American republic) the citizens of these states are kind, humane, generous, and, in a proportion to the whole population, equal to that found in most parts of Christendom—devout and exemplary Christians. No better friends have the slaves in any part of the world than are to be found in those states. Cases of harsh treatment, of severe punishment, of wanton disregard of their feeling—are exceptions not the rule.

The colonization movement had begun as a coalition of interests. On one side were the philanthropists who grieved over the plight of the poor blacks. On the other side were politicians, most of them slave-holding Southerners, who wanted to get rid of what they considered a useless and troublesome minority. When the arguments over slavery grew fiercer, the majority of philanthropists turned to the abolitionist cause, leaving the colonization movement in the hands of the politicians. These were by no means all zealous slavers. The greatest liberal of his age, Abraham Lincoln, wanted to keep the two races apart. 'Such separation, if ever effected at all,' he said in 1857, 'must be effected by colonization.'

Right to the outbreak of the Civil War and for several decades afterwards, the American Colonization Society continued to send parties of emigrants to Liberia. Southern plantation owners made wills granting liberty to their slaves on condition that they emigrated to Africa. The former President Madison left two thousand dollars to the society. But after 1835 there was no vigour left in the colonization movement, for most Americans realized that the coming crisis—the question of how blacks and whites could live in one land—was too large to be hidden away on the West Coast of Africa.

Chapter Six

In 1847, after twenty-five years as a colony, the tiny settlement of Liberia became a sovereign state and held its first election for a president. Liberian orators like to invest these events with the glory and excitement of a struggle for independence. In fact there was no struggle; independence was thrust on, rather than won by, the citizens of Liberia. The American Colonization Society, hard up for money and mauled by its anti-slavery foes, was anxious to lose an expensive responsibility. The United States Government had enough troubles at home without taking on more troubles in Africa. The British in near-by Sierra Leone thought that they had enough, even rather more than enough of a colony on this insalubrious coast. The citizens of Liberia took control of the country, largely because there were no other takers.

The end of the 1830s was marred by native wars and by rows between Monrovia and the smaller American settlements. The American Colonization Society in 1839 changed the constitution to give more power to the executive in Monrovia, and the title of governor to the agent, Thomas Buchanan. Governor 'Big Cannon', as he was known because of his prowess in war, was the last white ruler of the colony, which he treated with small respect. The members of the Elective Council, he wrote in January 1840, 'went so far in their folly as to declare they would do nothing until I should yield at least the right of vetoing'. He complained in confidence to the society 'that the great error in our system of government is the large infusion of the principle of democracy'. Fever, the fiercest democrat on the coast, removed Governor 'Big Cannon' in 1841. His place was taken by Lieutenant-Governor Joseph Jenkins Roberts, later the first President of Liberia and the most illustrious statesman in the nation's meagre history. He was also the first black leader.

Roberts's blackness was political rather than physical, for he was, at the darkest, octoroon. He was described at about this time as a slightly-built, handsome man, with a very English-looking face, brown hair, blonde moustache and grey eyes. It is true that his face turned sallow in later life—but so do the faces of most Europeans who spend a long time in West Africa. In the United States of today, a Negro of Roberts's colour would doubtless describe himself as a black, but Roberts himself used the phrase 'man of colour'.

Governor Roberts, like his descendants today, belonged to the aristocracy of the colony. Born in Norfolk, Virginia, in 1809, he came to Monrovia at the age of twenty with two younger brothers, one of whom became a doctor, the other a bishop. Joseph Roberts went into trade, at which he proved very successful. He became a sheriff, trained as an officer in the militia, and led one of the forays against the natives. His pronouncements as governor during the 1840s reflect the solid beliefs of the Liberian bourgeoisie. He stood four-square for sobriety: 'Some will no doubt curl the lip, and say that we have no cause for alarm in Liberia, that a more temperate people exists nowhere ... I admit this to be true, but why drink at all?' He regretted the lack of imprisonment for debt. And like so many rich traders in both Liberia and Sierra Leone, he disapproved of other people who tried to grow rich by trade: 'The greatest hindrance to our successful agriculture in Liberia is the ruinous desire of most of our people to become wealthy in a very short time ... they become traders, and in nine cases out of ten, from their unacquaintance with a system of which they have had no previous knowledge, in a few years they become bankrupts.' In spite of such admonitions to the Legislative Council, Roberts was tolerant and benign and found 'great occasion to rejoice in the general welfare of the colony.' Visitors to Liberia were much impressed by its leader. The American Commodore Perry said in a message to Washington that Roberts and Governor Russwurm of Maryland were 'irrefragable proof of the capability of coloured people to govern themselves'.

Although Maryland and Liberia were still separate, Governors Roberts and Russwurm pursued a common policy with regard to the outside world, and imposed an identical import duty of 6 per cent. The British merchants plying the coast resented this duty and tried to evade it. When a Sierra Leonean ship was seized by Liberian customs men, the British at Freetown sent a gunboat to Grand Bassa and seized a Liberian vessel. The British Commodore Jones wrote to Roberts in 1844 that the right to impose dues could only be exercised by sovereign and independent states. 'I need not remind your Excellency', he went on, 'that this description does not yet apply to "Liberia" which is not yet recognized as a subsisting state, even by the Government of the country from which its settlers have emigrated.' Roberts mildly replied that 'to some extent this may be true.' He recognized the British case; and the British, to do them justice, were well disposed to Liberia. 'Our intercourse with British officers has been of the most friendly character,' Roberts reported, although he complained of certain merchants. The attitude of the British Government, implicit in Commodore Jones's letter, was that disputes over import dues could easily be resolved if Liberia were to declare independence.

The Liberians, however, did not want independence if it meant losing financial help from the American Colonization Society. They hesitated until 1846, when the directors of the society virtually told the colonists to proclaim their sovereignty. A convention was called at Monrovia in July 1847 to draw up a constitution and make a public declaration of independence. Both documents are clear and sensible pieces of work. The framers of the constitution were probably unwise to rule that the President, the Representatives and half the Senate would have to stand for election every two years, as this invited constant political turmoil. Moreover, with hindsight, it seems unfair that the benefits of the constitution applied only to townspeople—the settlers from America—and not to the natives of the interior. Later, when the settlers extended their influence into the hinterland, the contrast between the two groups resulted in much injustice. But at the time of the constitution, the overwhelming majority of the natives lived in separate systems of politics. Liberia, as conceived in the constitution, was not the entity on the map today but merely a handful of coastal settlements.

Sir Harry Johnston, who wrote the best history of Liberia, complained of the choice as a national flag, of the Stars and Stripes, but with only one star. 'No combination of colours has been done to death in the same way amongst the nations of the world as red, white and blue,' Sir Harry wrote, and offered his own design for a future flag. This showed the white star on a green background, representing the forests of Africa. He coloured the stripes alternately black and yellow, to represent the coastal Negroes and Muslim tribes of the interior. For good measure, Sir Harry added an extra white stripe as a symbol of thanks to the white people of the United States, Britain and France for their acts of kindness, and to recognize 'that the Black Republic of the West Coast of Africa by no means excludes white enterprise or energy from its territories'. Sir Harry, when he wrote these words, was hoping to put his own enterprise and energy into planting rubber in Liberia. His business venture failed; and the Star and Stripes of Liberia, now fluttering as a flag of convenience on hundreds of foreign ships, remain unalterably red, white and blue.

Independence, although not dearly won, was greeted with general excitement. On August 24th, 1847, the day of raising the new national flag, 'old men seemed to have renewed their youth, and youth itself moved with a more buoyant and elastic step.' At nine o'clock, the governor and his staff assembled at the courtyard while the troops moved up to the Central Fort. At the Methodist Church old Colonel Elijah Johnson, one of the heroes of 1822, stood to attention beside the flag at the altar. Later, 'a large number of ladies and gentlemen assembled at an evening entertainment, composed of the rich products of their own luxuriant soil, where patriotic toasts and gallant sentiments were drunk in the very purest water which Monrovia afforded.' The day is still a national holiday but, in modern times, the ladies and gentlemen drink their copious toasts in the very purest whisky that the Scottish Highlands afford.

154

Governor Roberts was elected first President in October 1847, and inaugurated in January of the following year. His most urgent task, during the first months of office, was to get Liberia recognized by foreign powers. The United States Government, not wanting a Negro diplomat to be accredited to Washington, refused its recognition until 1862, during the Civil War, when Lincoln was no longer frightened of white susceptibilities. Britain, a long-time friend of the colony, was the first country to acknowledge it as a sovereign state. In 1848, President Roberts went to London, where he signed a treaty of friendship and commerce with Palmerston and met philanthropists such as the Bishop of London and Lord Ashley, who raised funds to help Liberia in its war against the slavers. President Roberts was received in the royal yacht by Queen Victoria, who presented Liberia with a transport ship and a four-gun sloop. The queen, to the end of her life, took an affectionate interest in the Negro republic; the Liberians returned this affection. One meets Liberians to this day who believe Queen Victoria is alive, while others pay her the compliment of asserting that she had Negro blood.

France, which had started a settlement on the near-by Ivory Coast, soon followed Britain in recognizing Liberia. The new state was therefore secure from encroachment on both sides until, as happened many years later, the imperial powers started to covet this enclave of sovereign Africa. Holland and Prussia gave recognition in 1849, followed by Portugal, Austria, Denmark, Sweden and Norway, Brazil, Haiti, Hamburg, Bremen and Lübeck.

Liberia was not the first black country to win her independence. The Empire of Ethiopia had existed for thousands of years behind the daunting battlements of her mountains and ravines. In Haiti, rebel African slaves had won a bloody but lasting sovereignty. However, Liberia was the first black state to adopt the ideas of government of the advanced white world. It was, and still is, run on the principles of law, elective democracy and the rights of the citizens. Liberia, as we shall see, has not lived up to the hopes of her forefathers—few countries do—but she has retained for 120 years at least the form of a constitutional government.

The white Americans, British and Europeans who visited Liberia at the time of her independence, showed no special surprise at the idea of a black republic. Yet when Ghana, Kenya and the Ivory Coast were given their independence during the 1950s and sixties, the white world split in debate on whether these countries could work. On the one side were those who said that the blacks were not yet capable of self-government; on the other side were those who insisted on instant freedom. This argument did not really gain strength until the colonial age in Africa. During the 1840s there were few white settlements north of the Cape; the European Powers saw no reason to turn their trading stations into expensive colonies. Therefore they felt no jealousy of a black republic. Suspicion of black self-government, and with it hostility to Liberia, did not arise until the end of the nineteenth century when most of the continent had been chopped up into colonies. Liberia got its sovereignty in 1847 because the white Powers, at that time, had no reason to fear an example of black competence. Had Liberia asked for her independence in 1947, rather than 1847, many people would no doubt have said that it was not yet ripe for self-government.

PART THREE

Chapter One

When MacCarthy (the greatest governor of Sierra Leone) was killed in 1824, he left his colony in good shape. Trade flourished; the British Navy each year brought thousands of recaptured slaves to be educated and civilized by the British missionaries; and Sierra Leone had established subsidiary colonies in the Gambia and on the Gold Coast. Yet it was not till the end of the century that Britain expanded this embryonic empire in West Africa. Sierra Leone, for about fifty years, remained an isolated settlement on the coast; and when at last Britain was seized by the itch for empire, its older colony was overshadowed in influence by the Gold Coast and Nigeria.

Sierra Leone was static but never stagnant during the nineteenth century. It grew, it developed and even, from time to time, throve; but it never fulfilled the early dreams of the Saints as a beach-head for the civilization of Africa. The Saints themselves were largely to blame for this failure. Men like Sharp and Wilberforce had conceived Sierra Leone as a means of redeeming the black man from ignorance, heathenism and slavery. When the Anti-Slave Trade Act became law (in 1807) they hoped that the Royal Navy, working from Freetown, would manage to put an end to the traffic. In fact, British efforts to stop the slave trade may actually have increased it. As a result of the cotton boom in the southern United States, and the growing demand for plantation slaves in Cuba and Brazil, there was still a flourishing market for the slaver. The Royal Navy could not get a conviction against the slavers unless they could prove that slaves were on board, so the slavers, when faced with capture, would simply throw the slaves overboard to the sharks. A British commodore complained in 1822 that the slave trade could not be reduced while certain countries in

Europe gave it informal protection. In 1830, the British Commissioners of the Mixed Court at Freetown reported to London that the traffic in slaves was actually on the increase. 'In 1837, the courts condemned 27 vessels,' writes W. E. F. Ward, a modern authority on the subject, 'but in that year, 72 vessels left Havana for the African coast, and 92 vessels, in spite of the law, succeeded in landing a total of 46,000 slaves in Brazil. The Navy was still merely a nuisance.' The British Saints understood this. For every slave recaptured and landed at Freetown, many others were shipped to servitude in the Americas. The British Saints, like their counterparts in the United States, came to see that the only way of stopping the slave trade was to stop the institution of slavery. They therefore lost interest in Sierra Leone.

The British Government, also, had little interest in the colony, or indeed in the whole of West Africa. Later in the century, when the surplus of capital had created the need for more markets and more tropical raw materials, Britain joined eagerly in the 'scramble for Africa'. But until, roughly, the 1880s, Britain was anti-imperialist in her thinking. Governments saw no purpose in colonizing these fever-ridden coasts, still less in opening up the forest of the hinterland. British traders did not need the authority of the government but made their own arrangements with the chiefs. In the 1860s, Sierra Leone extended its sovereignty to some territories to the east, but this was done to tidy the border with Liberia and not from any policy of expansion.

If Sierra Leone achieved little during the nineteenth century, she was nevertheless an object of great outside interest. In this small colony, over a hundred years before the 'wind of change', black people took part in the management of a modern state. Black businessmen, doctors and lawyers (above all, lawyers) competed as equals with whites. There were black officials, at one time a partly-black governor, as well as the first black bishop, Samuel Adjai Crowther, and knight, Sir Samuel Lewis. The white Victorians, always alive to social as well as racial distinctions, talked of the new phenomenon of 'black gentlemen'. Then, as now, they discussed whether the Negro race was capable of

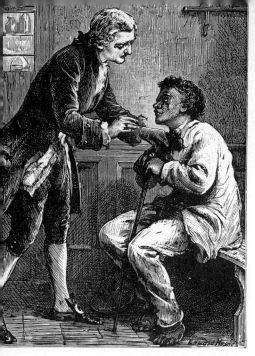

Above: Granville Sharp, 1735-1813,
philanthropist and founder
of Sierra Leone.
(*Radio Times Hulton Picture Library*)

Left: A Victorian impression of Granville Sharp's
meeting with the slave Jonathan Strong.
(*Mary Evans Picture Library*)

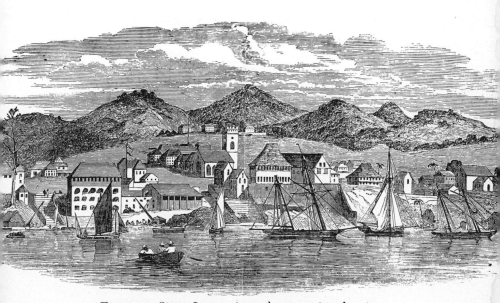

Freetown, Sierra Leone. An early engraving showing
St. George's Church before it was enlarged into the Cathedral.
(*Mary Evans Picture Library*)

Zachary Macaulay, Governor of
Sierra Leone 1793-99.
(Radio Times Hulton Picture Library)

Left: Yehudi Ashmun, classical scholar turned trader; the virtual creator
of Liberia. Right: Joseph Jenkins Roberts, President of Liberia 1849-55,
and subsequently first Principal of Liberia College.

Bishop Samuel Crowther, the recaptive slave who became the first black bishop and a symbol of the progress of Sierra Leone. *(Church Missionary Society)*

Sir Samuel Lewis, influential leader of the Creole bourgeoisie of Sierra Leone in the opposition to English rule.

Sir Richard Burton.
'Not the first, but the fiercest
critic of Sierra Leone.'
(Radio Times Hulton Picture Library)

Monrovia, Liberia, at the turn of the century. The President and Prime
Minister marching in state (under umbrella), with the old
executive mansion in the background.
(Paul Popper)

Early photograph of the boy's compound, Bo School, Sierra Leone.
(Foreign and Commonwealth Office Library, London)

A nineteenth-century missionary bishop bringing spiritual enlightenment
to the hinterland of Sierra Leone.
(Church Missionary Society)

Left: The heyday of British colonialism: a group at Hill Station, Sierra Leone, in the early years of this century. *(Royal Commonwealth Society Library)* Right: Street scene in a Sierra Leone port, 1923. *(Radio Times Hulton Picture Library)*

A versatile shopkeeper in Freetown, 1931.
(Radio Times Hulton Picture Library)

Marcus Garvey, leader of the
American Back-to-Africa
movement in the 1920s.
(U.P.I.)

President Tubman, President of Liberia from 1944 to the present day,
at the inauguration ceremony for his sixth term of office.
(U.P.I.)

Stamps issued to celebrate the granting of
Independence to Sierra Leone in 1961.
(Church Missionary Society)

One of the main streets in modern Freetown.
(United Nations)

self-government, and this argument grew acute during and after the Civil War in America. Both sides in the argument cited Sierra Leone as evidence for their contention, and gave very different descriptions of life in the colony.

The black ruling class in Sierra Leone during the nineteenth century was formed from the recaptured slaves. Between 1807, when the slave trade was declared illegal by Britain, and 1863, when the last shipload of slaves was put ashore at Freetown, about fifty thousand recaptives, or nearly one thousand a year, were found a new home in the colony. Although the first recaptives had to fight for a place in society, they soon outnumbered and later absorbed the descendants of the original settlers, the Nova Scotians and the Maroons. They were encouraged or even obliged to live in villages outside Freetown, were frequently apprenticed on terms very like serfdom, and there were many cases of gross cruelty to recaptives. 'It is to be feared', wrote a missionary at the village of Hastings, 'that many of these poor apprentice girls fall a sacrifice to the lusts of those who ought to protect them, and are compelled to that sacrifice through bodily fear.' A lady missionary said that in one village the authorities would not let an apprentice be buried without an inquest, nor allow the report of a death unless the body was shown. As late as 1855, Governor Kennedy reported to Parliament that many apprentice children were sold up-country as slaves.

Many recaptives protected themselves by joining societies for mutual help. These 'companies', as they were called, were sometimes formed of shipmates aboard the slavers, but more often they corresponded to tribes or peoples from which the recaptives had come. The most numerous of these two peoples were the Yorubas, nicknamed Akos, from what is now western Nigeria, and the Ibos from what was recently Biafra.

The brighter recaptives learned English, adopted some Christian faith and claimed full rights as citizens of the colony. Young recaptive men attended the missionary college that opened in 1827 at Fourah Bay. An Ibo teacher, who had been flogged by a village administrator, brought a successful action to prove that he had the same rights as anyone else in the colony. Recaptives with adequate education were soon permitted to sit on juries. The whites in Freetown, who had long complained of settler and Nova Scotian jurors, complained even more vehemently of the recaptives, above all the Yorubas, who were said never to pass a verdict against one of their own race.

Many enterprising recaptives left their smallholdings in the villages and went to Freetown to trade. Working individually, or through their 'companies', they bought trade goods from the captured slave ships and sold these to stalls or small shops. The Yorubas, who were then nicknamed the 'Jews of Africa', and the Ibos, who are so nicknamed today, proved particularly skilful at commerce. These merchants relied on cheap labour from the recaptive apprentices, whom they normally chose from among their own tribe. By 1840 an 'Akoo' contractor, Isaac Pratt, was successful enough to employ a Nova Scotian carpenter, and a tax list for 1853 shows seven recaptives among the nineteen richest landowners in the colony. Some of the settlers and Nova Scotians resented the rise to power of the recaptives, or 'captives' as they still insisted on calling them. Many Maroons went back in disgust to their native Jamaica. However, most of the three original colonizing groups were soon intermarried and merged with the much larger group of recaptives. The recaptives, in turn, copied the manners and attitudes of the earlier colonists. By the 1850s all four groups had come to be known by the general name of Creole. The Creole historian Dr Arthur T. Porter writes that by 1870 all distinctions between them had been almost completely obliterated.

The Victorians, who relished tales of people rising from rags to riches, particularly savoured these histories of the former slaves who made good. Some recaptives made good at astounding speed. A Nube boy-slave, John Ezzidio, was set free but penniless in 1827, educated himself, got a job as a merchant's agent and by 1841 had saved enough money to buy a substantial house in George Street. He became a devout Wesleyan, travelled to England, sat on the Board of Health and won a seat in the colony's first

Legislative Council. Like many successful Creole businessmen, he was a great signer of protests and petitions, a guardian of Creole dignity against the aspersions of white people. The goods he sold included ladies' shawls and silk stockings, gentlemen's suitings, patent-leather boots, mixed biscuits, patent medicines, sherry, port and stout. The man, like the goods he sold, was solid Victorian bourgeois.

The Yoruba Syble Boyle, who had taken his name from the H.M.S. *Sybille* that rescued him and from Dr Boyle his first master, was of a scientific bent, again typically Victorian. At the Sierra Leone Industrial Exhibition of 1865 the French from Senegal carried the highest honours, but Boyle did the colony proud with examples of country cloth and medicine. 'In articles manufactured from vegetable fibres he stood unequalled,' an admiring observer wrote, also praising the photographic equipment. As an old man, Boyle belonged to the 'Upper Ten' of the colony, and his house in Trelawny Street, according to Christopher Fyfe,

> displayed the standard he and his friends aspired to. Its pedimented windows, iron-work balconies, pillared upstairs drawing-room with a bust of Queen Victoria and a large gilt mirror over the fireplace imitated the kind of house being built in rich bourgeois quarters in Europe. There he could entertain the Colonial Secretary or the leading European businessmen in the sort of surroundings they aspired to themselves.

The first Freetown lawyer to be called to the London Bar was a Maroon, John Thorpe, who stayed on in England until his death. His achievement was soon repeated by a number of other Creoles, including recaptives. The first three doctors from Sierra Leone were all the sons of recaptives, of whom the most famous, James Africanus Horton, soon made his name in both medicine and in literature. Like all Freetown medical men and like most Freetown non-medical men he held strong views about health on the West Coast of Africa,* but his argumentative nature expressed

* These views are discussed in the next chapter.

163

itself best in politics. A doughty defender of Creoles against their foreign critics, he claimed that 'it cannot be shown in the world's history that any people with so limited advantages have shown such results within fifty years.' He called for an extention of the Sierra Leone franchise, the establishment of a Freetown municipality and the appointment of a health officer. He favoured independence, on the Liberian model, but with a monarchical system of government. 'As in the Gambia, a republic is unsuited to the taste of the people ... It will never have among the native inhabitants, who have always looked up to their king, the same influence and effect.'

Dr Horton's interests ranged further than Sierra Leone. In his book, *West African Countries and People*, he produced an interesting and informed account of life along the coast. His remarks on his native Iboland are fascinating for the way they foreshadow modern ideas about the Ibos and Biafra. 'The Egboes', for so he spelt their names,* 'are considered the most imitative and emulative people in the whole of Western Africa.' Their kings might be dethroned for any excessive use of power and their women 'hold a very superior rank in the social scale'. Their religion, Dr Horton maintained, was 'Judaism, intermixed with numerous pagan rites and ceremonies' and even claimed that the Egboes stemmed from the lost tribe Heber or Eber.† On the map in the front of Dr Horton's book, the territory of the Ibos, east of the lower Niger, is clearly marked 'Biafra'.

Dr Horton observed that many Creoles had left Sierra Leone to take up civil or military jobs in the Gambia, Gold Coast or Lagos, which Britain had occupied in 1861.

Besides this [he went on], they are to be found in every part of the coast sighing after gold in the capacity of merchants, traders and clerks—in the French colony of Senegal; in the rivers Gambia, Casamanza, Nunez, Pongas, Sherbro and

* He risked confusing the Ibos or 'Igbos' with the 'Egbas' of Mid-West Nigeria.
† Although the Ibos, in modern times, have frequently been compared to the Jews, the Judaic legend is more often attached to the near-by Ibibio people. See Barry Floyd, *Eastern Nigeria* (Macmillan, 1969), p. 26.

164

Gallinas; in the Liberian Republic; in the Gold Coast; in the Kingdom of Dahomey; in Lagos and Abeokuta; in the Niger; at Bonny, Old and New Calabar, the Cameroons, Fernando Po, the Gaboons and the Islands of St Helena and Ascension.'

The first Sierra Leone settlers in the eighteenth century had gone down the coast to trade. The Creole traders of the mid-nineteenth century ventured much farther abroad. The majority of them were recaptive Yorubas or men from the Niger delta, who could exploit their knowledge of local languages to parley and trade with the natives. In 1839, a body of twenty-one Creole merchants petitioned the Freetown government for help in starting a colony on the coast west of the Niger. This help was refused but, notwithstanding, sixty-seven people went down the coast in a private capacity. By 1842, as many as five hundred recaptives had gone back as businessmen to the land of their origin. In the 1850s it was believed that this exodus had reduced the population of Sierra Leone by thousands. In Lagos alone there were several hundred Sierra Leone Creoles, who rivalled the whites for good government jobs such as chief clerk and collector of customs. Freetown merchants of Ibo origin sailed up the Niger to trade in the great market town of Onitsha.

Most of these merchants were Christians who made the effort, or at any rate the pretence, of spreading the faith as well as making money. The Church Missionary Society, which at first had confined its work to redeeming recaptured slaves, began looking around for new fields of endeavour, so that by 1874 the Reverend Henry Seddall could write that 'Sierra Leone is not now so much a mission station as the headquarters for the extension of African missions.' The role of Sierra Leone Creoles in the development of British West Africa is personified in the life of the first black bishop and former slave Samuel Adjai Crowther.

Adjai, to use his original name, was born about 1810 in what is now Mid-West Nigeria. This area at the time was ravaged by slaving wars. Some time in 1822, Adjai was tilling the fields with his mother, two sisters, an infant and a cousin, when they were set upon by marauding soldiers. Adjai was captured before he could use his bow and arrow, then taken off into slavery. He was bartered, first for a horse, then for a bag of tobacco, and finally led to the coast to be sold to the foreign slavers.

> Men and boys [he later recalled] were at first chained together with a chain of about six fathoms in length, thrust through an iron fetter on the neck of each individual and fastened at both ends with padlocks. In this situation the boys suffered the most. The men, getting angry, would draw the chain most violently, as seldom without bruises on our poor little necks, especially the time of sleep, when they drew the chain so close to ease themselves of its weight in order to lie more conveniently, that we were almost suffocated or bruised to death.

At one moment he tried to strangle himself—a sin he regretted in later life.

The future bishop, with hundreds of other slaves, was put on a Portuguese slaving vessel, which no sooner got out to sea than it was seized by ships of the Royal Navy. The rescued slaves at first feared their rescuers even more than their captors, and Adjai was dreadfully scared by the sight of a hog's carcass and heaps of cannon balls. 'The former was supposed to be the flesh and the latter the heads of the individuals who had been killed for meat.' The fear passed, and during the two and a half months that Adjai stayed on board he became a favourite with the seamen and probably learned some English. After only six months at Sierra Leone, where he lodged with an English missionary couple, Adjai was able to read the New Testament. The missionaries took him to England, had him baptized and named after an English divine, then found him a job as schoolteacher, in a village near Freetown. In 1827 Samuel Adjai Crowther became the first pupil at Fourah Bay College, the Church Missionary Society foundation.

The principal of the college was a Bavarian, Charles L. F. Haensel, a martinet who did not allow his pupils to get above themselves. Young Crowther and his classmates went barefoot throughout the week, but on Sundays were made to wear boots for the three-mile walk to church. They found wearing boots an agony, and as Crowther was afterwards to recall: 'After losing sight of the college we sat on the gate, took off the shoes, walked barefoot, and only put them on at the porch of the church ... But after some months we invested in the purchase of boots ourselves and were careful to buy those that made noise and creaked as we stepped with them, to our great delight and the admiration of our pupils.' These pupils also admired Crowther's suit of blue cloth, waistcoat and white stockings, as well as the beaver hat he wore on Sundays.

Dr Haensel insisted that all the pupils kept diaries in which they described their day's work, writing about themselves in the third person. The entry by Crowther for March 22nd, 1828, records an important step towards manhood:

> When Samuel Crowther brought last week's journal to Master, Master desired him to put the word 'Monitor' under his name. He also told him what the word meant, namely, not one who 'rules' over others, but one who 'reminds' others. And he said, he wished that everyone in the Institution should be a Monitor to his brethren, but he would call Samuel so in particular, because he was the oldest, and would look to Samuel that he should remind the other boys whenever he saw them do that which is not good, or when they did not do that which is good.

On leaving college, Crowther married a recaptive girl and went back to work as a teacher in one of the villages near Freetown. As a mission teacher and as a Yoruba, Crowther was doubly interested in missionary work to the Niger. He believed, like his missionary colleague J. F. Schoen, that Sierra Leone would become 'like Jerusalem of old, a centre from whence the word of God will go forth to many a benighted tribe of Africa'. But an expedition into the Niger territory would be too expensive and too dangerous for the Church Missionary Society to mount on its own. The missionaries and their backers in London therefore pressed the British Government to support them in this venture. The Whig governments of the 1830s were opposed to any annexations in Africa but they did look favourably on the promotion of commerce and Christianity. The anti-slavery agitators like Buxton were eager to mount an expedition and helped, in 1839, to persuade the Government. Lord John Russell, announcing the Niger expedition, said its aim was to achieve the abandonment of the slave trade and 'the admission for consumption in this country on favourable terms, of goods'.

The Niger expedition set sail in 1841, with two Church Missionary Society men, Schoen and Crowther, acting as missionary and interpreter. The progress of the two ships up the huge and mysterious river was much less hazardous than the voyagers had expected. Some of the natives were sulky because they were not offered rum by these pious Englishmen, but most were civil and curious. Crowther, to judge from his journal, took rather a supercilious attitude to these, his heathen countrymen, as when he remarked that a visiting chief 'marched about on the quarter-deck, with apparent satisfaction at having white men for his friends'. The only threats to the expedition were river mosquitoes and fever. Nearly a third of the Europeans died in the last two months alone and of all the men on the expedition, Crowther alone was not touched by illness. 'He was a born traveller,' wrote his friend and biographer, Jesse Page, 'a little man, with nerves of steel, upon whose constitution neither lagoon nor mosquito could leave any deadly germ.' This physical toughness, as much as spiritual strength, explains Crowther's long career as a missionary in the bush.

After the Niger expedition, Crowther was sent to England to be ordained. Back in Sierra Leone, he became a famous preacher both in English and in Yoruba, and although some of his fellow countrymen denounced him as an apostate, even Muslim Yorubas listened to his sermons. In 1847, Crowther returned to Yorubaland as a missionary. Soon after arriving he rediscovered his mother and sister, whom he had not seen since the family had been torn apart by the slavers, twenty-five years before. 'When she saw me she trembled', Crowther wrote of his mother. 'She could not believe her own eyes. We grasped one another, looking at one another in silence and great astonishment, while the big tears rolled down her emaciated cheeks.' His mother was to become Crowther's first convert.

During the next twenty years, Crowther roamed over Yoruba-land and set up a mission at Onitsha, the principal Ibo town. Although Britain still did not contemplate forming a colony on the Niger, there was big public interest in this, the most populous region of Africa. The Liverpool merchants sailed up river behind the Creole missionaries. Queen Victoria and Prince Albert summoned Crowther for a discussion on how to destroy the Lagos slave trade, and listened, impressed, to the Lord's Prayer in Yoruba. The *Church Missionary Intelligencer* of May 1864 wrote that the native church and missionaries had proved so successful that 'to delay any longer the native episcopate would be unduly to retard the development of the native church.' The Archbishop of Canterbury appears to have taken the hint, for the following month, on June 29th, 1864, Crowther was consecrated a bishop. Special trains ran from London to Canterbury and there was scarcely room for the crowd in the cathedral. Among the many old friends who came to honour Crowther, was Admiral Sir H. Leeke who, as a young officer forty-two years before, had rescued and befriended the frightened slave, Adjai.

Bishop Crowther served in the Niger territory until his death in 1891. His biographer truly remarked 'how much the political as well as the commercial interests in the Niger owed to the Bishop.' The Creoles of Sierra Leone played a big role in transforming West Africa, but Sierra Leone itself grew increasingly less important. When slavery and the slave trade ended, no more recaptives were landed at Freetown. As Britain, France and Germany carved up the territory of the coast, new ports were opened and new towns were built that outstripped Freetown in commerce and importance. The Gold Coast and Lagos, that once had been ruled from Sierra Leone, had grown by the 1890s into rich and thriving

169

colonies in their own right. Creoles from Freetown, living abroad, adopted the citizenship of their new home. Freetown, the 'Athens' or the 'Jerusalem' of West Africa, lost its intellectual lead when universities and mission colleges were founded in Nigeria and the Gold Coast.

Some Freetown Creoles went abroad because they felt frustrated in their own colony. Even during the last thirty years of the century, when the Creoles were at the height of their influence, they never wrested political power from the Englishmen. It was a principle at Whitehall that the Governor of Sierra Leone should be appointed from outside. No Creole, however distinguished, was ever offered the job, and the only coloured governor, William Fergusson, was a West Indian military doctor. This discrimination against the Creoles was almost certainly based on colour prejudice. Yet Fergusson, in his one year as governor before dying of fever in 1845, proved such a success that even the Reverend Thomas Eyre Poole, a pompous and bigoted army chaplain, was generous in his praise of him:

> Mr Fergusson, the Governor at that time, received me with ease and urbanity. His manners were perfectly unaffected; a rare exception to the general bearing of Africans and coloured people, when raised over their European neighbours; and in carriage and conversation he was gentlemanly. He said and did everything without vanity or pride; a feature in his public character which is rarely to be met with in those who have rule in small colonies. In figure Mr Fergusson was tall and well made; of an intelligent and amiable expression; and the manly bearing, inseparable from and belonging to, those only who have followed for years the military profession, gave to his whole appearance the stamp of a superior man ... I addressed Mr Fergusson as 'His Excellency'. Touching me good-naturedly on the shoulder, and calling me aside whilst a pleasing smile of amiable humility lit up his countenance— 'Mr Poole,' he said, 'you will oblige me by not calling me His Excellency. There is no occasion for it. I have lived here for

many years and am better known as "Mr Fergusson". Drop it if you please.'

Although Poole concedes that Fergusson as a governor had 'never been surpassed, probably not equalled', he accepts as a matter of course that white men should be preferred for office.

It is not considered the best or wisest policy by those who, from local and practical experience, and not from mere hearsay are entitled to some credit for their opinions and judgements in these things, to place either Africans, or men of colour over Englishmen in any department; when, amongst the latter, men can be found equal in ability and integrity to discharge public duties.

This policy appears to have influenced governors of Sierra Leone in appointing people to office in the colony. Although the British Government declared in 1830 that white officials were to be slowly replaced by blacks, this process was never advanced but indeed slightly reversed. For example Norman Macdonald, the governor who succeeded the West Indian, Fergusson, insisted during his six years of office that Africans were unfit for office, and he resisted urgings from Whitehall to appoint them. Sir Arthur Kennedy, who served two long spells as governor, was in principle ready to give jobs to Africans but in practice gave them only unimportant jobs. At the same time he made jobs more attractive to Europeans by obtaining them bigger salaries and six months home leave every two years. One governor who really wished to advance the Creoles, was John Pope-Hennessey, an Irish Catholic radical who arrived in 1872 after a stormy, eccentric career in the Far East. 'Whenever it can possibly be done,' he wrote to the Earl of Kimberley, 'I would strongly recommend dispensing with the services of Europeans on this coast. Fortunately this can be done, and to a greater extent than is generally imagined. It is no disparagement to the other members of the Legislative Council to mention the fact that the two ablest members of that body are both pure negroes.' Whether or not this was meant as disparagement, such an attitude did not endear Pope-Hennessey to the Europeans. His generous championship of the coloured races made him just as unpopular with the whites in Sierra Leone as it had done previously with the whites in Hong Kong and was to do later with the whites of the West Indies. Uncompromising and tactless radicals like Pope-Hennessey did no more to advance the Creole cause than the grumpy conservatives who were the normal run of governors. Pope-Hennessey was a hero to the Creoles, who still remember his name and his sympathy to their cause, but partly because of his dangerous popularity he was given a new job after a year at Freetown.

If the Creoles never ousted the whites from the places of power in the colony, they did for a time run its commerce and professions. According to Dr Porter, the period from 1870 to 1900 'can indeed be called the apogee of Creole civilization and ascendancy'. By 1867, the Freetown lawyer William Rainy could tell an anti-slavery conference in Paris:

> There are a few leading English merchants but the native merchants occupy a very high position. The retail trade is almost entirely enjoyed by them, and they are enabled to give their children the inestimable benefits of a liberal education in England. They have established an excellent newspaper in Freetown... the *African Interpreter and Advocate*, and a number of missionary schools receive their support.

In 1876, the college at Fourah Bay was affiliated to Durham University and therefore became the first institution in West Africa with the power to award degrees. The Creoles may have been weak in the government of the colony but were powerful in the Freetown Corporation. Their aspirations, achievement and pride are well summed up by the career of Sir Samuel Lewis, the first Creole knight.

Samuel Lewis, born in 1843, was the son of a Yoruba who had been freed at Sierra Leone in 1828. William Lewis followed the usual road to success, becoming a Wesleyan, then a shopkeeper, a wholesale merchant and even a ship-owner. He refused, on

172

sectarian grounds, to let his son Samuel study in London on a scholarship from the Anglican Church, but in 1866 he was able to pay for this education out of his own pocket. Samuel Lewis became the third Sierra Leonean barrister and by far the most prosperous and respected, attracting big retainers from Creole merchants and European business firms. At the height of his fame he was said to command up to one hundred guineas for an opinion alone, and his services were requested as far down the West Coast as Lagos. His style in court could be cutting and dangerous. 'I prefer to destroy you with your own sword,' he once told opposing counsel, 'and then destroy your remains with mine afterwards.'

Although Lewis sometimes served as acting Queen's Advocate, and frequently took briefs for the colony's government, he did not take and apparently was not offered a permanent government post. His passion for public affairs found its obvious outlet when the Legislative Council was formed in 1863. Lewis was one of the first unofficial representatives, and held this seat for twenty years. Although jealous of Creole privileges—he once forced an acting governor to abandon a bill that threatened the freedom of newspapers—Lewis was never against the government for the sake of it. He served three times as mayor of Freetown and only gave up because he did not want it imagined that he was the only Creole fit for that office.

Sir Samuel, as he became in 1896, was pleased to be called 'more English than the English themselves'. A zealous patriot, he helped to finance the Golden Jubilee fête of 1887. Like many rich men in Freetown and Monrovia, he constantly preached the need for the encouragement of agriculture and he set up a model farm that, of course, lost money. However, this farm enabled Sir Samuel to live in the style of a rich country gentleman. On Lewis's fiftieth birthday, in 1893, Governor Fleming and thirty-seven other guests came to his party by chartered steamer and were met at the wharf by Lewis's private hammock-bearers. When Lewis and his family were carried to Sunday church, as many as eighty Mende labourers marched in procession behind them. Lewis, a Wesleyan, married his first wife, a Roman Catholic, in St George's Cathedral, which is Anglican—but the most prestigious church in Freetown.

Sir Samuel Lewis played an important part in the turbulent politics at the turn of the century. Having lived through the finest years of the Creole ascendancy, he witnessed the start of their decline. A moderate and an anglophile, he realized only late in life that wealth, respect and even a knighthood could not bring him real parity with the English. Black gentlemen do not achieve black power.

Chapter Two

'The town itself is picturesque. It rises from the water's edge and gradually creeps up the sides of the surrounding hills, with its white dwellings and prolific gardens; whilst in the distance, emerging from high woods, appear the country mansions of white gentlemen, with patches of ground devoted to the produce of coffee and fruit.' So wrote F. H. Rankin, who spent eight months in Sierra Leone in 1832 and gave an agreeable picture of the colony. But even those who detested it most had to admit its natural beauty. The mountain of fierce greenery, slashed by scars equally vivid red earth, stands out unparalleled from the flat, dark mangrove swamps that fringe the rest of the West African coast. Even the city of Freetown, during the nineteenth century, was often praised for its charm, and sometimes its beauty.

> The style in which the houses are generally built [Rankin continues] throws an oriental character over the view; they are as often of wood as of stone, and are washed white or yellow; piazzas, with pillars at due intervals, support the verandahs, and secure a shady walk in the open air even during mid-day; the verandahs exhibit rows of jalousies, a kind of Venetian blind painted green; and the roofs, principally formed of layers of thin dry wood called shingles, project to a great distance, with wide eaves.

An English lady, who also wrote a book on the colony, felt that 'spacious as the piazzas are, and even lofty, to me they had at first an *attic* appearance, caused not only by the roof sloping down until it reaches the top of the outer windows, but by its consisting merely of the planks on which the slates are nailed.' Both writers were struck by the broad Freetown streets that burst each rainy season into rich meadows of grass, flowers and indigo. Only the cattle, sheep and goats that browsed in front of the houses prevented this vegetation from blocking the traffic.

The dress of the Freetown populace was even more vivid and strange. The scarred and ugly Krumen preferred to go about naked, to the intense disgust of the missionaries. The Muslim traders from the interior were conspicuous, then as now, by the elegance of their long blue robes. The Creoles dressed somewhat after the English fashion. Since nakedness was the badge of a slave, an abundance and even an excess of clothes was seen as the proof of freedom. The wealthier men wore jackets, waistcoats and trousers of cloth, sometimes torturing themselves with suits of wool because this was more 'English' than cotton. Top-hats and spats were often seen in the last decade of the century. One visitor in the 1880s wrote a fictional account of the colony, in which he made mock of

> *Such* clothes. Stout negresses in the latest fashions from 'home', compressed into tube-like dresses of vivid colours, exchanging the time of day in the most elaborate language with black gentlemen of Grandisonian manners, clad in long and tight black frock-coats, with enormous white shirt cuffs gorgeously linked, high collars, bows or fold-over ties of parrot tints and lemon or lavender kid gloves, and chimney-pot hats which they took off with a flourish. Their boots were of patent leather with pearl-buttoned uppers.

No account of Sierra Leone, from its founding until the present day, has neglected to mention its piety. Wesleyans, Baptists and more exotic sects like 'Lady Hunting Tom's Collection' (for so its devotees called Lady Huntingdon's Connection) vied with each other in fervour. At innumerable churches and chapels, all day and most of the night, the Lord's Word was preached, chanted, calypsoed and yelled. Sabbath observance was so absolute that a Scottish missionary, hearing the great hush, felt ashaméd to recall the profanity of a Scottish Sunday. An American man of God, who visited one of the recaptive villages that had been built out of the jungle, said that on Sunday 'a calmness reigned, as solemn and profound as had done six years before, when nothing was heard in the wilderness but the softly creeping tread of the leopard when preparing to spring on his prey.'

St George's Church, later Cathedral, represented the spiritual might of British colonial government, but the slow pace at which it was built shamed many zealous Anglicans. Begun by MacCarthy in the early 1820s, it was still not complete in 1837 when the authorities, to save money, ran up 'an ugly brick wall in the centre, for the purpose of appropriating one half of it to religious duties, and the other to public office'. The church might have been finished earlier had not succeeding governors chosen to tinker about with the architectural style. Round windows replaced the original pointed Gothic and the first tower, thought too small, was pulled down to make room for a larger. The military chaplain, Poole, while officiating at St George's was impressed by the native choristers in white surplices but discovered, on glancing at the decalogue, that the seventh and eighth Commandments were incorrectly placed. 'How long this gross error has been permitted', Poole could not tell; nor presumably could the white congregations who sweated and dozed in the steamy heat of Sunday services.

The piety of the Freetown blacks was not always matched by sobriety. One Wesleyan 'God-palaver house' stood opposite to a building of at least equal popularity, a rum-house. 'These two fashionable resorts seem to be upon cordial terms, playing into each other's hands as it were. A tide of votaries flows backwards and forwards; the languid spirit seeks from spirituous energy a spiritual fervour.' In 1848 George Thompson, an American missionary, was upset by the bibulous habits of the devout. 'At Krootown Chapel I could not commune with them on account of the *alcoholic wine*', and he did not have much success in obtaining signatures to a pledge. 'The baptist minister (a coloured man) drinks freely, and although he would not sign his own name, he went round with the papers to get others.' However, this missionary managed to make the grog sellers writhe at one of his sermons, and got children to join him in singing 'Away, the bowl'. He blamed the depravity on his native America and even his native state of Ohio: 'This town and country are very much cursed by America. An untold amount of *tobacco* is brought here, and sold very high. But the ARDENT SPIRITS! Oh! the *seas* of it that are imported from my native land ... the other day I counted 50 barrels together, just landed from the same state that sent me here to preach the gospel.'

Pious foreigners were often enraged by the sexual attitudes of the colony. Black Christian men thought it natural to take 'country' wives while the women enjoyed freedom to leave a cruel or stingy 'husband'. 'The morals of Freetown', wrote an American, 'are *fearfully* bad ... The abomination is not committed under the cover of midnight—it is done at noonday.' Even midnight was not always cover, as one learns from a rather hilarious court case that took place in 1827. A Maroon trader and Methodist preacher, William Thorpe, had been charged by a carpenter with adultery. The plaintiff's counsel summed up the case in a plea which deserves to be quoted at length:

> The defendant, gentlemen, I am instructed to say, is verging towards the decline of life; to have arrived at these years, when the hey-day of the blood might well be expected to have gone by, and that, while he preached morality, he would find no constitutional impediment to prevent him practising it.
>
> [But the Reverend Thorpe, the counsel continued ...] sent a lad to call Mrs Polly Bernard to his house. You must know, gentlemen, that Mr Samuel Thorpe then lived (and for aught I know does now) in the same street and within a short distance of the dwelling of my client, but which was then occupied exclusively by his wife. The object of thus sending for Mrs Bernard by the defendant, is alleged, I am informed, for the simple purpose of making his bed. It is really astonishing that this gentleman could not be content to have his bed made by some of his men servants; that he did not hire a

female considering his ample means. Now the real object for which Mrs Bernard was thus called to the house of the defendant became soon apparent. After her ingress the light ceased to throw its shade through the casement ... the windows and doors were closed upon the guilty pair. Too much cunning generally defeats its own intention: not far distant from this scene of unhallowed pleasure stood the keen eye of jealousy, watching the progress of the night in order to preserve what custom had made her consider as her own, Yes, gentlemen, Mrs Samuel (another intimate acquaintance of the Rev. Samuel Thorpe) ... rushed to the house ... and ... attacked Mrs Bernard. Only conceive, gentlemen, what a fine figure for the painter and the moralist was here exhibited; at the dark hour of night, two married women fighting most lustily in the bed-chamber of the pious defendant; while he (taken by surprise) kept pacing his piazza, unable to recollect what he had best do, and trembling with fear that the indiscreet uproar would lead to his exposure.

The wretched Thorpe was fined fifty pounds but he must have suffered even worse punishment from the wrath of the two squabbling women.

The scold's bridle was introduced to the colony only two years after its founding; Sierra Leone ever since has been infamous for its shrewishness. Even the Reverend Poole, in an unconsciously comic passage, describes how he was victim of such a 'palaver'. Having rejected the too-familiar approach of one of his black women neighbours, Poole reaped the savagery of her injured pride. 'There was no abuse which was too bad for me and she appeared to believe she could never give me enough of it.' He tried to avoid her and, when this failed, took a summons to silence her by law, but even in this he was foiled: 'The quarrelling and railing were succeeded by not less noisy, but more excusable vociferations. A religious meeting of some kind was held three or four times a week in her hut; when what with the screaming and invocations of the Deity, I was delivered from one evil for another equally bad.' Sierra Leonean women were also famed for inquisitiveness. People returning home would find a girl inspecting their wardrobe; diners would look up to see a 'black face, calmly observing through a window the whole process of nutrition'.

The enemies of Sierra Leone dwelt on the passion for litigation. It is true that many lawyers used cheating methods to win their cases, especially to win a case for a black against a white man. There were no doubt many instances when a black jury, through prejudice, brought an unjust conviction against a white. In no country are lawyers or juries perfect. Prejudice was all the more likely in Freetown where black people were given the duty of exercising the law but not the power of making it. This sense of frustration helps to explain the bumptious, querulous manner of the Creoles, so different from the courtesy of the Gold Coast or Nigerian people.

The whites during the 1830s numbered probably less than a thousand, of whom three-quarters at least were in the government or the army. But few as they were, they ran Sierra Leone and set an example, of sorts, to the Creoles. They were not the cream of the cream, these Englishmen, who went to the fever coast in search of a fortune. Indeed, to be accurate, few were actually Englishmen. Macaulay, MacCarthy, Campbell, Findlay, Macdonald, Kennedey are the names of the first six governors that spring to mind. 'It is a curious circumstance', wrote one visitor to the Colony 'that in Sierra Leone, the whole of the white residents, with few exceptions, bear Scotch names.' Some Africans too had spotted the tribal distinction, and Krumen were heard to refer to the Scots as 'bush Englishmen'. It was not till the end of the century that intelligent men were specially chosen for jobs in the Colonial Service. In Sierra Leone, as late as 1885, there were only two white men, apart from the doctors, who carried degrees from a university. Probably most of the British were debtors, adventurers, men who had failed in other colonies or disgruntled officers from the army or navy.

Few white ladies followed their husbands to Africa. The ten or a dozen in 1837 mixed little among themselves, partly because their houses were far apart and 'partly from etiquette, which even here intrudes to split the number already so small into different circles'. One of the ladies referred to here was Mrs Melville, the wife of a judge, who wrote a charming account of her residence in the colony. Living high on the hill, close to the site of the present-day college, she does not appear to have mixed much with her neighbours, and her book is preoccupied with servants' chit-chat, country walks and observations of flowers, ants, birds and the odd, more exotic chameleon. Mrs Melville wrote that: 'The most unpleasant thing about the wet season is the impossibility of getting out to take proper exercise', because of the danger of sudden rain and having to run home at 'railway speed'.

Another white lady, Mrs M. Church, praised the racecourse and its 'half barb' horses with 'slender clean legs, blood-red nostrils and arched necks'. Unfortunately they had been trained as racers and were therefore unsuitable for a lady rider. After 1850, when the tsetse fly came to the colony, few horses of any kind could survive and the upper classes, both white and black, relied on hammocks or palanquins for their transport.

'No theatre can be supported', wrote one of the whites with a sigh; 'indeed, no plays could be performed excepting such as contained Othellos and Orinocos only.' As a matter of fact he was wrong. Some twenty years later, in 1857, the garrison officers and their wives gave an all-white production of *Othello*. The perform-ance had a curious sequel when the commanding officer, who had taken the role of Othello, shot and killed 'Cassio' in cold blood, and only escaped the gallows by dying in prison first. Quarrels like this were frequent among the whites, who often settled their differences by duelling on the racecourse.

Although the military stayed apart in boorish isolation, most whites until the end of the century mixed easily with the Creoles. Many missionaries and traders married black women. Creoles, like Michael Jarrett, a doctor, and J. B. M'Carthy, a barrister, married English girls they had met while studying and brought them back to Sierra Leone. Moreover, until the end of the century there was no stigma attached to affairs between whites and blacks, and little hostility to the children. Governor MacCarthy, who liked black girls, had a number of illegitimate children. So did Governor Findlay, whose anti-black prejudice stopped at the bed. Charles Heddle, the richest and one of the most respected Creoles, was white on his father's side. When a new missionary girls' school refused to give places to illegitimate daughters of white men, its motive had nothing to do with morals. The authorities were short of space and said that white men could afford to provide a school of their own. It was not till the end of the century, when more white wives started to join their husbands from Britain, that the colony started to frown on Creole 'sick-nurses' and 'housekeepers'.

Drunkenness was the characteristic and most embarrassing fault of the whites. Sailors, released for a day or two from the tyranny of below decks, would lurch from rum-shop to rum-shop, before going to sleep in a doorway or on the grass. One author describes with a wince the sight of a ship's mate 'reeling towards the wharf through the principal streets, bent double and roaring incoherent sentences; a Krooman and a Joloff were assisting him on either side, and grinning with amusement at the abuse which he heaped upon them for daring to take hold of a white, although unable to stand without their support.' The most respectable Europeans were accustomed to drink beer and claret at breakfast—indeed they believed it necessary for their health. A newcomer during the 1880s would find himself offered an evening cocktail of gin and brandy and curaçao, whereupon, according to one report, he feels himself 'the wittiest of men, and West Africa—especially if the moon is shining and a few stars are out, and the scent of the frangipanis is strong—seems not half a bad country after all.' But eventually, warns this moralist, the newcomer goes the way of the rest. 'There are only about ten out of forty here who are not more or less drunk every night. In the daytime they consume porter and bottled beer, fiery sherry and tots of rum or whisky besides the uncounted cocktails ... Most of the men here drink from sheer funk, to keep away the dread of fever, which comes like a thief in the night.'

Fear of the fever was partly just an excuse for a drink—but the fear was real nevertheless. The nickname 'White Man's Grave' was given to Sierra Leone in the early nineteenth century and it was used as the title of three books and countless articles on the colony. The nickname lingered into the present century so that even today, when Sierra Leone is mentioned, people sometimes say: 'But isn't that very unhealthy?' Sierra Leone, in Victorian times, was almost a synonym for pestilence. Even those who travelled around West Africa regarded Freetown with unique terror. 'It being generally considered a very sickly place to the whites', said one American visitor, 'very few European or American captains desire to stay any longer there than is really necessary for the transaction of their business.'

There is no doubt that Sierra Leone in the nineteenth century was unhealthy for white people. Two years was the average term for a governor, many of whom survived the fever only to die soon afterwards because of their weakened condition. Sometimes the death rate was dizzying. Turner succeeded MacCarthy in February 1825 and was dead by March the next year. His successor, Sir Neil Campbell, praised the Sierra Leone climate and blamed the mortality of the troops on intemperance: he died of the fever in August next year. Sir Neil's successor, Denham, survived in office only one month, and Denham's successor, Lumley, died after two months and was buried with two other governors under a plum tree in the garden. Lumley's successor, Ricketts, went off his head but made his escape to England. The wag, Sydney Smith, remarked at this time that there were always two governors of Sierra Leone, one going out, one coming back; while *John Bull* magazine, which detested the Saints and their colony, said that the governors had to be sent out in triplicate, like dispatches.

Statistics show a jump in the death rate in certain years, for example 1836, 1837, 1844 and 1847. One of the worst years, 1859, began with intense heat in the early months while the rains did not begin until July. The deaths that year were 1,939 against an average of about 500, so that more than 1,000 deaths can be attributed to disease. Tradition says it was in that year that the vultures first visited Freetown, where they are now as common as pigeons are in London. In 1872, one in four of the white population died of fever. It is not always clear from what disease people died. Measles, smallpox and dysentery could be recognized. Most Europeans probably caught malaria during their first or second rainy season; many died from this, which they called simply 'fever'. The ravages of the very bad years were due to yellow fever, the murderous 'Yellow Jack'.

Everyone in Sierra Leone had his pet way of preventing and curing the fever. Some thought it necessary to get up early and avoid the midday sun. Others, with truer instinct, feared the hours of dawn and dusk, although they thought the disease was carried by mist and not by mosquito bites. A naval commander, who had been asked by Governor Campbell to breakfast with him at eight, 'excused himself by saying that he made it an invincible rule on the coast of Africa, not to land before ten'. Most people agreed that excessive drinking was dangerous but the Reverend Poole recommended 'a judicious and properly regulated use of wine and ale, and even brandy, if of good quality'. He referred unconvincingly to the death of a 'missionary, of what persuasion I cannot say, who fell a sacrifice to the advice of some enthusiastical water drinker'.

The chaplain liked his drink and persuaded himself it was good for him. He also liked early rising and hearty breakfasts: 'In the tropics you must rise early if you would preserve your health and enjoy the most invigorating, indeed the only invigorating part of the day ... Beefsteaks, mutton-chops, curry and similar substantials and seasoned dishes supply the first repast of the day; these are improved by the famous bitter ale.' The delicate Mrs Melville also favoured a big breakfast of 'highly seasoned dishes (smoking under covers) of meat, fish, fowl and vegetables; pickles and sauces are handed round as at dinner, and the wine decanter stands vis-à-vis to the water-jug; claret and ale are in readiness.' Most whites favoured exercise but not to such excess as those twelve men who, Rankin reports, played cricket on the racecourse at 98°F. in the shade. 'Abundant wines and liqueurs were on hand for refreshment and hospitality. They left the cricket ground, burning with fever voluntarily sought; and after a fortnight only one is said to have been living.'

If the means of preventing the fever were useless, the cures sound actually dangerous. Quack medicines were imported from London; bleeding was recommended for many years; one pregnant woman with fever survived a large dose of mercury. The Nova Scotian nurses, described by Mrs Melville, sound as though they had learned their trade from Sarah Gamp:

> Provided you let them have wine and spirits *ad libitum* by day and night, they testify their gratitude, as soon as you begin to recover, by recommending you to breakfast off Westphalia ham; and instead of doling out the prescribed tea-spoonfuls of Madeira, will dash nearly half the contents of the decanter into your glass, with a liberality that speaks more for their readiness of doing as they would be done by, than for their skill and common sense.

The Creole doctor, James Africanus Horton, rightly blamed the climate for the unhealthiness of Freetown. But he insisted that outside Freetown, Sierra Leone was 'one of the healthiest spots in the whole western coast of Africa. The high and lofty peaks invite, but in vain, the inhabitants of the low, steam-vapoury Freetown.' He recommended the Europeans to wear cotton cloth, to eat light breakfasts and to avoid unripe fruit. Nothing was so injurious, he insisted, as 'the habit of some men in the tropics, on opening their eyes in the morning, to have a "good stiff shot of brandy".'

Horton and others rightly observed that the low land was more dangerous than the sea, but they did not realize until the end of the century that the low land, with its patches of stagnant water, was dangerous because of mosquitoes.* Indeed Rankin had stated, with more facetiousness than scientific accuracy, that 'mosquitoes are not frequent ... since, according to report, the climate of Sierra

* Horton was obsessed by the question of what happened to 1,825,000 gallons of urine shed annually by the people of Freetown.

Leone is too deadly even for these persecutors of the human race, the offspring of pestilential marshes.'

It was fitting that Sierra Leone, the White Man's Grave, should be used as the testing-ground for the prevention of malaria. Sir Ronald Ross, then Major Ross, had realized from his research in India that the disease was probably spread by *anopheles*. Needing further proof for his theories, he went to Sierra Leone with a team from the Liverpool School of Tropical Medicine. On December 15th 1899, he reported back to the Colonial Office on his cautious but nevertheless sensational findings. He had discovered that two species of gnat could spread the disease; that the larvae of these two species lived mostly in small pools of water; and although he did not rule out the possibility that malaria could be spread by other means, he explained why he thought this unlikely. He summarized his suggestions for the prevention of the disease as the obliteration of breeding pools by draining, the destruction of larvae, the building of houses on stilts and the use of window screens and mosquito nets. The historian of Sierra Leone, Christopher Fyfe, has added a caustic footnote to this chapter in medical history: 'Joseph Chamberlain (the Colonial Secretary) in his public speeches professed great interest in tropical medicine — but neither he nor his under-secretaries troubled to read this epoch-making report when it was sent to the Colonial Office.'

Fyfe, always eager in the defence of Sierra Leone, suggests that it did not deserve its unhealthy reputation. Others had made the same argument in the nineteenth century. 'The mortality amongst European residents in the West Indies is without doubt in a much greater ratio than in Sierra Leone, but it is much less recognized. In our African colony, whose population scarcely counts a hundred individuals, each fills an ostensible and important station. Each death is noted … ' Far from living in terror of death, few Europeans even bothered to go to church on Sundays; 'Where are they? They are enjoying the easy hours, released from the cares of the week; riding on the racecourse, sailing on the bright estuary to Pirate's or Cockle Bay, or chatting at home.' Rankin quoted the jocose remarks of a senior government officer: 'After our hospitality it will be most ungrateful should you make known in England the healthy climate of the colony, or endeavour to remove the impression derived from old tales of horror; for you might thus lessen our salaries, and cut down our pensions, so properly awarded to men who came here to sacrifice themselves to a cruel climate for the public good.'

The whites in Sierra Leone were annoyed by this passage in Rankin's book and sniffed that he had not been long enough in the country to see a serious outbreak of fever. But his statement contained much truth. Sierra Leone was no more unhealthy than the West Indies, Madras and Calcutta, or indeed the rest of the West African coast. If more white people died in Sierra Leone than in Gambia, the Gold Coast or Lagos, it must be remembered that more white people lived there. The Colony's fame as the White Man's Grave must be attributed, at least in part, to its enemies in Great Britain, of whom the most famous and rancorous was Sir Richard Burton.

Chapter Three

I have been east and west, north and south, ascended mountains and dived in mines, but I never knew nor ever heard mention of so villainous, sickly and miserable an abode as Sierra Leone. In short I know not where the devil walks but his direction, or poste restante, is at Sierra Leone.

(From *The Life of a Sailor* by F. Chamier)

Sir Richard Burton, the explorer, scholar and man of letters, was not the first, but the fiercest, enemy of Sierra Leone. Critics in Britain and Africa had railed at the little colony since its founding in 1787. Some disliked the Saints and therefore disliked their political protégé, while others, the slave traders, the sugar, tobacco and cotton merchants, distrusted Sierra Leone as an ultimate threat to slavery. On the other hand, the extreme anti-slavery agitators, just like their friends in America, felt that a colony for recaptive slaves diverted attention away from the goal of abolition. Tories disliked Sierra Leone for being a philanthropic colony based on the dangerous, democratic idea that all men were created equal. The Liberals and the Left disliked it because they did not want it used as the base for a British Empire in Africa. These attitudes, even those that appear contradictory, had crystallized by the mid nineteenth century into a general and virulent prejudice which Sir Richard Burton undoubtedly shared before his three-day visit to Freetown in 1862. His account of the colony appeared the following year in *Wanderings in West Africa*—a book whose repercussions are felt in Sierra Leone to this day.

Burton at the best of times was inclined to be cantankerous; and 1862 was one of his bad years. Fame, wealth and personal happiness were still eluding him. The British public, ten years before, had acclaimed the journey he made to Mecca and Medina disguised as an Arab. More recently he had discovered Lake Tanganyika, and he still boasted, erroneously as it turned out, that he had found the source of the Nile. He had published successful books on expeditions to Harar in Ethiopia, to Salt Lake City and into the underworld of Arabia and India. A linguist unequalled in Britain, a relentless collector of anthropological facts, a witty if crabbed writer in prose and verse, and a man of demonic personal fascination, Burton recognized—and let others know—his genius. A commissioned officer seconded to consular work and to expeditions, he had quarrelled sensationally with the army, the Foreign Office, and most of his fellow explorers. Seven months before his trip to West Africa, Burton had married Isobel Arundell, the romantic and maddening woman who had worshipped him when a young girl, and was to honour him after death by destroying all his manuscripts that she thought improper. Burton was not an easy husband. A restless, essentially solitary man, he fretted under Isobel's protective adulation. A recent biographer, Fawn M. Brodie, suggests that Burton may have been impotent from the syphilis he had caught in Arabia. Certainly there is evidence in some of his poems and other writings about this time that he suddenly felt old and spent. These feelings, whatever their cause, were exacerbated by setbacks in his professional life. He and Isobel, as Arabists, had cajoled the Foreign Office to give Burton the consulship in Damascus, but because of the enmity of the many officials whom Burton had savaged in his dispatches he was sent instead to the remote and pestilence-ridden Spanish island Fernando Po, in the Bight of Biafra. The climate was too bad for white women, Burton said, and he left the protesting Isobel in England; perhaps half of him was glad to be free from her often cloying solicitude.

'A heart-wrench—and all is over', Burton began his account of the voyage to West Africa. Poor Isobel described the same parting in page after page of despairing lament. She knew, just as well as Burton, how strong a chance there was that fever would take him away for good. But Burton's grief seems to have found relief in rage. Quite apart from his other grievances, he nourished a special hatred for Africa and claimed that 'in the various degrees of intellectuality, the Negro ranks between the Australian and the Indian—popularly called Red—who is above him.' He deplored the fact that 'our black friend now boldly advances his claims to *egalité* and *fraternité* as if there could be brotherhood between the crown and the clown!' The Negroes, it must be admitted, were not the only race whom Burton despised. He was against Slavs, Jews, most Indians, and even, at times, his own fellow Irishmen. There were even some Africans whom he disliked less than others. Thus he approved of the Mandingoes, the Somalis and the Gold Coast people, but hated the Yorubas and the Ibos. Reading Burton, one sometimes wonders how much of this Negrophobia was genuine and how much designed to annoy the Evangelicals and the Liberals. At the time of Burton's appointment to Fernando Po, the civil war was raging in the United States and, if he did not actually side with the Southerners, Burton appeared to think they would win. His *Wanderings in West Africa* is dedicated to 'The True Friends of Africa—not to the "Philanthropist" or to Exeter Hall'—where the anti-slavers met. Both an atheist and a Tory, Burton derided those well-meaning Christians who took a sentimental view of the Africans.

Burton went to Africa prepared to detest Sierra Leone, and nothing about the journey had tended to change his ill-temper. He left Liverpool on a grey misty day and his connection with his 'beloved land concluded with a further demand of £6 2s. for baggage'. On board he complained of the noise of the crew, the lack of stewardesses ('even black women would be better than nothing') and worst of all, the wine. 'The claret is black strap, the hock is sourish, the champagne all syrup, the burgundy is like the house Burgundy of the Reform Club—meat as well as drink; the Moselle *sent son perruquier*; the sherry is a mine of bile; and of the port—the less said the better of "such strong military ditto".' The vessel stopped for a day each at Madeira, Tenerife and the Gambia in which brief time Burton found material for 172 pages of reportage, crammed with pedantic detail and arcane references—often in foreign languages. At all three places Burton saw much to deplore and little to praise. At Madeira the guides tried to cheat him, the tobacco was infamous and 'the ennui which [Madeira] breeds is peculiar; it makes itself felt during a few hours' stay'. Madeira was prison, he said, and a 'cockneyfied prison'. At Tenerife he admired the señoritas, but disapproved of the food, the wine and the camels—on which subject, needless to say, he was expert. At Bathurst, in true black Africa, Burton started to huff and puff his disgust into a state of absolute fury. 'The liberated Africans, principally Akus and Ibos, have begun the "high jinks" which we shall find at their highest in Sierra Leone. They have organized "companies", the worst of trading unions, elected head men who will become their tyrants, effected strikes, and had several serious collisions with the military. They are in missionary hands, which disciplines and makes them the more dangerous.' After a few jibes at abolitionists in 'England and Yankeedom', Burton suggested that Britain should drop her colony. 'And to those who would retain the Gambia, I wish nothing worse than a year's residence, or, rather, confinement there.'

Early in *Wanderings in West Africa*, Burton defended himself against the charge of making snap judgments:

> Despise not, gentle reader, first impressions, especially in a traveller. I am convinced ... that if a sharp, well-defined outline is to be drawn, it can be done immediately after arrival at a place; when the sense of contrast is still fresh upon the mind, and before second and third have ousted first thoughts ... The man who has dwelt a score of years in a place, has forgotten every feeling with which he first sighted it; and if he writes about it, he writes for himself and for his fellow-oldsters, not for the public.

Of course there is much to be said for the soundness of first impressions; but Burton frequently formed these impressions some time *before* his arrival.

Already on board ship, Burton had studied the conduct of two Sierra Leone Negroes who were returning home with their wives. 'One was a Jamaican shop-keeper, gifted with the usual modicum of intelligence, and a superior development of "sass", justifying the eccentric Captain Phil. Beaver in declaring that he would "rather carry a rattlesnake than a negro who has been in London".' The other Negro passenger, whom Burton called 'our Gorilla or Missing Link', was the son of Samuel Crowther, who, as Burton predicted with horror, was soon to be made a bishop. Burton accused both men of arrogance and pretentiousness:

> *Chez eux*, they will wear breech-clouts and Nature's stockings —*ecco tutto*. Here their coats are superfine Saxony, with broadest of silk velvet collars. The elongated cocoa-nut head bears jauntily a black pork-pie felt, with bright azure ribbons, and a rainbow necktie vies in splendour with the loudest of waistcoats from the land of Moses and Son ... There are portentous studs upon a glorious breadth of shirt, a small investment of cheap, gawdy, tawdry rings sets off the chimpanzee-like fingers, and when in the open air, lemon-coloured gloves invest the hands, whose horny reticulated skin reminds me of the cranes which pace at ease over the burning sand.

While crediting their wives with some charm, Burton said that both black passengers despised the very people from which they had come. Yet Crowther, in his books and in England, had cried up the majesty of the African kings. 'I have heard a negro assert, with unblushing effrontery which animates the negro speechifying in Exeter Hall, or before some learned society that, for instance, at Lagos—a den of thieves—theft is unknown, and that men leave their money with impunity in the storehouse, or on the highway. After which, he goes home, "tongue in cheek", despising the facility with which an Englishman and his money are parted.' Burton ended his remarks on his black fellow passengers by calling it 'a political as well as a social mistake to permit these men to dine in the main cabin, which they will end by monopolising: a ruling race cannot be too particular about these small matters.'

Freetown, from a distance, struck Burton as 'not unpicturesque, but the style of beauty is that of a Rhenish Castle, ruinous and tumble-down'. Nothing could be viler than the selected site and he blamed malaria for the failure to build on high ground. 'Men come out from Europe with the fairest prospect, if beyond middle age, of dying soon. Insurance officers object to insure. No one intends to stay longer than two years, and even these two are one long misery. Consequently men will not take the trouble to make roads, nor think of buying a farm, or of building a house upon a hill.' He deplored the lack of a marine parade and of adequate wharves; he derided the 'puny light house' and the 'contemptible jetty'. He described the 'mildewed cankered gangrened aspect of the decadent Europeo-Tropical settlements' and the 'little thatched hovels' of the natives.

Like every visitor to Sierra Leone, Burton was struck by the manifestations of piety; however, he did not approve of them. He jeered at the architectural deformities of St George's Cathedral. 'The cost was £150,000,' he exclaimed, 'not including a statue of Buxton (*the anti-slavery leader*) which, somewhat uncharacteristically, has shrunk into a shady corner ... Chapels there are in foison.' Like others, Burton remarked on the strict observance of Sunday but added his waspish footnote: 'All missionaries praise the African for his strict observance of the Sabbath. He would have 365 Sabbaths in the year if possible, and he would as scrupulously observe them all.' However, he claimed that piety had not produced real morality and he asserted that the Christian tenderness of the British Government had helped to debauch the natives. There lacked even the sanctions of truly primitive people down the coast:

In the Bights of Benin and Biafra, where the chiefs walk about with fetishman and executioner, there is still some manliness amongst men, some honour amongst women—the outward and visible form at least, if not the 'inward spiritual grace'. There the offending wife fears 'saucy water'* and decapitation; here she leaves the husband—the latter more rarely abandons the better half—with impunity. The women have become as vicious as those of Egypt, the basest of kingdoms.†

* Trial by sasswood: ordeal by poison.
† An Egyptian woman had given Burton V.D.

193

Theft is carried out to such an extent that no improvement is possible at Freetown which, as regards property, is the most communistic of communities.

Burton divided the 'darkies' into three rather arbitrary groups. 'First, the merchant, an honourable name, assumed by all who can buy half a dozen cloths and sit behind them on 'change, chatting and doing little else all the day. Second, the tailor, whose wife is certainly a washerwoman ... Third, the missionary, of whom the least said the better.' True, the one merchant, Syble Boyle, whose shop Burton actually patronized, he described as civil and honest— but then insisted that Boyle was 'an honourable exception'. Burton distinguished between the different types of 'darkies', if only to prove them dreadful in different ways. The settlers, Nova Scotians and Maroons were now too debased to compete with the more energetic recaptives, but these, he insisted, had only been sold into slavery because they were criminals. Of the two major races of the recaptives, Burton remarked that 'the Aku will do anything for money, the Ibo will do anything for revenge. Both races are intelligent enough to do harm—their talents rarely take the other direction.'

Although Burton attacked certain Sierra Leonean whites and mulattoes, his worst bile was spent on the Creoles—'these spoiled children, their puerile inept ways, their exceedingly bad language, their constant intoxication, and their disposition to quarrel on all occasions'. Although the Sierra Leonean was capable in some trades, only 'a perfect greenhorn on the coast will engage him in any capacity. The S'a Leone man is an inveterate thief; he drinks, he gambles, he intrigues, he over-dresses himself, and when he has exhausted his means, he makes master pay for all.' During his three days in the colony, Burton found time to study and then condemn the cemetery, the post office (where he was cheeked by the chief clerk), the prison ('conducted on philanthropic principles'), the journalism ('in the lowest stage of Eatenswillism'), a school (where they taught by rote) and above all the legal system.

'From the moment of our arrival "negro palaver" began,' said

Burton, describing a case where an Englishman had been fined fifty pounds for throwing a Negro out of the house. He repeated every old canard about the Sierra Leone juries and spiced the tales with his special malevolent wit.

The British Constitution determines that a man may be tried by his peers. His peers at S'a Leone are perhaps a dozen full-blooded blacks, liberated slaves, half-reformed fetishmen, sometimes with a sneaking fondness for the worship of *Shango*, and if not criminals in their own country, at least paupers clad in dishcloth and palm-oil. It is useless to 'challenge' for other negroes will surely take the place of those objected to ... The judge may be 'touched with the tarbrush' but be he white as milk he must pass judgment according to verdict, and when damages are under £200 there is no appeal ... Our forefathers never dreamed that the liberty and the institutions for which during long centuries they fought and bled, would thus be prostituted—be lavished upon every black recaptive, be he assassin, thief or wizard, after a residence of some fourteen days in a dark corner of the British empire. Even the Irishman and the German must pass some five years civilizing themselves in the United States before they are permitted to vote.

It was not true, of course, that a slave, recaptured fourteen days before could sit on a Sierra Leone jury. Like many pieces of information and anecdote in Burton's scurrilous book it was both untrue and unfair. Burton admits with a note of regret that he himself never experienced the Creole impudence that he treats as a known fact; and even the chief clerk's surliness at the post office sounds pretty mild in the telling. Perhaps he realized afterwards that his book had been not quite fair, for he gave a slightly different account of the colony after his second visit twenty years later. He was then British Consul in Trieste, but spent most of his time in voyaging round the Near East. For many years Burton had suffered from gold fever, and had already made some fruitless diggings on the Arabian side of the Red Sea. In 1881 he became convinced that he could strike gold and make his fortune in some little-known parts of the Gold Coast. Accompanied by a younger explorer Lovett Cameron, he set off once more to the continent that so repelled but attracted him. The two men caught fever after two months; the Foreign Office, which had expressly ordered Burton not to go abroad on commercial ventures, was furious; the mining survey, predictably, failed. Perhaps in an attempt to recoup their expenses, Burton and Cameron combined to write *To the Gold Coast for Gold*. Most of the book is unmistakably Burton's; indeed whole passages have been lifted unchanged from *Wanderings in West Africa* and *Two Trips to Gorilla Land*. Once again Burton described, with acerbic pedantry, the geography and the human life of the ports at which they called on the way. Once again, at Sierra Leone, he utters the same jeers at the 'darkies', presumably hoping that if the public enjoyed the jokes once they would enjoy them doubly when they read them twenty years later.

However, in this second account there are interesting alterations. The abuse of Crowther is omitted, perhaps on the assumption that now his father was a bishop he might be ready to sue for libel. After an uncharacteristic remark that 'it is better for both writer and reader to praise than to dispraise', Burton, aged sixty, came out with a statement that would have horrified Burton aged forty: 'Most Englishmen know negroes of pure blood as well as "coloured persons" who, at Oxford and elsewhere, have shown themselves fully equal in intellect and capacity to the white races of Europe and America.' The trouble, as Burton went on to explain, was that Negroes had not had fair play. While repeating most of his diatribe against Freetown, Burton admitted that here, too, things had changed for the better, 'physically by a supply of pure water, morally by the courage which curbed the black abuse. Twenty years ago to call a negro "nigger" was actionable; many a £5 has been paid for the indulgence of lese-majesté against the "man and brother ..." Now, thanks to a new law that civil complainants would have to prove themselves men of substance, the negro 'no longer squares up to you in the suburbs and dares the "white niggah" to strike the "black gen'leman".' Nor did he ever, except in the bilious imaginings of such Englishmen as Burton.

196

Several times, Burton expressed his astonishment at not observing things he had probably not observed when he was there twenty years earlier:

> There was none of the extreme 'bumptiousness' and pugnacious impudence of twenty years ago; indeed the beach-boys, nowhere a promising class, were rather civil than otherwise ... Nor did the unruly, disorderly African character ever show itself, as formerly it often did, by fisticuffing, hair-pulling and cursing, with a mixture of English and Dark-Continent ideas and phraseology, whose *tout ensemble* was really portentous.

Perhaps Burton had mellowed with age. Perhaps his fellow author, Cameron, not having seen the iniquities described by Burton, had mildly suggested, with proper respect to the older, more famous man, that he tone down some of his former, fiercer judgments. In *To the Gold Coast for Gold*, Burton (or possibly it was Cameron who wrote this passage) gave great praise to the Creole businessman, William Grant, for a speech he had made in England. It was Grant's complaint that the Negro was getting the wrong sort of education—one suited not to him but to Englishmen. 'He fancies', sad Grant, 'by the sort of education which you give him that he must imitate you in everything—act like you, dress in broadcloth like you. Then you see the result is that he is not himself; he confuses himself, and when he comes to act within himself as a man he is confused.' A dislike of Africans aping the Englishman partly explains Burton's preference for the Muslims. The Arab mosques he preferred to St George's Cathedral. He contrasted the buildings of Freetown, grey and mildewed, with the blue, yellow or whitewashed houses of Muslim Africa. Repeatedly he admired the dignity of the Mandingoes he met in Freetown, and laughingly he condoned their habit of kidnapping Creole children.

Burton's savage caricature of the Freetown Creoles, which is often distorted, crass and silly, had a lasting influence on the British public. As an African explorer and a distinguished scholar, Burton was regarded as an authoritative writer, whom critics assailed at their peril. The man who had convinced the Royal Geographical

Society that the White Nile flowed out of Lake Tanganyika, rather than out of Lake Victoria, was capable of putting over just as false an impression of the character of the Freetown Creoles. Burton's books also influenced other writers on Africa. The young W. Winwood Reade, who was to win fame with *The Martyrdom of Man* was, like Burton, a Tory, an anti-Christian and a romantic who preferred the primitive to the coastal Africans. 'If I have any merit', he wrote in introducing *Savage Africa*, 'it is that of having been the first young man about town to make any bona fide tour in Western Africa; to travel in that agreeable ·and salubrious country with no special object, and at his own expense; to *flâner* in the virgin forest; to flirt with pretty savages; and to smoke his cigar among cannibals.' Reade's facetiousness at the expense of the Freetown Creoles was almost as caustic as Burton's had been. He repeated the usual stories of corrupt juries, of laziness and of a Creole man 'dressed as if he had taken a bath in a rainbow'. When a porter who had carried his case demanded an extra sixpence 'for breaking the Sabbath', Reade was 'pleased to find that the labours of our missionaries had not been in vain'. When Reade returned to Sierra Leone in 1868 he wrote a much kinder description. 'There is a hardness and sourness in youth as in all unripe things,' he explained; '... I am not so fond of sneering and sarcasm as I was.' With all the wisdom afforded by six more years, Reade found that he liked the Freetown people. 'They are all rogues and beggars, to be sure, but some allowances must be made on their behalf; they are slaves or the children of slaves ... These negroes speak and write abominable English; yet, but is it not to their credit that they can speak and write English at all?'

Burton was also an influence on the extraordinary Mary Kingsley who by the time of her dismally early death was established as the greatest-ever writer on West Africa. She, too, was a rationalist and a conservative. She, too, although an able scientist, had gone to Africa with romantic yearnings. She, too, favoured the primitive even cannibal Africans over the urban Christians of the coast. She, too, made fun of the Freetown Creoles although her mockery was more kind than Burton's. Her racy, gushing, yet gawky prose—its character half genius and half gym teacher—is at its best in describing Freetown; as for example the turkey-buzzards on St George's Cathedral roof:

> ... The beauty of that edifice is very far from great, and it cannot carry off the effect produced by the row of these noisome birds as they sit along its summit, with their wings arranged at all manner of different angles in an 'all gone' way. One bird perhaps will have one straight out in front, and the other casually disposed at right-angles, another both straight out in front, and others again with both hanging hopelessly down, but none with them neatly and tidily folded up, as decent birds' wings should be. They all give the impression of having been extremely drunk the previous evening, and of having subsequently fallen into some sticky abomination— into blood for choice.

In his hostility to the coastal Africans, Burton was thirty years ahead of British colonial thinking. At the end of the century when Britain, for economic or geo-political reasons, began to push to the hinterland, Burton's ideas entered the normal currency. Lord Lugard took over the territory of the Muslim Fulanis and Hausas, respecting their institutions and exercising government only through 'indirect rule'. In the hinterland of the Gold Coast, the British once again fought and at last succeeded in crushing the fierce and courageous kingdom of the Ashantis. From about 1890, the year of Burton's death, Britain started to open up the interior of Sierra Leone. From then on in British West Africa, the power of the Creoles waned. British officials, professional and business men, working together with the chiefs of the interior, took over the management of affairs from the now derided 'black gentlemen'.

Chapter Four

Sir Richard Burton's contempt for the Freetown Creoles and his preference for the natives of the interior were regarded as odd, even indecent, when he voiced them in 1862 and again in 1882. By 1902, nearly twelve years after Burton's death, these views were the attitude of the British Government. The intervening twenty years had witnessed the 'scramble for Africa' in which the map of the continent had been redrawn. On the West Coast, Britain had seized the large and populous territories of Nigeria and the Gold Coast. The French had pushed their empire east from Senegal to the Sudan and had added more colonies on the coast. The Germans, newcomers to the imperial business, got Togo, the Cameroons, Tanganyika and South-West Africa. The French and Belgians carved up the Congo lands, while Britain in eastern and southern Africa acquired the Sudan, Kenya, Uganda, Nyasaland, two Rhodesias, several protectorates and the defeated Boer republics. During the last decade of the nineteenth century, the British moved into the hinterland of Sierra Leone. In the war of 1898 between the British and dissident inland tribes, the Creoles were disliked and distrusted by both sides. They lingered on, as a separate and rather pathetic group, until the middle of the twentieth century; but their power and spirit were broken; the fond experiment of the Saints was knocked over and trampled during the scramble for Africa.

The British invasion of Egypt in 1882 provoked the race for African possessions; yet Britain herself was a slow and reluctant competitor until over a dozen years later. Her anxiety over the Nile concerned Mediterranean safety and the link with her Far Eastern empire. 'The great question of British interest', was the Suez Canal, Gladstone said. In defence of this interest, Britain extended her influence to the Sudan, the Red Sea and even as far as Kenya. But black Africa, and especially West Africa, was of little interest to the British Government. Gladstone and his Tory successors wanted free access for British trade, but not if this meant annexing the hinterland. Britain already obtained most of her tropical raw materials from the East and from Latin America, and did not regard West African produce as economically interesting. The merchants of Liverpool and Manchester, who handled most of the West Coast trade, were not yet a powerful lobby in Westminster.

British trade policy in West Africa had been based on a tacit agreement with other commercial powers that none of them should upset the present arrangement. The occupation of Egypt changed all that. Bismarck's Germany, bubbling with new-found national pride, accepted the move as a challenge. France, still smarting from her defeat in Europe, was eager for *gloire* in Africa and the Far East. King Leopold of the Belgians lusted after the wealth of his massive estate in the Congo. All three got the go-ahead for their plans at the conference in Berlin in 1884 when Africa was chopped up into spheres of influence. Only Britain still refused to get interested in West Africa. She encouraged British traders, such as Goldie in Nigeria, to establish private treaties with the chiefs, but she did not want the government to take on the trouble, and still less the cost, of physical annexation. Britain already possessed an enormous empire which few politicians were interested in augmenting. British public opinion derived its ideas of West Africa from Sierra Leone, the White Man's Grave. Few in England were bothered when France started to snap up the African hinterland. As Mary Kingsley, herself a keen expansionist, was ruefully to observe:

You will often hear in England regarding French annexation in Africa, 'Oh! let her have the deadly hole, and much good may it do her.' France knows very well what good it will do her ... She knows Africa is a superb training ground for her officers ... and the next time she tries conclusions with one of us Teutonic nations, she will be armed with men who have learned their trade well on the burning sands of Senegal, and they will take a lot of beating. We do not require Africa as a training ground for our army; India is as magnificent a military academy as any nation requires; but we do require all the Africa we can get, West, East and South, for a market, and it is here we clash with France; for France not only does not develop the trade of her colonies for her own profit, but stamps trade at large out by her preferential tariffs . . .

The martial French had long since explored the upper reach of the Niger, and had drawn up a treaty with Fouta Djalon that threatened to cut off the hinterland of Sierra Leone. This move caused unease in Freetown. The Creole bourgeoisie, who for years had gone down the coast in search of trade and employment, had recently turned their attention towards the hinterland. The trade of the colony had increased five-fold during the fifty years until 1880, and most of this was accounted for by Creole commerce up country. Creole men, and the formidable lady merchants, had set up posts at river heads in many remote districts. Visitors to 'native' huts noticed signs of Creole influence such as 'a few cane-bottomed chairs, a fir centre table with cover, a small side table [and] a couch of plain deal with cotton print cover'. The missionaries, too, did good business. A pious Iowan windbag, Daniel Flickinger, who had spent thirteen years in the Sherbro and bagged only two conversions, claimed that thousands were coming to church in the 1880s, possibly awed by his newly awarded title, United Brethren Bishop of Germany and Africa. The Manchester textile merchants must have been favourable to the bishop, who was tireless in his efforts to stop the native infants from going naked.

As the Creoles moved into the hinterland, so immigrants came into Freetown in search of work. The Creoles were grateful for this supply of cheap labour, but they accused the newcomers of burglary, dirtiness, witchcraft and making a row at night by drumming and dancing. Gangs of Creole louts would insult and beat up the immigrants, while even some of the bourgeoisie favoured this tough treatment of strangers. The eminent Creole gentleman A. J. Sawyerr is said to have told a meeting in 1886: 'There was a time in the annals of the settlement when a little Sierra Leonean might kick a Timeneh or a Soosoo with impunity. Nowadays we hear of Timeneh "strikes". Significant phenomenon, gentlemen; we must not consider ourselves safe and secure because we have a regiment at the barracks.'

Even a chief's son, Yarreh Kur, was not spared the contempt of the Creoles. As a boy at the C.M.S. grammar school, he was constantly teased—'Kur, Kur, Kur, Kur, Kroo, canoe'—so that his guardian had his name changed to Edward Carew. This teasing may explain why Muslims from up country changed their comfortable cool cotton robes for the bastard English finery of the Creoles.

In the mid 1880s, when Freetown was nervous about the French advance from the north, a severe commercial slump hit the colony. This was caused largely by a world-wide drop in the price of such staple Sierra Leone products as rubber, palm kernels, and palm oil. The Creoles attributed it to the 'tribal wars' in the hinterland. These were, in fact, really trade wars between chiefs who wanted to exercise control over the river heads, where traders gathered to buy goods from the interior. Although these wars may sometimes have hampered trade, they were, seen historically, a result of the greatly increased trade in palm oil that had upset the old trade agreements between the neighbouring chiefs. The quarrels were often exacerbated by Creole traders and English officials who intervened and tried to arbitrate without understanding the niceties of bush diplomacy and trade.

Most Creole merchants, in 1885, wanted vigorous action to suppress the wars, and to ensure the safety of traders. The Sierra Leone Association, representing the Freetown bourgeoisie, held a meeting which was attended by a thousand people, who adopted a resolution calling upon the colonial government to maintain peace by force of arms, to guard the trade routes with troops, to define the frontier with France and to send expeditions to open new areas for trade. Sir Samuel Lewis chose the time of the Queen's Golden Jubilee to make a public speech demanding expansion. He deplored attempts to conciliate 'the semi-barbarous aggressors on British territory by the purchase of peace from them'. Many Creoles at this time spoke of the need to redeem the 'natives' from savagery. The Freetown Christians, who for nearly a century had ignored the ways of the hinterland, now deplored the horrors of slavery, cannibalism and such murderous gangs as the Leopard and Crocodile Societies.

Sir Samuel Rowe, who returned in 1885 for a second term as governor, was cool to the Creole demands for expansion. He toured up country and tried to make peace between quarrelling chiefs, but he knew that aggressive policies would not be well received in London. For one thing it was considered impolitic to control an area where slavery was still practised. More important still, there was not enough money. Sir Samuel Lewis, like most of the Creole community, believed in 'peaceful annexation financed by an imperial loan'. Sir Samuel Rowe, faced in any case with a deficit, favoured import duties or straight taxation.

The Creoles agreed to an *ad valorem* duty but were resolute against taxes. Sir Samuel Lewis and A. J. Sawyerr, a bookseller and politician, favoured instead a cut in government officers' pay. Feeling ran high in the Freetown press, and a local poet, J. T. Macfoy, put his argument to the tune of 'God Save the Queen.'

> No more taxation's paws
> On out beloved shores
> Shall e'er alight;
> Lewis's forensic force
> Sawyerr's placid discourse
> The monster's horrid jaws
> Have broken quite.

Some of the whites in Sierra Leone derided the Creole unwillingness to pay tax, and they too put their point of view through doggerel in the newspapers.

Here's a pretty go my lads, whatever shall we do?
There ain't no money in the box an' things is looking blue.
The Governor he works all day to make the two ends meet,
But three and two will not make six by any juggling feat.
  With a hocus and a pocus and a quantity of rot,
  A Sawyerr and a lawyer and the Colony to pot.

Although white Freetown merchants had joined the Creoles in
calling for expansion to the interior, there were others who looked
on the colony as a destructive influence. This view was expressed
by John M. Harris, who had traded for twenty years at Sulyma to
the south, where the government of Sierra Leone had recently
started a customs post. His thesis was that the policy of raising
money by import duties instead of by tax, and therefore raising
the price of goods for sale inland, was a tax on the people of the
interior, a cause of war and a great injustice. He accused the
colony of

> annexing outlying districts that have been hitherto inde-
> pendent under their native chiefs, with the view of taxing their
> trade, while (beyond some paltry stipends of mere nominal
> amounts, paid to the chiefs) it proposes to confer upon the
> districts so annexed no advantages whatever in return, either
> in the form of security to life and property, which ought to be
> the first duty of a Government that levies taxes, or in the
> formation of roads and other conveniences for the traffic which
> is taxed.

Far from conferring security, Harris argued, the customs duty
actually fostered wars:

> Trade rivalries and jealousies, though not the final and alleged
> cause of outbreak, are always at the bottom of some wars.
> And these heartburnings are certainly not lessened when the
> chiefs of the interior find that those on the coast have been
> induced, or forced, to submit to payments which increase the
> cost of everything they use. These people have laws and

customs of their own, well known and enforced by the *porroh*, or sacred traditions of their country, which have come down to them from their forefathers.

Any chief who made a treaty without the consent of the others would become an object of enmity and attack.

From twenty years of friendship with many chiefs, Harris believed that they wanted British protection. What they received was taxation that led to wars, which were followed by brutal punitive raids by Sierra Leonean troops who burned down villages and fired shells into the sacred groves. 'What is really objectionable', Harris concluded, 'is the system of partial annexation, which neither leaves the country alone nor takes it over entirely.'

Mary Kingsley guyed the British colonial policy as 'a coma interrupted by fits'. This eccentric lady was a partisan of the Liverpool and Manchester traders, and she argued their case with vim, if not with utter consistency. As she explained in one of her two mammoth books:

> My idea is that the French method of dealing with Africa is the best at present. Get as much of the continent as possible down on the map as yours, make your flag wherever you go a sacred thing to the native—a thing he dare not attack. Then, when you have done this, you may abandon the French plan, and gradually develop the trade in an English manner, but not in the English manner *à la* Sierra Leone.

She wanted to open up the interior, but for the benefit of the British traders and not the Sierra Leone Creoles.

The African traders and imperialists went unheeded until 1895, when Joseph Chamberlain was made Colonial Secretary in the new Unionist Government. Like Mary Kingsley, he wanted to snatch land for Britain in Africa, but his motives were subtly different. His friends, enemies and the history books called Chamberlain a radical, although the title means little. He believed that the world's economic system was moving towards protectionism; he had borrowed from the socialists a belief that the state should contribute to public welfare; he believed that both these principles could be maintained by an empire. Although much has been made of Chamberlain's middle-class Birmingham background, his principles were like those of Bismarck, the Junker aristocrat.

Chamberlain was greedy for what he called the 'undeveloped estates' of Africa. He complained that the Liberal governments, with their doctrine of laisser-faire, had allowed too much of the continent to fall to rival powers. Helped by Sir Charles Dilke, another imperialist, Chamberlain rushed to catch up in the race. He gave a charter to Goldie and encouraged him to seize land in Nigeria. He egged on the Gold Coast Government to crush the stubborn Ashanti. Last and, it must be admitted, least, he encouraged a policy of expansion in Sierra Leone. Paradoxically it was in Sierra Leone, the smallest and least significant of the three colonies, that Chamberlain's imperialism resulted in disaster.

The governor of Sierra Leone fated to execute Chamberlain's policies was a professional soldier, Colonel Frederic Cardew, who had come to the colony in 1894. Colonel Cardew had spent twenty years in India, five in South Africa and had fought against the Pathans and Zulus. A plump-faced man with bulging eyes and a great meaty neck, his tunic buttons straining to hold in his chest, Cardew looked like a caricature of the plethoric ex-India colonel. Curry-tempered he was, but Cardew, untypically for his kind, was both devout and a strict teetotaller. This last may account for the outstanding physical energy that enabled him, at the age of fifty-five, to begin the first of a series of treks through the hinterland of his colony. It was his purpose to turn the 'sphere of influence' into a British protectorate where the chiefs would still hold authority, but under the guidance of Freetown. This policy, that he had seen and approved in Zululand, was later formulated by Lugard into the theory of 'indirect rule'. During his first year in Sierra Leone, Cardew reorganized the Frontier Police, who had been formed in 1890. He tightened up discipline, dismissed or imprisoned policemen who had abused their office, and started up schools for recruits. He supervised the Sierra Leone side of a boundary agreement drawn up by the French and British Governments.

And he pursued his favourite plan for the construction of a railway.

There had been talk of building a railway since 1872, but no capital could be found to take the risk. Under pressure from the Liverpool Chamber of Commerce, the government had sent two surveyors to explore some of the likely routes. Cardew believed that the line should run east through the territory most rich in oil palms, and this advice was ultimately to be taken. The Legislative Council was excited about the plan, and china plates were sold in Freetown showing the governor's head with a train running round it. The Liverpool Chamber of Commerce welcomed the plan when Cardew told them about it during his leave. However, no private investors would put up the risk capital for the venture unless it was subsidised by the British Government. It was fortunate for Cardew's plan that Chamberlain took over at the Colonial Office just at the time, in the middle of 1895, when the railway was being mooted. He approved the railway, the first in British West Africa, and put the Crown agents in charge of construction.

Cardew regarded tribal Africans as 'ignorant, superstitious and uncivilized' but he thought it his duty to protect them from the inroads of civilization, and particularly from the Creoles. This was already the policy of the Colonial Office. When the Creole J. C. Parkes, then head of the Department of Native Affairs, had suggested in 1893 that the protectorate should be run by Creole agents, the Colonial Office refused. One official wrote: 'But Mr Parkes is an exception and I don't for a moment suppose we could get half a dozen natives like him who could be trusted for this kind of work.' Another official added: 'We could not depend on them and they would be likely to get us into all sorts of difficulties. I should much prefer a couple of good European travelling Commissioners who should go about the country and settle difficulties, taking with them an escort of police.' Governor Cardew began by distrusting Creole officials; soon he came to distrust all Creoles, particularly traders, lawyers and journalists.

Like most new governors, Cardew enjoyed a brief honeymoon with the Creoles in which he approved of them and was approved.

He worshipped at St George's Cathedral, danced with their wives at balls in the Wilberforce Hall and went to (teetotal) receptions at their homes. Samuel Lewis and he were mutually admiring. The Creole praised the governor for his indefatigable work of travelling in the interest of the colony, and welcomed the opportunities for investment that Cardew's railway would shortly provide; in short he believed that the protectorate would soon enjoy 'the blessing' of Industry and Civilization. The governor, maybe pleased with this flattery, recommended Lewis for a knighthood.

The friendly Mr Lewis soon turned into a hostile Sir Samuel. The quarrel began over a legal issue concerning the status of the protectorate. Other disputes followed, and the two men were scarcely on speaking terms by June 1897 when Cardew himself was awarded a knighthood. By this time, Cardew was quite disenchanted with Creoles. His Queen's Advocate had been caught taking private money; his Creole secretary had deceived him; and two Creole postmasters were found out in graft. He regarded the Creoles of the interior as swindling land-grabbers who traded in guns and rum; those in Freetown were swindling lawyers or bitchy, anonymous journalists. Like many Sierra Leone governors who had planned to advance the Creoles, Cardew soon came to rely only on Englishmen. He stopped appointing Creoles to the Legislative Council, which anyway was becoming feeble.

The protectorate was proclaimed in August 1896, under authority of a British Act of Parliament. The chiefs had not been consulted and the proclamation was issued only in the colony. The colony at this time had a population of roughly 73,000, while the protectorate, covering 40,000 square miles, had nearly a million inhabitants. Yet the Creoles of the colony still did not appear to understand that they might one day be swamped by the people of the interior. Even Lewis, while making the legal point that the chiefs had not been consulted nor given assent, seems personally to have welcomed the protectorate.

The uprising in the protectorate in 1898 came to be called the 'Hut-Tax War', and must largely be blamed on this method of raising revenue. Although Cardew was the man on the spot, and therefore directly responsible, it was part of Chamberlain's West African policy that the interior should be opened up by railways and an expensive force of administrators and police paid for partly by a house tax on the natives. A similar tax was levied in the Gold Coast, and the fact that it did not provoke a war there was due more to luck than wisdom. Certainly Cardew himself believed in the house tax. He believed that the colony was too poor to pay for the development of the hinterland and that, anyway, there was much cash in circulation within the protectorate. 'In the first place I believe the natives will prefer to pay in coin (rather than goods),' he wrote in a dispatch to London, 'and in the second that it will very soon be, if it is not already, within their ability to do so. My experience in Zululand, where I used to collect hut-tax and where after the first year it was paid in cash, leads me to this conclusion.' He proposed a tax of ten shillings for houses with four rooms and five shillings for houses with less. This was considered reasonable by other British officials. G. Braithwaite Wallis, who had come to Sierra Leone as Assistant Inspector, wrote:

In Liberia, every male over twenty-one years and residing within the Government's sphere of influence, has to pay in tax at the rate of six shillings and threepence per annum and there is no difficulty in collecting it. In Basutoland the rate was ten shillings in 1885, and since then there has been an increase; and in Natal every Kaffir pays about two pounds per hut. So the tax of five shillings which was being imposed in the Sierra Leone Protectorate was not unreasonable and by no means out of the power of a majority of the inhabitants to meet.

Governor Cardew told the Colonial Office that some opposition to the tax might be expected. Although confident that he could deal with this, he reminded the government that if they feared the consequence of a tax, they could finance development out of imperial funds. The government did not take the hint, as Cardew hoped they would not. For it is clear from Cardew's writings that he wanted the tax, not just as a source of revenue, but as an instrument of development, and above all as a way of obtaining labour. 'In Zululand', Cardew recalled, 'after the first year of the imposition of the hut tax, in which some of the Zulus paid in cattle, they always paid in cash. The chiefs used to send their young men to the labour fields at Kimberley and Natal to earn the fourteen shillings—not five—per hut, which they had to pay.' Almost everywhere in Southern and Central Africa, the colonial governments imposed (and indeed still impose) a tax, payable only in cash, to force the Africans into the labour market. As Cardew was later to write, in justification of the tax:

The products of the Protectorate are only just now beginning to be developed by the construction of a railway, by improved roads and other means of communication, and by the intro- duction of capital in the form of trading and development companies. There is every possibility, therefore, of the re- sources of the Protectorate being doubled within a reasonable time, and in the meantime, as an additional source from which to pay the house tax, there are increasing demands for labour —which the natives furnish, and for which they are paid at a high rate—not only in Freetown, where many hundreds are daily employed, but for the carriage of provisions and supplies for the troops, Frontier Police and other Government establishments in the Protectorate; for the construction of the railway which is now advancing into the Protectorate, the annual account of which is at least £16,000; and lastly, for the trading and other companies that are in course of being formed for the development of the Protectorate.

Payment of the tax was not to begin until 1898, but from the time of its announcement, late in 1896, there was uproar from the protectorate. Many chiefs complained, often untruthfully, that they had not the money to meet the demand. At one meeting in Government House, after Cardew had explained at length why he was introducing taxation, one chief said 'he couldn't under- stand how Queen Victoria could lack money when her head was stamped on every coin.' More seriously, many chiefs believed that the new law divested them of the ownership of their property and that the tax was a kind of rent to the government. A petition from six Temne chiefs, for example, read: 'We are not able to pay for our own houses, because we have no power and no strength to do so.'

The hut tax was announced as one part of a special protectorate ordinance. Other provisions also worried the chiefs of the interior. They feared that the power of the governor to take over 'waste and uninhabited lands' was a threat to their ownership of ancestral estates. They objected, with good reason, to having to pay a two-pound licence to trade in their own country. They feared that the ordinance would undermine their authority in the tribal courts and would even prevent them from beating their wives. Most objections to these provisions, as to the hut tax itself, were based less on genuine grievances than on misunderstanding. In this respect, Cardew must take the blame for pushing through his reforms too fast and without consultation. Like so many Englishmen, he could not grasp the bush African's deep respect for justice and the consequent need for patient explanation. The chiefs were quite agreeable to a British protectorate and, as it turned out, they were able to pay the tax. After the uprising, the British journalist, E. D. Morel, who belonged to the Kingsley school of thought, made a pertinent comparison between the taxation methods employed in Sierra Leone and those in neighbouring Guinea:

> A poll-tax was applied in French Guinea in 1897 ... It has been peacefully collected. Was this the result of overwhelming military strength? Not at all, for although French Guinea is now about three times the size of Sierra Leone, the military, or rather the police force of the French Protectorate is a little over half what it is in Sierra Leone. The 'show of force' theory has, therefore, been conspicuous by its absence ... [Morel then put his finger on what had gone wrong in Sierra Leone] 'The tax in French Guinea is a poll tax, the tax in Sierra Leone is a property tax. In the one case there was no interference with native land tenure; in the other there was indirect interference with native land tenure.

Anger mounted throughout 1897. When the tax came into effect at the New Year, active and passive resistance broke out all over the protectorate. Chiefs announced their refusal to pay the tax, or even to trade with the white men. The Frontier Police replied with displays of force and sometimes with personal violence. 'An unmistakeable sign of the way the wind was blowing', C. Braithwaite Wallis later wrote of a journey through Mende country early in 1898, 'lay in the fact that on arriving in several of these towns, the greater part of the inhabitants would bolt incontinently into the bush. Nowhere was I hospitably received.' The first fighting broke out in the Temne area of Port Loko, north of Freetown, where the chiefs had threatened death to anyone paying tax. A government force tried to persuade the chiefs and, when this failed, arrested five of them, sentenced them to hard labour and sent them by boat to Freetown jail. These events were reported up river to Bai Bureh, the main chief of the Kasse area. This burly, drunken, but highly intelligent man had already caused trouble in 1894, when an expedition was sent, unsuccessfully, to arrest him. In February 1898, another party of 'Frontiers' once again went to arrest Bai Bureh and once again failed. The 'Frontiers' retreated with casualties, whereupon violence broke out in many parts of the nothern protectorate.

Sir Frederick Cardew, as he had become in 1897, proved incapable of averting the war. Neuralgia, shingles and insomnia had combined with the psychological horrors of Freetown to make him suspicious and querulous. He became increasingly tetchy about the complaints of the chiefs and increasingly favourable to a show of force. The time and energy that should have been spent on the problems of the protectorate were wasted on petty spats with his British colleagues. In particular, he disliked Colonel the Hon. James Caulfield, Commander of Troops and deputy governor. On January 15th, 1898, when the two men should have been pondering on the military threat to the colony, Cardew instead wrote to Caulfield:

Sir, Referring to our conversation yesterday on the subject of your appearing at the Council without your sword and during which you called in question my right to ask you to wear it, I have the honour to inform you that, apart from the fact that I think it only proper that an officer in uniform, when acting in his official capacity, should wear his sword and further that his doing so when attending Executive or Legislative Council is in consonance with the dignity of those assemblies, it has been the custom for the last 28 years and I believe from time immemorial for the Officer Commanding Troops to appear at Council with his sword on, and that, under these circumstances, I trust you will conform to the custom which has so long prevailed, and that I may have your assurance that you purpose doing so as a departure from it cannot have either my concurrence or sanction.

This preposterous tiff, which ended by Caulfield sulking and not turning up at the council meetings, recalls Mary Kingsley's remark about a colony (which I feel sure was Sierra Leone) where 'the officials even carry on their personal quarrels on government paper in a high official style, when it would be better if they put aside an hour a week and went and punched each other's heads'.

The Temne troubles in February had come as a reaction to the hut tax. The uprising in the Mende territories south and east of Freetown reflected a widespread distrust of the protectorate. The rebel chiefs, using the secret Poro societies, arranged a simultaneous attack through the whole Sherbro, Mende and Gallinas countries. Hundreds of aliens, whites and Creoles were slaughtered, sometimes with frightful cruelty. Missionaries and traders living in isolated posts had no warning of the revolt and no way of escape from its violence. Those who managed to reach a boat and flee to the safety of Freetown gave blood-curdling accounts of their experiences. Enraged by these atrocity stories, the British reacted with equal savagery.

Several hundred whites and Creoles were killed in the first few days of the uprising. At most times, such an outrage would have meant a sensation in Parliament and instant punitive action against the responsible governor. Fortunately for Cardew, the Hut-Tax

War had to compete for coverage in the newspapers with a number of other uprisings and wars that had broken out the same year. Thanks partly to Mr Chamberlain's policies, there was simultaneous trouble in Somaliland, Swaziland, the lower Niger, Borneo, New Zealand and Uganda, not to mention the threat of war with France over control of the upper Nile. The Hut-Tax rising could therefore be put down with the minimum of publicity.

The details of the campaign are of little interest, for the outcome was never in question. The Mendes of the east proved brave, but because of their habit of charging in open country against machine-guns, they were scarcely even troublesome to the British. Shooting them down, in the words of a young British officer was 'grand sport'. Bai Bureh in the Temne country was a much more subtle campaigner and gave the British a long run. His troops would dig trenches and build stockades at ambush points in front of the British forces, then open up at close range with their trade guns. When pressed, they would disappear in the bush. The Temne warriors loved their chief and he earned the inevitable compliment from one of the British officers: 'He's a poor benighted 'eathen but a first-class fighting man.' Bai Bureh fought until October when most of his men grew hungry and fled. The old chief was a realist, so, accompanied by a fiddler and a flagon of palm wine, he gave himself up to the British troops, saying: 'De war done don.'

When peace was restored, the Freetown Government turned to the punishment of the rebels. The Temnes like Bai Bureh had been guilty of armed revolt, but not of any atrocities, and were merely banished abroad for a few years. To punish the murderers in the Mende country, the government brought over an English barrister to go round the country on a special assize with five Creole tradesmen as assessors. This deputy-judge, George Bonner, found that most accused were guilty of murder according to the law, but those young men who were merely obeying their chiefs, he recommended to mercy. 'Later on,' he afterwards wrote, 'when I got back to Freetown after two months of Assizes, I regretted to find that a number of "boys" whom I had recommended to mercy, had not been reprieved but had suffered the last penalty.' However, only eighty-three men were hanged compared with more than a thousand who had been massacred.

Many Englishmen favoured far more ferocious punishment. After describing the torture of an Englishman which had left him 'a mere mass of quivering, mutilated flesh', C. Braithwaite Wallis doubted 'if any political adjustment called a "pacification" or any punishment inflicted by us on the ringleaders in this rising subsequently, could possibly atone for crimes like those. Surely the British had been justified had they wiped out every black the country through.'

Others, more generous, saw that the natives of the protectorate had rebelled under provocation. For example, Lieutenant J. Stewart, who served with the West African Regiment during hostilities, blamed the revolt on the hut tax, the behaviour of white officials and the bullying methods used by the Frontier Police. This view was expounded with gusto by famous writers on Africa such as E. D. Morel and Mary Kingsley, who likened the tax to those greased cartridges that had sparked off the Indian Mutiny. Their arguments made an impression on Chamberlain, who decided to send out a special commissioner to look into the cause of the war and the general state of the colony. The man chosen, Sir David Chalmers, had served ten years as a judge in West Africa, including a spell at Sierra Leone, and one doubts whether he went to his task with a quite unprejudiced mind. From his arrival in July 1898, he was on bad terms with Cardew and ready to blame him for what had gone wrong.

Those who condemned and those who excused the rebels of the protectorate agreed in blaming the Creoles for the part they had played in the war. Cardew accused the Creoles of responsibility for the war by provoking the natives not to pay the hut tax. There had been articles in the Creole press that attacked the tax, and these had found their way up country, but there is no evidence that the Creoles incited the natives to disobey. If so, they were very incompetent provocateurs, for almost everywhere in the Mende territory the Creoles were the first victims of the massacre. 'They used to say the Sierra Leone people were the children of the Governor,' said one survivor of the uprising, 'and it was through us that the Governor knew they had money to pay the tax, and if we are all killed the Governor will not follow us to make them pay tax.' The natives frequently referred to the Creoles as 'white men', or 'white man's piccin' or 'Englishmen'. Some blamed the Creoles for stirring revolt; others, like Lieutenant Stewart, blamed them for arrogance and swindling. 'There must be some truth in the last,' he went on, 'for look at the vindictive and barbarous way everything Sierra Leonean—whether human beings or property—have been dealt with.' The same logic in Russia in 1919 blamed the Jews both for leading the communists and for having, by their financial avarice, provoked the revolution.

The Creoles in Freetown regarded the war with a mixture of terror and fury. They were terrified of the fate they would meet if the natives stormed into the city; they were furious with Cardew for trying to blame the revolt on them. The newspapers vindicated the Creole cause with counter-attacks on Cardew and his administration. These articles still further inflamed the governor's hostility. Sir Samuel Lewis, almost alone of the Creole bourgoisie, had volunteered for service in the militia, but he too defended Creole honour against Cardew's accusations.

Meanwhile Cardew did his best to cut down the power of the Creoles, above all in the judiciary. When Bonner had gone on his assize through the Mende country, he had taken Creole assessors because of the physical difficulties of taking a twelve-man jury around the bush. He was critical of these assessors, whom he accused of trying to convict every prisoner. Afterwards the assessor system, introduced as a temporary convenience, was kept on as a permanent institution. The jury system, so long a bulwark of Creole power, was abolished for all non-capital cases in 1898. A further ordinance imposed the hut tax in the colony as well as in the protectorate. Cardew still further sapped the influence of the Creoles by barring them from the Legislative Council and not advancing them in office. As J. D. Hargreaves writes in his biography of Sir Samuel Lewis: 'Leaders of the African bourgeoisie,

217

like Lewis, were no longer welcomed as collaborators in the process of improvement from above, and the day of the democratic politician drawing power from below had not yet come. Till it did, the pace of the colony's political progress was regulated by the Protectorate.' In April 1899, Sir Samuel Lewis boarded the railway train that he had so long advocated, only to find himself punched by a British soldier who wanted Lewis's servant's seat. Sierra Leone had become just another colony.

The final battle of the Hut-Tax War was fought in London in 1899, when Chalmers delivered his report. As expected, this was a condemnation of Cardew. The report put the blame for the war on an unfair tax and the failure to familiarize the chiefs with the constitutional changes. It accused the Frontier Police of brutality, adding that many were 'runaway slaves—generally the idlest and worst-behaved of a household'. It exonerated the Freetown press and the Creoles in general from any responsibility for the revolt.

The Chalmers report, although true in many respects, was partisan in tenor, and unfair on certain points. In his reply, Governor Cardew accused Chalmers of having put leading questions to witnesses and then misreported their evidence. He defended the Frontier Police, the hut tax and the railway by pointing to the progress they had already brought to the colony. Although Chamberlain studied the Chalmers report and heard arguments in its favour from Mary Kingsley, he decided at last, in the manner of all politicians, to believe the facts that fitted his previous prejudice. In a long speech to the House of Commons he repudiated the Chalmers report, and expressed his confidence in Cardew's administration. A few hours earlier, Chalmers had done what so many others had quickly done after serving Sierra Leone for good or ill. He had died.

PART FOUR

Chapter One

For the first twenty years after her independence, Liberia was a flourishing and respected state with a thriving economy. Her native coffee, the famous *Liberica*, was grown on plantations beside the St Paul's River and sold to Europe and the United States. There were enough large farms of sugar-cane to keep one steam-mill and three ox-mills in constant operation. Cotton was grown beside the Junk River, and it was from Liberia that the first palm kernels were shipped to Europe. One settler wrote back to America in 1851 that, provided you had a house built and a garden planted,

> if you will but work two hours in each day, you cannot fail to do better than by working the whole day in America. You can raise sweet potatoes, yams, cassava, cotton, coffee and all other vegetables ... If a man plants ten acres of coffee, in four or five years he will realise a handsome income. Coffee requires very little labor, and is of more value than anything America can produce from your labour in twenty years ...

These were not empty boasts, as is seen from Liberia's export trade. By 1870 about fifty small coastal ships of between thirty and eighty tons had been built in the docks of Monrovia. Larger ships, owned and manned by Liberians, carried the Lone Star flag as far as New York and Liverpool. These successes are all the more admirable when one thinks how small the country then was. On the 286 miles of coastland with a hinterland stretching back only forty-five miles there were no more than 10,000 Liberians of American origin. Probably there were less than 7,000. Moreover, one must remember that most of these settlers were ignorant former plantation slaves from the southern United States, who were patently not of the stuff from which pioneers are made.

'Many friends of colonization think that this simple material is too rude for Africa,' wrote G. W. Hall, a settler, in 1857, 'and they would choose in its stead the more polished freeman of Northern cities, quite forgetting that in a new country the sturdy labourer is equally as indispensable as the man of education and refinement.' However, Hall goes on to regret that 'free coloured men of the North do not more often turn their attention to Liberia ... They can not, will not, emigrate to such a country, with clod-hopping slaves, clad in linsey-woolsey, and just redeemed from Massa's plantation.'

Most foreign visitors in the eighteen fifties and 'sixties praised Liberia, often comparing it favourably with Sierra Leone. Indeed, Liberia had the distinction of being one of the very few parts of the world to be praised by Sir Richard Burton, who stopped off at Cape Palmas after his famous stay in Freetown. Nothing about the country can have prejudiced him in its favour. It was run by educated blacks; it was widely renowned for its piety; and its settlers had come from a country that Burton called 'Yankeedom', whose flag, the Stars and Stripes, he described as the 'Oysters and Gridiron'. Indeed, Burton himself admitted that his knowledge about Liberia was confined to 'the dictum of an American skipper as regards Uncle Tom's refuge for the Destitute, namely, that in years to come the baboons would be putting off to trade with Liberians' skins.'

Needless to say, Burton enjoyed his jokes at the expense of the Liberians. On meeting some pious white missionaries who were eager for a Northern victory in the American Civil War, Burton delighted in telling them 'not without an irrepressible chuckle', about the Southern victory at Bull Run. But Burton was pleased with the cleanliness of the hotel, the diligence of the workmen and the courtesy of the Liberians, whom he called 'men of colour' rather than 'niggers'—his usual word.* Sometimes one gets the impression that Burton was praising the Liberians only so as to still further malign the hated people of Freetown. He noticed 'wonderful to relate, black carpenters at their benches and black

* He did, however, refer to Liberia as 'the Yankee-doodle, niggery republic'.

coopers—I saw nothing of the kind at S'a Leone—hard at work, refitting old casks for new palm oil'. And when Burton tried to recruit a gig's crew and two servants, the aspirants for the jobs behaved decently; 'they did now crowd upon us, and when told to go away, they went. At S'a Leone there would have been an action—at least a summons.' Liberia, in Burton's view, had benefited by being colonized from the autocratic United States rather than easy-going Britain. 'Civilised and perfectly capable of managing and utilising their wild congeners, the colonists appear in a most favourable light after the semi-reclaimed Akus and Ibos, their northern neighbours.' Burton then refers to the plan, put forward by President Roberts and turned down by the British Government in 1854, that Liberia should annex Sierra Leone. Burton thought this a good idea: 'I doubt not that, if permitted, they would soon effect important changes. Liberia is a Republic, that is to say, she is pretty far gone in the ways of despotism—the only fit government for "Africa and the Africans".'

Burton's disciple, Winwood Reade, also visited Liberia and made it the butt of some anti-Yankee jibes. The House of Representatives at Monrovia reminded him of the parent body at Washington. 'Spittoons are provided in both establishments, and frequently made use of; feet are put up on the tables.' He praised the leaders of Liberian society for their good education and intelligence but accused them of prejudice against genuine Africans. One Americo-Liberian remarked to Reade how odd it was that men in Africa had wool rather than hair while the sheep had hair rather than wool. Reade liked Liberia but predicted, rightly, that it was bound to run into difficulties for want of labour and capital. 'I shall always remember with pleasure', he said, 'my visit to Liberia; it is a quiet, respectable, well-ordered community; but if any American negroes should happen to read this book, I advise them to stay where they are; and I think that the greatest blessing that the American Colonization Society can confer upon the Africans is to vote its own dissolution.'

The political life of Liberia until about 1870 was as orderly and healthy as its economic life. President Roberts was re-elected in

1849 and for every two years until 1855, when he handed over the candidacy to the equally admirable General S. A. Benson, the vice-president. In this first spell of office, which was not to prove his last, Roberts continued the work of pacifying the native tribes and exterminating the slavers. He went to Europe in 1854 and was well received by the press and the politicians, above all in England, where he arranged for the minting of Liberia's first coins. Out of office, Roberts still played a leading role in the country's political life. He led the expedition to rescue Maryland shortly before that province was merged with Liberia. In 1857 he was appointed first principal of Liberia College, and in 1862 served on a six-month mission to Europe. The two main parties, during their first twenty years, frequently changed their titles and their policies, but the real dividing-line was colour rather than politics. The mulattoes, led by Roberts, held power throughout against the growing jealousy of the 'pure' blacks. The hostility between the two groups was to explode in 1871, as we shall see in the next chapter.

The chief concern of Liberia from the middle part of the century was the establishment and safeguarding of frontiers. In the early years there had been no threat from the neighbours. The French had a settlement on the Ivory Coast but showed no interest in extending it, while the governors of Sierra Leone, with rare exceptions such as MacCarthy, were horrified at the thought of enlarging their unloved and troublesome territory. When President Roberts first went to Britain in 1848, the Bishop of London and other philanthropists had raised £2,000 for Liberia to buy the Gallinhas territory north of the Mano river and to stamp out the Spanish slavers there. But when Liberia went ahead with this policy, by purchasing and occupying territory to the north, the British Government changed its view and claimed the land for itself. The rise of the palm-oil trade had made this once-barren region attractive to European traders. One Englishman in particular, John Myers Harris,* had set up business between the Mano and the Sulima rivers. In 1860, the Liberians reminded Harris of their political rights, which he as firmly rejected. He claimed that

* See also Part III, Chapter 4.

Liberian customs dues would upset the trade of the interior, while Liberia claimed that Harris himself was engaged in some form of the slave trade. President Benson sent a coastguard boat to seize two schooners belonging to Harris, who promptly appealed to Freetown. The British responded by sending a gunboat to seize the schooners back and continued to give their support to Harris. Recognition by the United States in 1862 gave diplomatic strength to Liberia but she still felt a need to secure or extend her frontiers. This motive and the lust for trade explain the series of journeys into the hinterland that were made in the 1860s. Liberia has so often been blamed for ignorance and neglect of the interior that it is right to record some of these now-forgotten journeys.

The Earl de Grey and Ripon, the President of the Royal Geographical Society, had much news from Africa to put in his annual address, given on May 28th, 1860. Speke and Burton had just returned from their epoch-making and quarrelsome trip to Lakes Tanganyika and Victoria. Livingstone was still busy in the southern part of the continent, while Du Chaillu, a young American, was bringing the first reports from gorilla land. Yet the President, pushed as he was for space, gave generous mention to the discoveries of two men named Ash and Seymour, from the 'remarkable African republic of Liberia'. These explorers, although untrained in trigonometric reading, claimed to have reached the city of Quanga, 287 miles from Monrovia, 384 from Grand Bassa and two weeks' march from Sierra Leone. Although the city has not since been traced,★ their account has the ring of veracity. Quanga itself was a walled town, 2,500 paces in circumference, with five gates from which roads led to other cities. The explorers, who had been well received, praised the beauty of the women, their white cotton cloth and their rich, gold ornaments. Earl de Grey reported in this same speech that two more American Negroes, Campbell and Delaney, had travelled in Nigeria and Liberia, while a fourth, Alexander Crummel, had gone up the River Cavalla.

The Proceedings of the Royal Geographical Society for 1861,

★ These mud and thatch towns were frequently abandoned or destroyed. Sometimes their names were changed.

the following year, gave the sad news of Seymour's death while undertaking a second journey. 'As one of the generally unfortunate class of persons of mixed African race', Seymour had lacked the advantages of an early education, but had made up for this by perseverance and energy. Although Seymour had not pretended to give very accurate latitudes and longitudes, his reports on the character of the country, its soils and productions and its commerce and civilization were accurate and intelligent.

One Liberian, Benjamin Anderson, should in justice rank with the greatest explorers of Africa. A pure black, born in Liberia, he received a good education, entered the Civil Service, and spent two years as Secretary of the Treasury. On leaving this office in 1866 he went to the United States, where he met many philanthropists who were interested in Africa. Several of them suggested that Liberia should send an expedition into its hinterland to map out the region and lay down the boundaries of the state. Anderson said he would make the journey himself, whereupon funds were raised to pay for the porters, trade goods, presents and equipment, the last including a sextant, two thermometers, two small night and day compasses, 'one tolerably good watch' and an artificial horizon. Before setting out Anderson tried to recruit an educated companion, but found that the young men he asked 'preferred the safe, soft grassy streets of Monrovia to an expedition into the heart of their country'. On February 14th, 1868, Anderson started the journey from Monrovia that was to keep him more than a year in the interior. The *Narrative of a Journey to Musardu*, which was published in 1870 in New York, is a short book compared with the tomes by Burton, Stanley and Livingstone. It is not remarkable as a work of science. The town Musardu, in the Mandingo country, has not been identified in modern times, so that Anderson cannot be called a great discoverer. He was, however, one of that handful of travellers and explorers who was also a writer of genius. This narrative is the funniest, most vivid and most enjoyable of all the books I have read on African exploration. It has the additional fascination that Anderson, being himself a black, could mix with the primitive Africans in a way impossible to the white explorers. Unaffected, with none of the snobbish airs sometimes put on by civilized Africans, Anderson treated everybody he met on a basis of human equality. Most white explorers looked down on the Africans as a grown-up looks down on a child; the good ones were patted and patronized, while the naughty ones were chastized. Anderson reacted to people with normal human responses. Those who were friendly and kind he liked. Those who were hostile he disliked and wanted to fight. His attitude to the natives of the African interior was the attitude of an Englishman to the natives of Ireland or France.

His black skin did not safeguard Anderson from the usual hazards of African exploration. He had scarcely gone ten miles from Monrovia when all his Kroo carriers, except for the headman, Ben, ran away for fear of the Dey people. Anderson replaced them with a team of Congoes.* Although he was aiming due north into Mandingo country, Anderson made a detour north-west to avoid what he had been told was a very unfriendly area, but the detour carried him to the still more unfriendly Bessa Town. King Bessa himself was a greedy brute who resolved to delay the Liberian and to rob him of his stores. He provoked a strike among Anderson's porters, frustrated his efforts to hire a guide, and constantly wheedled or threatened him for more presents. 'Drunk he gets every day', wrote Anderson, 'and after the first two or three hours of excess are over, he finally sobers down to that degree at which his avarice is greatest and his regard for other peoples' rights least ... I will not relate all the circumstance of his lashing an old slave until his cries drew the tears of all who stood by nor his stamping in the breast of one of his slaves until death ensued, on account of some slight offense.'

At last, Anderson set out on his own to the neighbouring town of Bopuru, which appeared to be the capital of the region. He made friends with the local Mandingoes—who, as everywhere in Liberia and Sierra Leone, were the important traders—Muslim priests, the schoolteachers and civil servants. The Mandingoes

* The Congoes were recaptive slaves, put down at Liberia by U.S. naval ships. The name was given to many slaves who did not come from the Congo region.

urged Anderson to be patient while they tried to recover his goods by diplomatic means. 'But I utterly refused,' wrote Anderson in his narrative, obviously making fun of his own hot-headed behaviour, 'I would talk of nothing but soldiers, cannon, the burning of Bessa's town and other furious things.' Eventually, as so often in Africa, diplomatic pressure succeeded where threats had failed, and the wicked King Bessa returned the goods and the now more obedient carriers. In the meantime, Anderson had been able to study the ways of the Condo people and get to know their delightful King Momoru.

The kingdom at this time had been much impoverished by a trade war farther inland between the Boozie and the Barline people. King Momoru was indignant that because the new administration down in Monrovia had not yet sent him a 'book' or message of greetings and had not attempted to settle the war, it had therefore fallen on him to act as mediator, to win the friendship of both sides by sending presents of salt, and finally to intervene if one of the parties proved obdurate. Anderson felt ashamed on behalf of his fellow Liberians

> that we leave to an untutored barbarian the quieting and settling of interior difficulties, while we remain ignorant of their very existence ... Yet it is a fact that this royal barbarian, without revenue, and without any of the resources to which we pretend, by following the policy of interfering in all interior concerns, is better known and has greater influence from Boporu to Musardu, and even beyond, than the civilised Republic of Liberia; and this is done by sending a few sticks of salt, accompanied by a friendly request or a threatening mandate.

The Condo people felt great respect for Dru-kau, as they called Monrovia, and imitated some of the coastal ways. The king had a frame house, with a piazza, a kind of veranda, around it, as well as chairs, beds, bedsteads, looking-glasses, scented soap and cologne. He was intrigued by Anderson's surveying equipment and took such a fancy to the stereoscope that Anderson finally gave it to

him. Anderson was full of praise for King Momoru's patience and
good sense as judge of his people's lawsuits:

> But the king sometimes takes recreation from the severe affairs
> of life at which time he is apt to enliven the hours of vacation
> from business with a glass of gin or whisky, and then he goes
> playfully around the town attended by his people. It happens
> that his caprice is as innocent then as his gentle disposition is in
> his sober hours; for he hurts no-one, only going from house to
> house, joking with and receiving little presents from his
> friends. Sometimes he attempts to dance, or to act some war-
> like feat; but want of youth and a rather fat body· mar the
> practice. One day he insisted on the performance to his no small
> discomfiture. He mounted upon an earthen hill, with a spear
> in each hand, in order to charge down in warlike style; starting
> in full tilt he came sprawling to the ground with such violence
> as to scarify the royal bosom in a most unseemly manner.

Much as Anderson liked the king and the friends he made in the
Mandingo colony, he was anxious to press on to Musardu. After
the usual troubles with guides and porters, Anderson got to
Zelleki, where the only pleasant person he met was King Momoru's
daughter, who shared her father's jovial disposition. When Anderson left the village, 'she marched out before me, with my musket
at shoulder-arms at a military pace, imitating what she had seen at
Monrovia the last time she was down there with her father.' At
Dalazeah, Anderson was impressed by the orderly and well-
tended farms of rice, corn, tobacco and cotton, while the Boozie
people, whom rumour called fierce and intractable, proved hospitable and courteous. They were astonished and overjoyed that
a 'Weegee', or American, should have come so far to visit them,
and they pleaded with Anderson to dress up in his foreign clothes.
'To please them, I did so,' Anderson wrote. 'I had not shaven for
three months, and when I made my appearance in the 'Merican
cloth, together with an unshaven face, the women and children
fled in every direction from the fearfully bearded Weegee.'

Others, more bold, remained. Anderson soon was serenaded by

229

twelve girls praising him, in advance, for his generosity, and, later, chiding him for his stinginess:

> The ungenerous little rogues ought to have remembered that it was through my liberality that they were enabled to have all the fine brass buttons which they sported around their necks at the Zow Zow market. However I hope it will be considered that I have done the state some service, when I announce that I have labeled nearly all the pretty women in the Boozie country as the property of the Republic of Liberia, with its military buttons.

Other Boozies were more polite, even too polite, always eager to shake hands with a click of the fingers.*

> The slightest favour is repaid with an 'Emmamow'—Thank you. Do you dance or afford any amusement whatsoever, you receive the 'Emmamow'. Are you engaged in any labor or business for yourself or others, you are as heartily 'thanked' by those whom it does not in the least concern as if it were for themselves … My Congo carriers, who were nearly fagged out with the weight of their burdens, used to be annoyed with this kind of civility, that contained all thanks and no assistance, and the Boozie 'Emmamow' was often exchanged for the Congo 'Konapembo' (Go to the Devil), an exhortation not unreasonable where misery is prolonged by politeness, and where one having his back bent, burdened, and almost broke, has to be stopped to be thanked and to snap fingers half a dozen times.

Anderson was stunned by the fertility of the Boozie country, which was almost literally covered with fields of rice. Standing upon a hill one morning, he saw to the west the rice-hills enveloped in showers; 'succeeding that whole mountainsides of rice partly buried in vapour; next to that could be seen a brilliant sunlight, spread over the brown and ripening plain of rice below.'

* The handshake with a click of the fingers is still popular in Liberia even among the sophisticates of Monrovia. It is rare elsewhere in West Africa.

The Boozie men he described as clean, healthy and strong enough to hold a United States musket, bayonet fixed, at full arm's length in one hand. The women—always Anderson's favourite subject—were definitely to his liking, although he disapproved of the way they plucked part of their eyebrows and eyelashes. Anderson was amused to note that many Boozies looked like Monrovians: 'Most of our people are fond of deriving themselves from the Mandingoes. I am sorry to say that this Boozie type of resemblance does not confirm an origin so noble and consoling.'

After quarrelling with Beah, his shifty Mandingo guide, Anderson went on alone to Musardu, determined to find the way by questioning and by instinct. Far from meeting trouble, he was greeted everywhere with great kindness, and the roadside saleswomen plied him and his carriers with quantities of free nuts. 'On we went, munching ground nuts, snapping fingers and making friends, and occasionally consigning Beah to evil destinies.'

At Bokkasah, a cloth-market town of some seven thousand inhabitants, Anderson decked himself out in a Mandingo toga, and seems to have made many friends:

> We would fritter away the time in talking and singing, and I musically entertained several of my Mandingo friends with the beauties of 'Dixie'. We would then clap into our prayers, they repeating the Fatiha, and I repeating the Lord's Prayer. A young lady begged that I would write off this prayer for her, in order that she might have it to wear around her neck, as well as to have fillets made of it to bind round her temples, as she was sometimes troubled with the headache.

From Bokkasah, Anderson went to Ziggah Porah Zue, whose king, an ogre by repute, proved helpful and courteous to the stranger. Near Pellazarruh, Anderson came to a plain of iron ore so pure that the road leading through it was a polished metal path made smooth by the feet of travellers. At last, after nearly a year of travel, he reached the drier savannah lands where the Mandingoes lived.

Here the peculiar features of the country are visible for miles. The towns and villages seated in the plains, people on foot and people on horseback can be seen at a great distance, and have more the air of light, life and activity than many parts of the Boozie country, where the sombre gloom of immense forests conceals all such things.

He had at last reached Musardu in the Mandingo country.

Thanks to the recommendations of many Mandingo friends, the visitor from Monrovia was well received in Musardu and given the highest honours of the city. There were many salaams and much snapping of fingers. A minstrel sang, to the accompaniment of a harp, of Anderson's many virtues, his courage, his wealth and liberality; 'upon the last two he dwelt with loud and repeated effort.' The dry air had an invigorating effect on Anderson—and on his watches which, having been stopped by the damp, salt air of the coast, now began to tick away in a clear and ringing manner. Anderson watched parades of cavalry and of infantry; he became mildly involved in a local trade dispute, and studied with admiration the ladies' gold ear-rings, so large that they needed a leather band for support. The Mandingoes were disappointed that Anderson had not brought trade goods but were happy to hear his assurance that others would come from Monrovia. He believed that a trade route could be assured by establishing four forts: two of them in the Boozie and Barline country, for the purchase of country cloths, raw cotton, camwood, palm oil and rice; and two in Mandingo country, where gold, bullocks, horses and country cloth could be bought at a good enough price to cover the high cost of transport. Anderson added that these forts would also safeguard the work of the missionaries, but I guess that he wrote this to please his pious patrons. A humanist by temperament, Anderson always took care not to offend the Muslim principles of the Mandingoes, and he was much annoyed with one of his Congo carriers, a Baptist, who yelled out prayers at the top of his voice each morning.

Anderson would have liked to stay at Musardu, but felt obliged to get back to the coast and his family. Before the return journey, people warned him of the ferocious tribes he would meet on his way, but Anderson now knew not to believe these tales. He knew that nobody would attack him if he proved himself capable of replying in kind. Therefore:

> I became a moving arsenal. I walked through the whole Boozie country with my bayonet fixed in my musket, my revolvers belted so as to be seen and feared at the same time, my sword swinging and clanking at my side; and when, to prove my *prestige* in arms, I was asked to fire my revolvers, I would draw and blaze away, several barrels going off almost at the same time—a serious defect to be sure, but regarded in a very different light by my friends.

Anderson observed that most of the stories told of bloodthirsty tyrant chiefs were propaganda spread by the chiefs themselves to inspire respect, and to keep people away from their territory. The really bad chiefs, such as King Bessa, were the exceptions. Here again the Negro Anderson was more sensible than most of the white explorers, who published every rumour they heard of black magic, torture and cannibalism. It may be that the tribes through which Anderson walked were unusually peaceful and courteous, but I suspect that this friendly and tactful man could have travelled with equal safety and ease almost anywhere in black Africa. Even those few white travellers such as Livingstone, Mary Kingsley and Savorgnan de Brazza, who walked alone or with few companions, met with general courtesy in the bush. Those, like Stanley, who encountered hostility, were those who provoked and expected it.

Anderson's *Narrative* did not make him famous. The reading public for books about Africa wanted either horrific tales of bloodshed, cannibalism and witchcraft, or improving tales of black children lifting their eyes to Jesus. They wanted Stanley or Livingstone. They did not want this mild, undramatic book—by a black man into the bargain—who made his journey through 'savage' Africa sound so jolly and safe. Anderson in 1874 made one more journey into the hinterland of Liberia, but the government, which was then once more under the presidency of Roberts, would give him neither backing nor encouragement. Liberia turned its back on Anderson's friends in the hinterland, while most Mandingo territory, including the area of Musardu, was occupied by the French.

Chapter Two

We resemble those plants which we call 'life everlasting'—I
do not know their botanical name—whose leaves severed from
the stem, appear to survive apart from the whole plant, with
no connection with root or branch. They can be pinned up
against a wall or anywhere and yet appear to be green.

(Edward Wilmot Blyden on the Liberians)

The Chancellor of the Exchequer, William Ewart Gladstone, must
have been surprised, one morning in spring 1860, to get a letter
from an address in Monrovia. Its contents must have surprised him
still more. The author, Edward Wilmot Blyden, began with an
apology that he, 'an entire stranger, residing on a far off and
barbarous shore, and connected with a race down-trodden and
despised', should intrude upon the patience and time of so distinguished a statesman. He then went on to introduce himself: 'I
am a youth endeavouring to obtain an education. My tastes and
predilections—strange as it may seem for one in my circumstances
—are for classical literature. The love of languages is my pre-
dominating passion.' This passion was evidenced by the Latin and
Greek quotations contained in the letter, which praised Gladstone's
opposition to slavery, his stand over divorce in 1857, and above
all, his recent Budget. 'Your budget has demonstrated to the
world', wrote this man from one of the world's most unknown
quarters, 'that literary men *can* be able financiers, despite the
current opinion to the contrary.' Gladstone, the classical scholar,
was then politely asked for advice on his method of study: 'What
works you read and the order in which they were read. How many
lines did you read at a lesson in Virgil? How many in Homer?' The
letter ended with a request that Gladstone should send out 'a small

library' of a dozen books; the appended list was headed, tactfully, by Gladstone's recent Budget and his *Homeric Studies*.

After being assured by the Liberian Consul that Blyden was a young man of respectability, Gladstone wrote a kind reply to his African admirer. Gladstone's colleague, Lord Brougham, cited the letter during a slave-trade debate as an example of the capacities of the Negro—and a tribute to the Liberal Party's Budget. Their high opinion of Blyden was well justified, for this Negro schoolmaster, then twenty-eight, was to become a world-famous scholar and author, the greatest champion of his race in the nineteenth century, and also a statesman of influence on the destiny of West Africa. A man of Blyden's capacity would have risen to fame and importance in any country. In Monrovia, which was a village, his talents shone with an almost freakish brilliance. The history of Liberia from 1860 until the First World War, is personified in the life and work of Blyden.

Blyden was born in 1832 on the then Danish island of St Thomas, one of the Virgin Islands. Although slavery still existed, both Blyden's parents were free, his mother working as schoolteacher and his father as a tailor, in which trade Blyden was trained for five years. The Blydens lived in a Jewish part of the capital—Charlotte-Amalie—and Edward as a child used to play on Synagogue Hill. When about thirteen, he had the good fortune to get to know a pious white American couple, the Reverend and Mrs John P. Knox, who encouraged his natural instinct for study. By the time Blyden was eighteen, and already a qualified tailor, he wanted to train for the ministry, and tried to enrol at Rutgers Theological College, where Knox had taken his degree. The college and two others in the United States refused to admit him because he was a Negro. Hurt by these racial snubs, Blyden was also alarmed by the risks he ran as a Negro foreigner in the United States, with the Fugitive Slave Law in operation. This law, which had been passed during Blyden's visit, gave federal commissioners comprehensive powers to seize runaway slaves and free Negroes who could not give proof of their freedom. Rather than stay in the United States or go back to St Thomas, where there was no scope for ambition, Blyden sailed to Liberia, arriving early in 1851.

There was no job for a tailor in Monrovia, since people bought their clothes ready-made, but Blyden managed to earn a living as clerk, newspaper reporter and soldier. He enrolled as a part-time student at the Alexander High School, later as full-time student, then teacher and finally principal, which was the job he held at the time he first wrote to Gladstone. At twenty-four he had learned Greek, Latin, Hebrew, French and German and had published his first short book called *A Voice from Bleeding Africa*. This youthful but very well-written essay proclaimed the case that Blyden was to argue for nearly sixty years—that Negroes could and must take a pride in the history and achievements of their race. He claimed that most slave-holding whites could not match the 'intellectual and moral greatness' of many distinguished Negroes, and went on to list some of the heroes of the race. Toussaint l'Ouverture, the liberator of Haiti, was then and always Blyden's favourite, partly because of his pure Negro stock; but Blyden also included among his 'African geniuses' some very pale mulattoes such as Dumas, the novelist, and Alexander Pushkin, 'the favourite alike of the Emperor and the people'. A jealous pride in the Negro race went with fierce Liberian patriotism. The newspapers in Monrovia were soon enlivened by hectoring articles, written by Blyden, exhorting the citizens to their duty. Many Liberians took offence and regarded Blyden as a young nuisance, just as fifty years later their grand-children and great-grandchildren were to regard him as an old nuisance. Few prophets have had less honour in their own country.

In 1861, Blyden was sent by the government to try and raise money for Liberian education from British and American philanthropists. Before Blyden sailed for Britain in March, the young men of Monrovia entrusted him with a walking-stick, made of ebony and mounted with ebony and gold, to present to Lord Brougham for his services both to Africa and the Negro race. While in England, Blyden had to turn down Gladstone's offer of a university education. So heavy were his commitments to his country, Blyden wrote, 'that I cannot leave them to hold converse with the muses in England'. Their correspondence continued, however, and Blyden gave Gladstone intriguing reports on the Northern states during the Civil War. Few of the politicians, he wrote, were willing to free the blacks.

> The oppression is intensifying. In the District of Columbia, which has been freed by an Act of Congress, the Fugitive Slave Law is in active operation. Though Congress has acknowledged Liberian independence, I, as a citizen of Liberia, was not allowed to enter the House of Representatives during the session because I was a black man; and before I could leave that distinguished city, I was obliged to get a *white* man to vouch that I was a *free* man.

In a bitter article for the *Liberia Herald*, Blyden described the manifold injustices suffered by blacks, and declared that he 'would rather be a citizen of Marmora's town* with all its attendant disadvantages, than be compelled, as a black man, to live in this country'. A passionate believer in the colonization movement, Blyden was irked to find that most Northern Negroes took little interest in Africa. As a recruiting officer for new immigrants, he had much greater success in the West Indies, where hundreds of well-qualified people were eager to sail to Liberia.

Blyden's talents and hard work were rewarded in 1864 by his appointment as Secretary of State, a post that carried the duties of deputy president. Although Blyden did not stay long in this office, it fanned his interest in the problems facing Liberia and above all the opening of the interior. In *A Voice from Bleeding Africa*, Blyden had echoed the prejudices of the Christian coastal Negroes who saw their settlements 'standing like a chain of light along the benighted shore and spreading their civilizing and recovering influences among the surrounding degradation and barbarism.' During the 1860s, his attitude changed. The more Blyden heard and saw of the Muslims of the interior, the more he came to admire them as true, uncorrupted Africans. He started to study Arabic in his spare time; he paid a long visit to Lebanon and quickly emerged

* Benjamin Anderson's visit to the same town is described in the previous chapter.

as a serious Arabic scholar. Although Blyden never became a Muslim, he admired the religion and thought it well suited to Africa. Islam, unlike the Christian Churches, had never imposed any racial discrimination. Indeed, Negro Muslims had been prominent in the movement 'and their exploits are recognised in all the great Arabic works, not excepting the Koran. There is a chapter in that sacred book inscribed to a Negro, in which his wisdom and piety are specially dwelt upon and pointed out as the direct gifts of God.' Gradually Blyden developed his theory that the best hope for Africa lay with the Muslims of the interior and not with the westernized Christians of the Coast. Blyden, the Negro nationalist, and Burton, the white supremacist, had arrived by different processes at the same conclusion; indeed the two men read and admired each other's books. But while Burton regarded Islam as a whip to drive the vicious and indolent Africans, Blyden regarded it as a teacher to give them knowledge and dignity.

By his championship of the interior peoples, Blyden also furthered the interests of the blacks against the mulattoes. He himself was 'of ebony hue' and claimed a descent from pure black Ibo ancestors. West Indians, even more than North American Negroes, have always been sensitive to the different shades of colour, and sometimes there has been hostility between light and dark. The same division, as we have seen in the previous chapter, caused political bickering in Liberia. Blyden sided wholeheartedly with the blacks against the mulattoes, who were represented by ex-President Roberts. There were several points at issue between the two colour groups. The blacks wanted more immigrants from the West Indies. The mulattoes, fearing that educated newcomers would threaten their own monopoly of power, wanted immigrants from the southern United States. The blacks, who favoured opening up the interior, wanted government help for exploration, and it was Blyden who found the American backers for Benjamin Anderson's voyage to Musardu. The mulattoes, as Anderson mentioned in a mysterious aside, were opposed to his trip, feeling that new trade routes might shake their grip on the commerce of the country. This difference of outlook sparked off a long dispute over the site for Liberia College. The blacks, headed by Blyden, wanted a college some way inland, while the mulattoes wanted it in Monrovia. Ex-President Roberts, the president of the college, opposed Blyden's suggestion that Arabic should be taught, and then was accused by Blyden of keeping out pure black students. Blyden's prejudice was still further inflamed by the fact that he could not stand his wife, a poorly educated woman and, worse still, a pale mulatto. Convinced that the mulatto aristocrats were engaged in plots against him, Blydon now feared that they had a spy in his bedchamber.

The enmity between blacks and mulattoes broke out in 1871 with revolution, and ended with the violent death of a president and the forcible exile of Blyden. The crisis began in 1870 with the accession of President Edward James Roye, a pure black of Ibo origin, and a personal and political friend of Blyden's. President Roye, in his inaugural address, set out bold plans for the country's future. These included the establishment of a national banking system, mass education, the introduction of railways, the incorporation of near-by tribes and friendly alliance with distant tribes, such as those that Anderson had met in his journey the year before. To finance these projects, Roye sought and obtained a British loan of £100,000 on terms that were disastrous to Liberia and his own political future. The Liberian consul-general in London, an Englishman, arranged the loan through a bank of which he was an agent. Although the Liberians offered their future customs receipts as a surety, the bankers insisted on keeping £30,000 as discount and advance interest while the remaining money had to be paid back within fifteen years at an outrageous 7 per cent interest. Roye's enemies in Monrovia called his acceptance of this loan a piece of financial folly.

The argument between blacks and mulattoes centred around the length of Roye's term in office. The legislature in 1869 had agreed to a referendum on whether the presidential term should be increased from two to four years. The mulattoes had favoured this change, hoping that their candidate Payne would therefore have longer in power. The electorate had voted for the amendment but at the same time had voted for Roye, who now claimed the right to stay in office for four years. The House of Representatives, where the blacks were in the majority, accepted the change in the Constitution, but the Senate where the mulattoes were in control, refused to give its assent to the result of the referendum. A Monrovia correspondent of the *African Times* wrote in December 1870: 'Matters stand in a very serious condition here. The country is in a great uproar.'

For Blyden, 1870 was a year of hope and excitement to which he looked back in later life as a source of inspiration. Encouraged by President Roye, he visited Benjamin Anderson's friend, King Marmora of Boporo, where he founded a school with a teacher from Monrovia. Back on the coast, he lent his journalistic skill to the defence of President Roye and to counter-attacks on 'decadent mulattoes'. In his championship of President Roye, Blyden frequently praised him for having married a black woman, and he claimed that Mrs Roye was the first black First Lady. His admiration for Mrs Roye and his frequent visits to her, even when Roye was out of the country, encouraged mulatto gossips to hint at adultery. Soon hints swelled to accusations and threats of assault, until one day in May 1871 a mob of 'forty poverty-stricken and ignorant blacks' seized Blyden and dragged him through Monrovia with a rope round his neck. A friend intervened to stop the lynching, whereupon Blyden fled to Sierra Leone. President Roye condoned the forced exile of Blyden, probably hoping to divert hatred away from himself, but he, too, fell from power in circumstances of tragedy and high farce. Ex-President Roberts, having held a private election, declared himself to be President once again and returned to Monrovia on October 22nd, 1871, to barge his way into power. On October 26th, the Senate and House of Representatives met, declared Roye deposed, and had him thrown into prison.

The end to the story is not yet clear. The mulattoes and most historians of Liberia said that Roye escaped from prison, hurled a number of hand-grenades round the town, and in the confusion tried to board ship for Freetown, but was drowned in the surf by the weight of the stolen gold that was strapped about his body. There are flaws in this rather exotic story. In the first place, it is improbable that the new government would have put Roye in prison but allowed him to keep the gold. In the second place, only the most foolhardy man would have made a dash for his life weighed down by satchels of bullions. Lastly, Roye was an extremely rich merchant with plenty of savings in British banks, and therefore had no need of the loan money. Blyden reported that when Roye escaped from prison and went to wait for a boat, a mulatto shot him and later invented the drowning. For all one knows, Roye may have been murdered in prison. The mood of the country was turbulent at the time, and many people were killed by the angry mulattoes.

Blyden was not the sort of man to mope in political exile, and Sierra Leone offered an excellent field for his intellectual enthusiasms. Here just as easily as in Liberia, he could study the Muslims of the interior, experiment with African education and propagate, through the newspapers, his views on the Negro race. Blyden spent most of the rest of his life in Sierra Leone and, while remaining a loyal Liberian, he in some ways preferred the British colony. A great admirer of Britain, he welcomed her power and influence in West Africa. Moreover, he saw that Britain, unlike Liberia, had the wealth and manpower to open up the interior. His specific projects during these first years of exile were to send explorers into the hinterland and to found an independent African Church and a secular university. His suggestion that Benjamin Anderson should be hired by the Sierra Leone government as an explorer was described as 'very interesting' in Whitehall but, sadly when one considers the book that Anderson might have written, the proposed expedition was either turned down or forgotten. Blyden's efforts to start an independent African Church were frustrated for other reasons. Soon after leaving Liberia, Blyden was asked by the Church Missionary Society to teach Arabic at Fourah Bay College. Blyden was popular with the African clergymen but the white Bishop of Sierra Leone was shocked by his defence of the Muslim faith and inclined to believe the whispers of his adultery. Blyden's job at Fourah Bay, like so many jobs in his quarrelsome career, was suspended after a few months.

After his rebuff by the British missionaries, Blyden turned his attention to the idea of a secular university. He found a surprising supporter in John Pope-Hennessy who arrived in February 1872 as governor of Sierra Leone. A radical with no respect for authority, an Irishman who resented English pretensions, and a Catholic who disliked the Anglican Church, Pope-Hennessy listened to Blyden's ideas with sympathetic interest. However, he insisted that a university of the type Blyden proposed 'must be the work of the Africans themselves. There are so many monuments of benevolent failures in Sierra Leone, that the Government would shrink from undertaking the initiative of such an Institution.' To which Blyden replied that 'to leave the work of initiating the education they need to the Africans themselves would be to put it off indefinitely ... [because] all educated Negroes suffer from a kind of slavery in many ways far more subversive of the real welfare of the race than the ancient physical fetters.' Pope-Hennessy's keenness on the plan was tempered by his awareness that funds were short, that the Secretary for the Colonies was not interested and that Blyden was disliked by most of the whites in Sierra Leone. The dream of a secular university vanished after a year when Governor Pope-Hennessy was transferred to another post, and Lord Derby, the Secretary for the Colonies, who did not think Africans fit for office, decreed that 'we want no more black men'.

His proposals rejected, Blyden turned his reforming energies into journalistic polemics. A group of wealthy Creoles backed him in starting the *Negro*, which like all the newspapers for which Blyden wrote, soon built up an eager readership. The dominant theme of all Blyden's writing was the separate destiny and identity of the Negro race. He praised European nationalists such as Mazzini, Fichte and Hegel, believing that Negroes as well should one day unite in a nation. Like Burton, whom he resembled in character as well as ideas, Blyden accepted several spurious theories about the physical differences of the races. Although a partisan of the Negro races, Blyden was generous with his praise of other peoples, especially the British, Arabs and Jews. He admired the Jews so much that he suggested, five years before the suggestion was made by the British, that the Zionists should establish their Israel in East Africa rather than Palestine.

Blyden made several journeys into the interior of Sierra Leone and he also made friends with the Muslims in Freetown. The more he learned of Islam, the more he came to admire its role in Africa, and particularly its insistence on education. 'A man might now travel across the continent, from Sierra Leone to Cairo, or in another direction, from Lagos to Tripoli, sleeping in a village every night, except in the Sahara, and in every village he would find a school.'

He praised the simple devotion of the Muslim missionaries in Africa. 'They take their mats or their skins, and their manuscripts, and are followed by their pupils, who, in every new Pagan town, form the nucleus of a school and congregation. These preachers are the receivers, not the dispensers.' This was an obvious rebuke to the Christian missionaries, especially Blyden's enemies in the C.M.S., whom he accused of becoming the patrons of their disciples. Blyden had some use for the Roman Catholic Church which had produced his hero, Toussaint l'Ouverture, but he derided the achievement of the Protestants. Not one tribe, Blyden pointed out, had been converted as a tribe, while piety was confined almost entirely to city dwellers. 'The native populations of Sierra Leone and Liberia—the Timnehs, Soosoos, Mendis, Veys, Golahs, Bassas, Kroos, &c.—are still untouched by evangelical influence … The whole black population of these settlements who have made any progress in Christian civilisations have been imported—in the case of Sierra Leone, from other parts of Africa, and, in that of Liberia, from America.'

Some of Blyden's essays and tracts appeared as pamphlets or small books and soon won him widespread fame.* In 1887, a selection of Blyden's writing was published as *Christianity, Islam*

* This fame has endured, for as recently as 1960 two rare volumes of Blyden's work were stolen from the library of the British Museum.

and the Negro Race. Most reviewers praised the book and expressed astonishment that its author was Negro. 'As honest Englishmen,' said *The Times* reviewer, 'we should welcome the truth from whatsoever source it may come, and I am not sure but that Dr Blyden's book may not yet prove the greatest contribution of the age on the gigantic subject of Christian missions.' Everyone praised Blyden's style; the *Interior* of Chicago said that 'in the use of terse, vigorous and pure English, he is scarcely second to Macaulay'. However, certain Anglican papers, above all the *Church Missionary Intelligencer*, objected to Blyden's praise for Islam and the Roman Catholic Church.

After two years in exile, Blyden managed to patch up his quarrel with the government of Liberia, to which he returned in 1873. His arch-enemy, J. J. Roberts, who had once again become President, offered Blyden his former job as Secretary of State but Blyden instead started a school on the St Paul's River. His fear and hatred of the mulattoes had now matured into persecution mania.

> I live among an unsympathetic people (he wrote in 1875)—and, I regret to say, an unsympathizing family. My wife seems entirely unimproveable. She is of the mind and temperament of the people around her—sometimes, pressed as I am on all sides, I feel like making my escape to the interior and never allowing myself to be heard from again. Domestically speaking, this has been my life for years. My restlessness and my apparent fickleness is largely due to this. I am persecuted *outside* but more inside. Uncongenial, incompatible, unsympathetic, my wife makes the burden of my life sore and heavy.

One can guess from this anguished testament that Blyden's Christian, mulatto wife in Monrovia may in part have inspired his policy of building a pure black Muslim Liberia in the hinterland.

When J. J. Roberts, first President of Liberia and for more than forty years its most distinguished statesman, died in 1876, Blyden repeated one of the unofficial obituaries:

> Roberts is dead—so I am told.
> His greatest love was the love of gold.

If to heaven he's gone, angels, look sharp
As you may lose a golden harp.

President James S. Payne, who succeeded Roberts, belonged to
the same mulatto faction; nevertheless, he offered Blyden the
dignified, although unpaid, job of ambassador at the Court of
St James. In his year and a half in London, Blyden worked hard,
if without much success, to promote the interests of Liberia. His
three main tasks were to settle the border dispute with Sierra
Leone, to assure his country's creditors that Liberia would not
default on the Roye loan, and to attract foreign capital for a railway
to the interior. These aims were achieved—but many years later.
Meanwhile, Ambassador Blyden won a social triumph in London.
Since he had visited England six times before this visit, he knew
many leading statesmen, clerics and writers. He was guest once
again of his old friends Brougham and Gladstone; he impressed
the Conservative, Derby; talked with the queen and joined
the Athenaeum. Certainly Blyden, the black ambassador, had a
curiosity value, but there is no doubt that many intelligent Englishmen at the time had a genuine, friendly interest in Africa and the
Africans. Blyden himself was quick to detect the four classes of
Europeans that Negroes were likely to meet:

> First the class who are professionally philanthropic. These at
> the sight of the Negro, go into ecstacies over this 'man and
> brother', and put themselves to all sorts of inconvenience to
> prove to this unfortunate member of the human race that they
> believe God hath made of one blood all nations of men, & the
> second class is composed of those who, at the sight of the
> Negro, have all their feelings of malice, hatred and all un-
> charitableness excited, and who adopt every expedient and
> avail themselves of every occasion to give exhibitions of their
> vehement antagonism. The third class regard him with con-
> temptuous indifference, and care to exhibit neither favour nor
> dislike, whatever his merit or demerit. The fourth class con-
> sists of those who treat him as they would a white man of the
> same degree of culture and behaviour, basing this demeanour

altogether upon the intellectual or moral qualities of the man.

Like many intellectuals, Blyden had little talent for politics and administration but refused to recognize his deficiency. Returning to Liberia in 1880, he accepted the two jobs most closely concerned with his own special interest: the presidency of Liberia College, and the Ministry of the Interior, which held responsibility for the hinterland. The college was moribund at the time Blyden became president. Under the feeble, almost senile, control of J. J. Roberts it had become not so much a place of learning as a battlefield for the squabbling blacks and mulattoes. Under Blyden's presidency, the college flared into intellectual flame, winning renown and causing controversy as far away as America; but in the end its achievements were slender. Blyden was incapable of understanding that other people lacked his intellectual powers, so that the syllabus of the college was made to include not only Mathematics, Latin and Greek, but Arabic and local history. He complained at this time that:

> We have young men who are experts in the geography and customs of foreign countries; who can talk glibly of London, Berlin, Paris and Washington; know all about Gladstone, Bismarck, Gambetta and Hayes; but who knows anything about Musahdu, Medina, Kankan, or Sego—only a few hundred miles from us? Who can tell anything of the policy or doings of Fanfi-dereh, Ibrahima Sissi, or Fahqueh-queh, or Simoro of Boporu—only a few steps from us?

The question sounds reasonable, but there were many Liberians who suspected, with reason, that Blyden was cramming such subjects into the syllabus as part of his old campaign against the Christians and mulattoes. These fears were justified when Blyden gave all eight places to students of pure Negro blood and then attempted to push the mulattoes off the Board of Trustees. As president of the College, Blyden was not just cantankerous but constantly absent from duty in the interests of his second job as

247

Minister of the Interior. This ministry was responsible for negotiating the boundary with Sierra Leone, and it was during Blyden's spell in office that this old argument came to a head. By March 1882, the British had made it quite clear that they meant to annex the lands west of the Marfur river; they sent four gunboats to emphasize their intention. Blyden and the attorney-general, who had been sent to Freetown to treat with the British Governor, bowed reluctantly to imperial bullying. However, Blyden's many enemies in Liberia took the chance to accuse him of having been bribed by the British. He lost his ministry, was threatened with assault and went into exile at Cape Palmas. When he resigned shortly afterwards from the presidency of the college, it was observed that for all the excitement during Blyden's spell in office, not one student had graduated.

Blyden's last and most laughable venture in politics was his bid for the presidency of Liberia in the election of 1884. The oddity of this bid for office was that Blyden stood as candidate for the Republican Party, the mouthpiece of the mulattoes in Monrovia. Apparently the party leaders believed that by getting Blyden as their candidate and adopting some of his views they could win over the votes of the Blydenite blacks while keeping the loyalty of the mulattoes. Blyden, after convincing himself that party labels did not matter, ran a hearty campaign and was beaten two to one.*

From 1884 until his death in 1912, Blyden spent little time in Liberia. He did two more spells as his country's ambassador, first in London and then in Paris, on both occasions proving a social lion, but most of his time was spent in Freetown with frequent visits to other parts of West Africa. Blyden had now abandoned his wife for a pleasant and pure-black mistress, but the wandering urge provoked by his marriage persisted all his life. He made frequent trips to the United States, where he spoke on behalf of the colonization movement. Blyden had come to believe, with Jefferson, that Negroes and whites could never live in harmony.

* The voting figures were H. R. W. Johnson 1,438; Blyden 873. Blyden said afterwards that all intelligent Liberians had voted for him.

With cruel logic, he therefore welcomed every discrimination against the Negroes that might drive them to refuge in Africa. He no longer complained when he was turned away from hotels or restaurants. He approved of the Civil Rights Act of 1875 that gave effective support to segregation. He wanted laws to prevent sexual union between whites and blacks. He spoke against higher education for Negroes and against the appointment of Negro diplomats. It is hardly surprising that whites in the Southern states told Blyden that they had never before heard 'so wise, natural and satisfactory a solution of the race problem before them'. His popularity with the whites did not make Blyden popular with the Negroes, and this marred his recruiting for Liberia. His insistence that emigration should go through the American Colonization Society, which shared his prejudice against mulattoes and tried to exclude them from Liberia, meant that only that small minority with a claim to pure Negro blood were given the chance to emigrate.

Old age did not mellow Blyden. He spent the last twenty years of his life in constant, satisfactory wrangles with Protestant missionaries, wrong-headed governments and impertinent mulattoes. The rise of Lagos, late in the nineteenth century, offered Blyden a rich new field for quarrelling and politicking. A group of white ministers in the Niger Mission had suspended or dismissed a number of African ministers on what appeared to be racialist grounds. The Africans called on Blyden to help, and greeted him, on his arrival later in 1890, with lines of welcome picked out in luminous letters:

> Africa's destiny lay hid in night,
> God said 'Let Blyden be', and all was light.

The light that Blyden shed was to prove, as usual, uncertain. True, he urged the setting up of an independent African Church and criticized the arrogance of the European missionaries. However, his Christian hosts were shocked when Blyden received distinguished Muslims and addressed a mass meeting of Yorubas on the virtues of Islam. His praise for polygamy gave all the more offence since it was well known on the coast that Blyden kept a mistress. Blyden enjoyed being perverse. Although he campaigned for African dress and African surnames, he went on wearing his neat English suit and calling himself Edward Wilmot Blyden.

Blyden praised Liberia when speaking or writing abroad, but he was frank and critical when addressing his fellow countrymen. He blamed Liberians for

> attempting to rule millions of people, their own kith and kin, on a foreign system in which they themselves have been imperfectly trained, while knowing very little of the facts of the history of the people they assume to rule, either social, economic or religious, and taking for granted that the religious and social theories they have brought from across the sea must be adapted to all the needs of their unexpatriated brethren.

He blamed Liberians for thinking like Americans, for trying to impose American concepts of law and land tenure, for 'trying to work the land on the gang system, which we learned in America'. 'We are beating the air, the objects of the sympathy or the laughing-stock of foreigners,' Blyden declared, and he summed up his country as 'a little bit of South Caroline, of Georgia, of Virginia—that is to say—of the ostracised, suppressed, depressed, elements of those States—tacked on to West Africa—a most incongruous combination, with no reasonable prospect of success.'

Seeing so little prospect of success for his native country, Blyden suggested handing it to the care of foreign Powers. He admired the 'wonderful' European race and welcomed their 'scramble for Africa' in the last two decades of the century. On a visit to the Ivory Coast he was 'delighted with the results so far of French administration upon the life and prospects of the natives'. The Germans, who were newcomers to African imperialism, he called apt pupils who had already mastered the situation. But Britain remained his favourite Power, as he told a group of Liverpool businessmen:

> Liberia is a British Colony in everything but the flag. We have everything that the Union Jack symbolises, except its financial

significance. And this we are now appealing to you to assist us to get ... We consider it to be a great privilege to say 'We speak the language Shakespeare spake,' even if we cannot add, with regard to the whole of our population, 'we hold the truth and morals Milton held.'

Liberia at this time, 1905, was in serious financial and diplomatic trouble, which may have encouraged Blyden to ask for some kind of protectorate. His biographer, Hollis R. Lynch, says that Blyden 'might have reasoned that Liberia was in danger of losing its sovereignty anyway, and such sovereignty if forcibly taken away rather than voluntarily relinquished might be impossible to regain.'

Blyden's championship of the Negro race grew year by year more passive and pessimistic. Having accepted discrimination in the United States as a means of driving the Negro back to Africa, he now accepted it in Africa as the price to be paid for civilization. Hence, Blyden was one of the few West Africans who did not object to the exclusion of Negro doctors from the West African Medical Service. He ignored the increasingly unjust treatment of Africans in South Africa. He feared, not the arrogance, but the ignorance of the European. He distrusted those whites, whether liberal or racialist in their attitude to Africans, who wanted to change and distort the structure of African society. Mary Kingsley, who had confessed her belief in African inferiority, became the heroine of the black philosopher. 'Brief as was my acquaintance with her,' he told a meeting, 'I recognised in her a spirit sent to this world to serve Africa and the African race ... She dreaded, as Europe with further light will dread, the guilt of murdering native institutions and thus, if not actually destroying the people, impairing their powers of effective co-operation with their alien exploiters.'

Blyden's final years were passed in poverty and neglect. The younger Africans were out of sympathy with his pro-British ideas. Most of his old friends and colleagues, and most of his many enemies for that matter, were dead. Only a few Englishmen remained loyal to him in old age, and the British Government gave him a pension. Disenchanted with both Liberia and Sierra Leone, Blyden compared his lot with that of the classic philosophers. 'History repeats itself; the people kill the prophets: Cicero, Demosthenes, Socrates, must go if the unprincipled demagogues so will.' He died on February 7th, 1912, a few months short of his eightieth birthday.

Blyden would have enjoyed his own funeral, where the Christians and Muslims of Freetown vied in demonstrations of mourning, as each claimed Blyden's soul for their own. The funeral service was conducted by a Christian friend of Blyden's, but Muslim men carried his coffin to the graveyard at the racecourse, while in the procession children marched from every Muslim school in the city. At a banquet given him five years before, Blyden had made this curious prophecy: 'The African will build no monument. If his great men are honoured in that way, it will be by aliens.' After his death, a group of British residents in Freetown paid for the bust of Blyden that stands to this day in Water Street. His memory is not honoured in Liberia.

Chapter Three

The Liberians have no money, immigration is slack, they do not intermarry with the natives, and the population is decreasing; they acknowledge themselves that their prospects are gloomy in the extreme. Nothing can save them from perdition except the throwing open of the land; the free admission of European traders, and of negro settlers from Sierra Leone; or, in other words, the free admission of capital and labour.

(W. Winwood Reade in *The African Sketch-book*, 1873)

The history of West Africa at the end of the nineteenth century is best understood in Marxist terms. Contemporaries, such as Blyden, regarded the advent of imperialism and the consequent decline of Liberia as racial or political phenomena. The failure of the Liberians to open up the interior was blamed, by Blyden at least, on the foolishness of the mulatto leaders. In fact, as Reade had prophesied as early as 1873, the failure was due to want of labour and capital. From the end of the 1860s there was an ever-increasing demand in Europe for tropical African produce; this led to the introduction of low-cost scheduled European shipping lines. These soon killed off Liberia's merchant fleet which had numbered fifty ships during the 1860s. The big manufacturers of margarine, soap or coffee always preferred to buy from traders of their own country, so that Europeans were encouraged to venture into Liberian markets, in competition with the Liberian merchants. Cheaper shipping also caused a drop in the price of such African exports as ivory, palm kernels and palm oil. Liberian coffee, which had been the principal export, was faced by competition from the Brazilians, who had introduced the Liberian bean. By 1900 the price of Liberian coffee had dropped from twenty-four cents to four cents a pound, while the volume of coffee exported was down 50 per cent. Protectionism in Europe towards the end of the century hurt the Liberian farmers and traders still more. Beet sugar, introduced in Europe with colossal government subsidies, was as disastrous to the export of Liberian sugar-cane as competition from Brazil had been to Liberia's coffee trade. Lack of capital, rather than lack of interest, prevented Liberia getting her railway. Lack of troops, rather than lack of ambition, prevented her from claiming the rich northern savannah lands that fell, during this period, to France. Indeed, Liberia was so weak that only the mutual rivalry of the Great Powers prevented any one of them from annexing her.

The ruling class in Liberia feared the intrusion of foreign capitalism, yet realized that this was the only means of opening up the interior. Early in the twentieth century, a concession was granted to the Union Mining Company, most of whose ownership was British. In 1904 another British syndicate formed the Liberian Rubber Corporation under the management of Sir Harry Johnston, the scholar and adventurer who had founded the British colonies of Nyasaland and Uganda. Sir Harry proved a bad businessman, and one guesses that he had taken this job for the sake of working in Africa rather than from any hope of a fortune. The corporation was not a success, but Sir Harry's experiences in Liberia provided him with the material for his classic history of the country. Certain enemies wrote off *Liberia* as a disguised prospectus for the Liberian Rubber Corporation, but as Roland Oliver pointed out in his fine biography of Sir Harry Johnston,

> prospectuses do not usually run to 1,200 pages ... and the born prospectus-writer, one feels, would hardly have bothered to recount the history of the West African Coast from the times of Hanno the Carthaginian, to have printed careful facsimiles of the Vai system of handwriting, to have mercilessly badgered the authorities of the Natural History Museum into identifying his collection of Liberian scorpions and spiders.

Sir Harry gave an attractive picture of life in Liberia at the start

254

of the present century. He found the inhabitants courteous, law-abiding, at least as well read as the average English peasant, and dextrous enough to construct and work a telephone. Their faults, Sir Harry declared, were a love of frothy oratory, a zest for hair-splitting politics and too great an indulgence in alcohol and religion. Visitors to Liberia even today would agree with Sir Harry's complaint that Liberians 'have erected the Bible into a sort of fetish'. Although he thought that Latin and Greek were unsuitable for Liberia College, Johnston otherwise agreed with Blyden's critique of the country:

> If the author of this book were a Liberian, he would strive (within reason) to do everything as differently as possible from what is done in Europe, Asia, or America. He would try to be original. For instance, if he were the Principal of the Liberia College, he would resolutely exclude 'mortar boards' from the heads of the students, not only because they are an unsuit-able form of headgear, but because they happen to be the mode adopted in England and America. He would try to develop a special African architecture, an African school of painting. He would certainly study and develop the inherent musical talent evinced by many of the Liberian natives. He would attempt to domesticate the Red bush-pig, and not introduce Berkshire swine; the red Buffalo and not the English Short-horn; the Agelastes Guinea-fowl and not the Cochin-Chine.

The effort to pay off the Roye loan pushed Liberia deeper into a debt which amounted by 1900 to nearly a million dollars. The government had tried to regain solvency by imposing a poll tax, a land tax, a patent tax and a school tax, but little money collected for these ever found its way to the Treasury. In 1906, the Liberian Development Company, another organization run by Sir Harry Johnston, arranged a further loan of £100,000. Some of this was to pay off pressing debts, while the rest was to go on roads and the establishment of a bank. To secure this loan, the British were given first charge on the customs revenue and an Englishman was appointed inspector-general of Customs. Troops of the Sierra

Leone Frontier Force, under a British officer, were sent into the interior of Liberia to supervise the collection of taxes. The Liberian Development Company, which received a rubber and mining concession as part of the deal on the loan, spent most of the development money on building a short road and buying two cars to drive on it. The Liberian Government was later to complain that in return for selling a piece of its sovereignty it had received only £30,000.

The loan and the British Frontier Force were so unpopular in Liberia that the government turned for help to its first protector and friend, the United States of America. A commission, created in 1909, reorganized the Frontier Force under Negro officers of the United States Army, while white Americans took charge of the country's finances. In spite of these changes, debt piled upon debt until actual bankruptcy threatened in 1911. The Americans called in France, Britain and Germany, the principal trading partners of Liberia, and asked all three to appoint receivers. All revenues from imports and exports, the duties on rubber, and all poll-tax money were pledged to these foreign receivers, who were in fact the directors of the economy. Liberia had become almost a colony of the United States, but her servitude was less severe than that of Haiti, Nicaragua and Cuba, where the United States at about the same time sent marines as well as customs men to protect her nationals and her investments. Even the British Consul in Monrovia had to admit that the Americans running the Frontier Force were more popular than the men from Sierra Leone.

Under pressure from the United States, Liberia entered the First World War in August 1917, later sending some troops to fight in France. In 1918, a German submarine shelled Monrovia, and sank the solitary ship of Liberia's navy, that same *Lark* given by England in 1848. Economically, war was a disaster. Germany had been the country's major trading partner. Most of Liberia's goods were carried on German ships and her money was lodged in the Deutsche-Liberia Bank. The breach with Germany put Liberia still more in the power of America and, to a lesser extent, of Britain. From the First World War till the present day, the United States has been the accepted patron, banker and friend of this nominally independent country, although several other Powers have sought the rights of colonization. The British, during the 1920s, toyed with the idea of exercising protection. The French, at times, were menacing on Liberia's northern frontier. The Germans once or twice hinted that Liberia might be given to them as compensation for some of her former colonies. Even the Poles, who have never been good at running their own turbulent country, were eager to take on the job of running Liberia.

It was the destiny of Liberia to become not a colony of the United States, but of one American enterprise, the Firestone Rubber Company. The United States had pioneered the development and production of automobiles, but was still dependent on imports for the rubber used in tyres. 'We have 85 per cent of the world's automobiles,' said Harvey Firestone, the principal manufacturer. 'We use three-quarters of the rubber production of the world, and of what we use, about 80 per cent goes into automobile tyres. And we grow only a very small fraction of 1 per cent under our own flag.' To make matters worse, the British, who were the major producers of rubber, were tinkering with the market. When the world price dropped after the First World War, the planters in Malaya claimed that they could not get a return on their investment and therefore petitioned Winston Churchill, then the Colonial Secretary, to introduce a restriction on production. After talks with the Dutch, the other big rubber producers, Churchill pushed through the Restriction Act of 1922 which cut the production of rubber, bumped up the price and therefore, as Churchill pointed out, helped to pay Britain's war debt to America. In 1922, the American manufacturers of tyres, such as Firestone, had paid as little for rubber as fifteen cents a pound. In 1925 they were paying as much as one dollar, twenty-three cents. Understandably, they were enraged at Britain's exploitation of her monopoly. Firestone called the Restriction Act

a vicious plan which will result in making Americans pay exorbitant prices for their automobile tires ... What is more

257

we are threatened with an actual shortage of rubber ... With our tremendous automobile production, which is putting motor cars into every part of the globe, our demand for rubber will exceed the supply unless more rubber is planted ... An automobile without a tire is useless, and so is a tire without an automobile. And yet these two great industries depend absolutely upon the will of foreign countries for their lives. They depend on rubber and no rubber is grown on the United States. It is not so important to any other nation, for the life of no other nation is so dependent on the automobile as is ours.

Since the British proved intransigent, Firestone decided to plant and produce at least a part of the rubber he needed. Executives were dispatched to various countries whose climate made them possible for plantations. In Panama and in Venezuela there was insufficient labour. The Philippines, although an American colony, was disturbed by an independence movement. Guatemala was politically unsound and in southern Mexico, Firestone's son, who had gone to inspect some likely jungle, was expelled by a group of revolutionaries. Liberia seemed to be free of these defects. As Firestone later wrote: 'Liberia offered the best of natural advantages. The labour supply is indigenous and practically inexhaustible. The government welcomed our proposals and offered most advantageous terms and conditions. Liberians consider themselves more or less a protectorate of America and want American capital to develop the country.'

In December 1926, the representatives of Firestone and the Liberian Government had worked out the terms of an agreement by which the American company was given the rubber plantations of the defunct Johnstone corporation, as well as a ninety-nine year lease on a million acres of forest, the rights of harbour construction and the effective control of all the revenue of Liberia. Although some members of the Liberian Cabinet argued that by accepting these terms they would be 'running from a sword, France, and impaling ourselves on a bayonet (U.S.A.)', the majority approved of the American alliance. The vestiges of authority exercised by the British and French governments under the terms of the 1912 loan were removed and transferred to the Americans. The National City Bank of New York, which was the broker for the Firestone interests, took over financial control of Liberia through its subsidiary, the City Bank of Monrovia. Twelve thousand Liberians were taken on to the pay-roll of the company, where they were introduced to the marvels of modern technology, such as the first radio message from across the Atlantic. The drooling publicist of the Firestone Company, describing the radio link of Christmas 1928 wrote:

> It was one of those moon-flooded nights such as Africa alone may know; a canopy of stars stretching across the heavens. From the jungle came the boom of croaking frogs and a medley of night noises ... Then, clearly, came the sound of music, followed by the voice of Mr Firestone, conveying his New Year's message from his winter home at Miami Beach in Florida ... At his first words some of the women and the more timid souls among the men ran away, and a few never could be induced to come back. Others crawled under the table to see who might be hiding there, talking through the horns. The very bravest strode right up to the broadcasting apparatus to defy this new kind of witch ...

Relations between the Firestone Company and Liberia were not always so genial as the Firestone authors pretended. On September 11th, 1926, the British Consul reported with poorly disguised amusement:

> Discussions appear to have been continuing in an amicable manner recently, when last Saturday, Mr Cheek, who is here with Mr Harvey Firestone, lost his temper with their chauffeur and boxed his ears ... The boy immediately swore out a charge against Mr Cheek (and against a doctor who had intervened) and the Police proceeded directly to the house which they entered and searched and finally marched the two offenders off amidst considerable abuse to the Court.

Certain left-wing writers attacked the Firestone agreement. The itinerant pundit, Raymond Buell, said that the plan had 'all the objectionable features of the large plantation system in regard to native labour', while the young Nigerian author, Nnamdi Azikiwe, later President of his country, pointed out that when the British capitalist Lord Leverhulme had tried to obtain a ninety-nine year lease for his palm-kernel and palm-oil plantation, the British Government had refused him. It was evident that from the time of the Firestone agreement, effective government of Liberia had passed to the hands of the rubber company. 'Though a friendly spirit exists between the officials in the Government and those in financial control,' wrote George W. Brown, the historian of the Liberian economy, 'it is quite evident that the Superintendent of the Firestone Plantation, the Manager of the Bank of Monrovia and the Financial Adviser are the triumvirate of power.'

Chapter Four

What is Africa to me:
Copper sun or scarlet sea,
Jungle star or jungle track,
Strong bronzed men, or regal black
Women from whose loins I sprang
When the birds of Eden sang?
One three centuries removed
From the scenes his fathers loved,
Spicy grove, cinnamon tree,
What is Africa to me?
                    (From 'Heritage', by Countee Cullen)

The American Colonization Society continued to send out emigrants to Liberia until the end of the nineteenth century. A few prominent Negroes, like Blyden, continued to preach Black Zionism, the Back to Africa movement. The movement had languished just after the Civil War but stirred again during the 'seventies and 'eighties, as the whites regained supremacy in the South. Militant Negroes, especially those in the North, distrusted the Back to Africa movement, preferring to fight for equality in America. But even they were proud of Liberia. Some Negro Americans looked to southern Africa, especially after the news of gold and diamond strikes in the Transvaal and at Kimberley. An Ethiopian Church was formed with priests and congregations both in the United States and in the African townships of Cape Colony. A Negro sea captain, Harry Dean, sailed his ship to Cape Town where he regaled his brothers in the Ethiopian Church with outlandish tales of diamond trading, of founding a Negro colony in Pondoland, and of having purchased

Mozambique for a mere fifty thousand dollars. The British authorities, unimpressed, asked Captain Dean to leave the colony.

The initiative of the Jewish Zionists in the early years of the twentieth century revived and inspired the old Negro dream of returning to Africa from their exile. The prophet, leader and martyr of the new Back to Africa movement was a Jamaican journalist, Marcus Garvey, the first man to rouse the Negroes of the United States to mass political action. The Garvey movement, for all its many absurdities, was father to the Black Power movement, the Black Muslims, the Black Panthers, to Malcolm X, Rap Brown, Stokely Carmichael, Eldridge Cleaver and all those groups and individuals who believe in a separate destiny for the Negroes of America. Since the Garvey movement also revived the old Negro dream of mass emigration to Liberia, it was most important to the history of that country and therefore to this narrative.

Like many leaders of the United States Negroes, Garvey was born and brought up in the British West Indies. Both his parents were pure black, an important factor in Garvey's career, because in Jamaica there has always been rivalry between the blacks and the mulattoes. Garvey's father, who claimed descent from the Maroons, was a stubborn and bitter man, and Marcus's written memoirs of childhood have none of the warmth and humour that one associates with Jamaica. In 1901, when Garvey was fourteen years old, a white girl of his own age, who had been his friend and playmate since their infancy, was sent off to school in Scotland, and was told by her parents, in Garvey's own words, 'that she was never to write or try to get in touch with me, for I was a "nigger" '. Garvey became an apprentice to a printer, qualified in this trade, and then left his home in a northern town for a job in Kingston, the capital.

Garvey progressed to master-printer and foreman, but increasingly he was attracted to editorial work. In 1907 he led a strike but when most of his workmates went back to work, Garvey turned from union politics to the concept of black power through propaganda and organization. He practised public speaking and

262

writing articles; he travelled in Central and South America and visited Britain to study law and politics. Garvey never received any formal or disciplined education, as may be discerned from his writing, but he did learn the persuasive force of a simple idea, simply expressed. 'One God! One Aim! One Destiny!' were the principles of the Universal Negro Improvement Association (U.N.I.A.) that Garvey launched in 1914, 'to promote the spirit of race, pride and love; to reclaim the fallen of the race; to administer to and assist the needy; to assist in civilising the backward tribes of Africa; to strengthen the imperialism of independent African states'.

At this time Garvey was influenced by the meliorative and cautious ideas of the American Negro leader, Booker T. Washington. His first visit to the United States in 1916 was to study the Negro colleges that Washington had established. However, Washington was dead by the time Garvey reached Harlem; and with him had died the old Negro society. During the decade from 1910 and above all during the war years of 1917–18, black America underwent an economic, social and spiritual transformation which was to give Garvey his chance for power and glory.

The First World War, even before the entry of the United States, caused an industrial boom in the Northern states, to which half a million Negroes moved between 1916 and 1918. The Negroes in Chicago alone increased from 44,000 in 1910 to 110,000 in 1920. Northern industrialists offered free railway passes to likely recruits in the South, who had anyway been attracted by stories they heard of good wages and racial equality. A plague of boll-weevil that ravaged the cotton plantations in 1915 gave added impetus to the mass migration whose most famous result was the nationwide craze for jazz. Great Negro musicians, like Louis Armstrong, left the honky-tonks of Memphis and Nashville and New Orleans to play in the dance-halls, and later the speakeasies of Harlem, Detroit and Chicago.

Even during the rich war years, there was social unrest among the immigrant Negroes. Slum ghettoes and Jim Crow were harder to bear in the promised liberty of Chicago than in the familiar tyranny of the South. Although black labour was welcome in the boom time in the North, Negroes were the first to be fired at the hint of bad times. Radical Negro newspapers like the Chicago *Defender* encouraged the black urban masses to stand up for their rights. War service, too, brought a revolution in attitude among the 400,000 Negro soldiers who felt they were not getting justice from the society they defended. Negroes stationed in France found they were well treated by white people and asked themselves why the same was not true at home. The increased confidence and aspirations of Negroes inspired an answering fear in many white Americans. The Ku Klux Klan was reborn in 1915; many Negro soldiers were lynched during and just after the war; hatred, compounded by economic recession, burst out in the 'Red Summer' of 1919 with twenty-six race riots, including one in Chicago, in which thirty-eight people were killed. This was the mood of the American black community to which Garvey addressed his arguments in articles and speeches.

Garvey's message was fresh and appealing. He preached a pride in the colour black—black skin, black power, even a black God ruling above—and disdain for the mulatto half-caste. Some commentators argued that Garvey made a mistake by transferring West Indian prejudices to the United States, where there was less hostility between black and mulatto. The fact remains that before Garvey no Negro leader had won a response from the darker skinned, poorer and badly schooled Negroes. The traditional Negro politicians, many of whom were mulattoes, wanted only freedom and justice within a white America. Garvey was first to offer a vision of black people holding power in a black nation. He jeered at Negroes who hoped to advance thanks to the goodwill or patronage of white liberals; indeed, like recent militant Negroes, he claimed to welcome the Ku Klux Klan. 'I regard the Klan, the Anglo-Saxon clubs and White American Societies, as far as the Negro is concerned, as better friends of the race than all other groups of hypocritical whites put together.' He was the first, but not the last, Negro leader to play on jealousy and dislike of the Jews.

By 1917, Garvey was drawing big crowds to his speeches. The following year he started a weekly journal, the *Negro World*, a heady mixture of rhetoric, maxims, portraits of black heroes, and items of dubious news. The *Negro World* was soon selling throughout the United States, Latin America and in those African countries where it had not yet been banned.* Garvey loved to boast of the Negro numbers—'four hundred million Negroes cry out for ... justice.' In fact there have never been half that number, but Garvey cared little for accuracy. The sense of irrepressible quantity encouraged the downtrodden workers of Georgia, Costa Rica, Jamaica, South Africa and wherever the *Negro World* was read. Its revenue soared, in spite of the fact that Garvey refused the profitable advertisements for such 'race-degrading' goods as skin-whitening and hair-straightening compounds. Scores of thousands of *Negro World* readers also paid for membership of the U.N.I.A., which bought an auditorium in Harlem. In August 1920 Garvey launched a rally in Harlem that was to make him famous throughout the white and Negro worlds.

Garvey had always known the appeal of titles, pageantry and uniforms. His own robes of office as president-general of U.N.I.A. were a mortar board and academic cape—the badges of the learned man that Garvey so longed to be. The great convention of 1920 offered a fantasy of power to a powerless and unhappy race. Scores of thousands of Harlemites saw the big parade by men of the African Legion, dressed in dark-blue uniforms with red trouser stripes; the two hundred girls of the Universal Black Cross Nurses, the African Motor Corps and the Black Eagle Flying Corps. Few of the crowd, in that moment of pride, stopped to inquire whether the Black Eagles knew how to fly or whether the Black Cross nurses had any nursing experience. Distinguished Negroes, who should have known better, took part in the preposterous charades. Some accepted strange orders such as Knight of the Nile, or the Distinguished Service Order of Ethiopia. Others accepted

* The acting governor of Sierra Leone wrote to the Colonial Office in 1923 that the *Negro World*, 'although not absolutely prohibited, has been strictly controlled, and only a few copies have been allowed to circulate'.

high-flown jobs and even salaries of from three to twelve thousand dollars, as ministers of an unborn state, under Marcus Garvey, provisional President of Africa. Many years later, Garvey wrote that, 'with the exception of Bishop George Alexander McGuire, who was elected Chaplain-General, and Lady Henrietta Vinton Davis, who had remained faithful to her oath and the organization, not one of the elected officers was worth more than $1,200 a year as an office boy or lackey'. As a matter of fact, very few of them even got $1,200 a year because there was no fund voted to meet their salaries. A Sierra Leonean 'potentate', with his country's characteristic faith in litigation, later tried to sue for back pay, but most of the officers at the time were flattered by their awards. The Mayor of Monrovia, Gabriel Johnson, was so pleased by his title, 'His Highness, the Potentate', that he referred to himself as 'First Negro in the World' to the great vexation of President King, the genuine President of Liberia.

The convention demanded that Negro must be spelled with a capital letter;* it gave the movement its colours of red, for the blood of the race, black for the skin of the race, and green for the hope of a new life in Africa.† It was at this convention that Garvey first clearly proclaimed his programme of Back to Africa:

> We shall now organise the four hundred million Negroes of the world into a vast organisation to plant the banner of freedom on the great continent of Africa ... If Europe is for the Europeans then Africa shall be for the black people of the world... We are striking homewards towards Africa to make her the big black republic ... We say to the white man who now dominates Africa that it is to his interest to clear out of Africa now, because we are coming not as in the time of Father Abraham 200,000 strong, but we are coming

* The capital 'N' for Negro was soon adopted by newspapers that wanted to please their coloured readers, including, in 1930, the *New York Times*. The capital 'N' is now obligatory.

† 'Black Power soldiers in South Vietnam have a flag of red for their blood shed, black for the face of black culture and green for youth and new ideas.' (*Time* Magazine, September 19th, 1969.)

400,000,000 strong and we mean to retake every square mile of the 12,000,000 square miles of African territory belonging to us by right Divine.

These promises, like Garvey's messages of support to the Irish revolutionaries, were studied with nervous interest by the British and other colonial governments. The White House, too, was suspicious of Garvey who, although not a radical in the socialist sense, had the active support of such socialist groups as the American Communist Party.

A Harlem ditty made fun of the Back to Africa movement:

> Garvey, Garvey is a big man
> To take his folks to monkey-land.
> If he does I'm sure I can
> Stay right here with Uncle Sam.

Some Negroes were not just sceptical but hostile, as can be seen from this description of Garvey by Robert W. Bagnall:

A Jamaican Negro of unmixed stock, squat, stocky, fat and sleek, with protruding jaws and heavy jowls, small bright pig-like eyes and rather bull-dog face. Boastful, egoistic, tyrannical, intolerant, cunning, shifty, smooth and suave, avaricious; gifted as self advertisement; without shame in self-laudations ... without regard for veracity, a lower of pomp and tawdry finery and garish display.

Garvey replied with even more snarling attacks upon the integrationists and Uncle Toms, the octoroons and quadroons, the hair straighteners and face bleachers.

The man Garvey hated the most because at the same time he feared him the most was W. E. Burghard Du Bois, who spent most of his nearly one hundred years in working for the advancement of the Negro race. Du Bois's background and career were the antithesis of Garvey's. Born in 1868 with a mixture of French, Dutch and African blood, he was light-skinned, hook-nosed and, partly because of his Van Dyke beard, looked much less like a

267

Negro than a Dutchman in a cigar advertisement. He was given a fine education, first at Fisk and then at Harvard University, after which he turned to sociology. Although he studied the Negro slums, he did so as an outsider, who felt ambivalent to the race whose cause he had chosen to champion. At first he encouraged Negro businessmen, then turned to social democracy, and at last, in old age, to admiration for Russia. He was one of the founders and few Negro leaders of the National Association for the Advancement of Coloured People. His power and fame depended upon his skill as a writer. Witty, tolerant, rational, well read, he had just those qualities that Garvey lacked, and whose lack was perpetually to enrage him. Du Bois's *Crisis* magazine never attained the readership of the *Negro World*, nor rivalled Garvey's influence on the Negro masses, but Garvey, the self-taught man who posed for photographs in a mortar board and gown, was envious of the Harvard graduate. Perhaps Du Bois's reasonableness made his arguments all the more hard to stand. His praise for Garvey's sincerity was as maddening as his pity. 'All his life', Du Bois said about Garvey, 'whites have laughed and sneered at him, and torn his soul. All his life he has hated the half-whites, who rejecting their darker blood, have gloried in their pale shame.'

These delicate jabs had the no doubt intended effect of provoking Garvey to bellowing wrath. 'It is no wonder that Du Bois seeks the company of white people, because he hates black as being ugly. That is why he likes to dance with white people, and dine with them, and sometimes sleep with them, because from his way of seeing things all that is black is ugly, and all that is white is beautiful.'

Garvey's downfall was his attempt to set up Negro businesses and, above all, the Black Star shipping line. By registering his companies in the state of Delaware, where the laws of incorporation were lax, Garvey floated enormous enterprises with only a small sum of cash. He then used the *Negro World* as an advertising medium to sell hundreds of thousands of dollars of stock to supporters. The Black Star Line bought several ships, all of them old, over-priced and often unseaworthy. The *Kanawha*, a converted millionaire's yacht, earned only a thousand dollars during the eighteen months of its operation, but cost more than a hundred thousand to run. When the *Yarmouth*, an ancient freighter, docked at Havana with a consignment of whisky, it was found that the crew had guzzled the cargo. The Negro maritime adviser, and one of the line's least reliable captains, was found to be in the pay of the people who sold Black Star its ships. The treasurer of the company was a former railway clerk with only the slightest knowledge of book-keeping. Most of the senior staff, including those few who were either honest or capable, soon quarrelled with the cantankerous Garvey, who was already in litigation with several newspapers, his wife and many political enemies. Garvey's answer to difficulty was typical of the megalomaniac: he recapitalized his company for ten million dollars. As critics like Du Bois always attempted to point out to him, this larger capitalization merely meant paying an extra fee, and did not bestow sudden solvency on the company.

Even Garvey's enemies at the time did not say that he personally robbed Black Star and his various other businesses. He drew only part of his salary, while his personal spending was moderate. Garvey, just as much as his stockholders, gave his money in sacrifice to the spirit of Negro Power. The ugly, limping ships of the fatuous Black Star Line were to Garvey and also to hundreds of thousands of Negroes, symbols of the enterprise and the hopes of the Negro race. But Garvey's creditors and the officers of the law were not impressed by these dreams. In January 1922, he was arrested and charged with using 'fraudulent representations' and 'deceptive artifices' in the sale of stock through the mails. The trial produced much evidence of incompetence but none of criminal intent. As one biographer of Garvey wrote, the real crooks were not the Black Star directors, but those who had sold them junk. At his trial, Garvey made the characteristic mistake of conducting his own defence with interminable, ranting speeches in which he often referred to himself in the third person. 'Garvey is but a man. Garvey is but human. But Garvey must be destroyed, but in destroying the physical in Garvey, you cannot destroy the soul and I feel you, Gentlemen, will not do anything except that which is prompted by justice, truth; and the law.' The gentlemen of the jury, who had to sit twice the normal length of a trial because of such long perorations, found Garvey guilty. The judge passed a sentence of one thousand dollars fine and five years' prison.

It was while Garvey was out on bail and awaiting appeal on his sentence that he turned his energies and his still colossal influence to the Back to Africa movement. As early as 1920 he had opened talks with the government of Liberia and had sent out a colleague, Elie Garcia, to represent the U.N.I.A. Meanwhile, in the United States, Garvey started a fund for the reconstruction of Liberia, whose government, no doubt anxious to get its hands on the money, offered the U.N.I.A. 'every facility legally possible in effectuating in Liberia its industrial, agricultural and business projects'.

Garvey and the Liberians appeared, on the surface, harmonious. But Garcia, on his return from the 1920 visit, handed Garvey a secret report that was most unflattering to the Liberian leadership.

> Liberia [it began] although a very rich country in natural resources is the poorest place on the face of the earth and actually the people are facing starvation. This condition is due to many facts, first the strong repulsion of the Liberians for any kind of work. There is no cultivated land in the Republic and RICE which is the national food is imported from England and other places and sold at a fabulous price, although it can be produced in enormous quantities there.

The Americo-Liberians were, in Garcia's view, a despicable group living on government graft, and frightened of competition from newcomers. 'This fact is of great importance', Garcia warned, 'and I dare suggest that words must be given to anyone going to Liberia in the interest of the U.N.I.A., to deny firmly any intention on our part to enter into politics in Liberia.' Nor should the U.N.I.A. reveal its plans for bettering the natives of Liberia for

> as it is, the Americo-Liberians are using the natives as slaves, and human chattel slavery still exists there. They buy men or women to help them, and the least little insignificant Americo-Liberian has half a dozen boys at his service—for he, himself, will not even carry his own umbrella in the street, said article has to be carried by a boy, and so, for the smallest parcel. When in Monrovia I went to a store and bought 7 yards of khaki to have 2 pairs of trousers made. The merchant wrapped the khaki and gave it to me. As I was stepping out of the store my companion (an Americo-Liberian) said to me: 'Why I don't suppose you are going to carry this bundle yourself?' 'Why not?' said I, 'it is a very small parcel.' He answered that it was not the custom in Liberia for any gentleman to carry parcels, therefore the usefulness of having slaves.

It seems that the Liberian Government did not learn for several years of Garcia's damning report. President C. B. D. King and Edwin Barclay, his Secretary of State, kept up at least the appearance of friendliness towards Garvey. Both men were pure blacks of West Indian origin and did not share the prejudices of the paler Americo-Liberians. They both expressed pleasure when, late in 1923, Garvey dispatched a team of experts to start on construction work in the Maryland province of Liberia. It was proposed that in August 1924 the first 30,000 emigrants would be sent from the United States—on ships of the Black Star Line—to settle in townships prepared for them by the experts. Acting-President Barclay once more welcomed the Garvey plan and appointed the Chief Justice, James D. Dossen, to co-ordinate the work of the U.N.I.A. and the government. As late as May 2nd, 1924, Dossen wrote to the U.N.I.A.:

> I am glad to learn that you are busy working out our Plan and that you hope to dispatch your first colonists in September, next. We shall stand ready to co-operate with you on this side,

in putting over the enterprise successfully. We entertain great hopes that working upon this line, you will accomplish much good in promoting the growth and industrial development of the Republic of Liberia and securing the Liberty, Independence and Protection of the millions of Negroes now under foreign domination.

Within two months the Garvey plan had been killed. Some ships carrying goods for the U.N.I.A. settlement were attached for debt by Garvey's creditors, and on June 30th, 1924, the Liberian Government unexpectedly warned all steamship companies that 'no members of the movement known as the Garvey movement' would be permitted to land.and the steamship companies would be held responsible for removing them. The government followed this up by expelling the group of experts who, in any case, were quarrelling with the U.N.I.A. over the slow receipt of money. In vain, Garvey petitioned the Senate and the House of Representatives of Liberia. In August 1924, Edwin Barclay signed a note from the government of Liberia, declaring it 'irrevocably opposed both in principle and fact to the incendiary policy of the Universal Negro Improvement Association headed by Marcus Garvey, which ... does not appear to be bona fide and has in addition a tendency adversely to affect the amicable relations of the republic with the friendly states possessing territories adjacent to Liberia.'

The most likely explanation of this sudden change of policy is that members of the Liberian Government had seen Garcia's rude report on the country, made in 1920. It could be that copies of the report had been leaked to them by some U.S. agency hostile to Garvey. Other Garveyites, noting Barclay's remarks in the message of August 1924, thought that President King had been influenced by the British and French Governments. The British, certainly, were suspicious of Garveyism, feared the *Negro World*, and opposed the Back to Africa movement. The Senegalese Blaise Diagne, a member of the French Senate and an unofficial spokesman on African affairs, had warned Garvey not to expect support from the natives of French Africa. When President King visited

Freetown in January 1925, Governor Sir Alexander Ransford Slater congratulated him for 'slamming the door on spurious patriots from across the Atlantic'; the French signalled their thanks by making King a Chevalier of the Legion d'Honneur. Garvey himself put the blame on his arch-foe Du Bois, who was sent by the United States as representative at the inauguration ceremony in January 1925. Although Du Bois had been critical of the Back to Africa movement, he pointed out that he could not be held responsible for decisions taken in Liberia six months before his arrival.

Garvey's plans for Africa, like his plans for the Black Star Line, were wrecked by excessive ambition. He talked of millions returning to Africa when only hundreds were ready to go. American Negroes would give money and moral support to a Back to Africa movement, just as Jews supported the founders of Israel, but few Negroes or Jews were prepared to leave the United States for the unfamiliar, uncomfortable life of a pioneer. By exaggerating the scale of the emigration, Garvey made enemies of the Liberians, who were ready to welcome a few useful immigrants, but feared the arrival of thousands or millions. A smaller, more cautious Back to Africa movement might have benefited Liberia and given the Negroes in their diaspora a pride and interest in their African origins. But smallness and caution were foreign to Garvey's nature; he thought in capital letters and exclamation marks; his every project was wrecked by his megalomania.

Early in 1925, Garvey lost his appeal on the mail-fraud charge and was taken to prison in Atlanta. 'When I am dead,' he wrote with the tone of a martyr, 'wrap the mantle of the Red, Black and Green around me, for in the new life I shall rise with God's grace and blessing to lead the millions up the heights of triumphs with colours that you will know ... ' His sentence was commuted in 1927, and Garvey was shipped to Jamaica where he tried with some success to revive the U.N.I.A. More quarrels and writs were to follow, one shorter prison spell and ever-increasing bitterness. In 1935, he removed his headquarters to London where, friendless and almost forgotten, he died in 1940. The news of his death was announced by mistake several days before it occurred, so that Garvey, so proud of his future place in history, spent the end of his life reading newspaper obituaries describing his own descent to obscurity.

A survey of Negro Chicago, *Black Metropolis*, records that in 1938 'only a corporal's guard' of faithful Garveyites still met in their shabby Liberty Hall. The authors quote a domestic servant speaking of U.N.I.A.: 'All I know about Garvey is that he wanted to form the coloured people into some kind of union and have us all go back to Africa and form a country of our own. That was a good idea.' But a relief worker asked: 'Why should the coloured people go back to Africa? There ain't nothing for them to do over there.' A businessman accused the Garveyites of running away from the coming fight in their own country. A barber's-shop lounger said of the Back to Africa movement: 'There ain't no boulevards in Africa.'

The dream of Back to Africa lingered on. One curious convert to the idea was that arch-anti-Garveyite, Du Bois, who fell in love with Africa during his visit to Liberia. 'The spell of Africa is upon me,' he gushed. 'The ancient witchery of her medicine is burning my drowsy, dreamy blood ... There is sunlight in great globules and soft, heavy-scented heat that wraps you like a garment. And laziness; divine, eternal, languor is right and good and true.' The laziness that Du Bois so admired was perhaps more remarkable in the gentlemen of Monrovia than in the slaves and labourers whom they employed. Later in life, Du Bois retained his affection for Africa but tempered it with some unromantic Marxism. As a very old man in the 1950s he went to live and at last to die in Nkrumah's Ghana.

A group of Black Muslims settled in Liberia as recently as the 1960s, and now run one of the best icecream shops in the capital. Most Negroes in the diaspora with an interest in the Back to Africa movement have turned their interest from Liberia to more belligerent countries. The struggle of Ras Tafari, the Emperor Haile Selassie, against the Italian army in the 'thirties, inspired the Rastafarians, a Caribbean religious sect, with overtones of African

274

Irredentism. Some Black Power leaders* have gone to Guinea, a radical state, and the refuge of Kwame Nkrumah, who once confessed that 'of all the literature that I studied, the book that did more than any other to fire my enthusiasm was the *Philosophy and Opinions of Marcus Garvey* ... '

The problems of the Negro in the United States are just as difficult and harsh as they were in Garvey's day. The same arguments rage about their destiny. There are integrationists in the Du Bois tradition and those like Garvey who want black power. Marcus Garvey, for all his folly, had understood one big truth: 'The prejudice of the white race against the black race', he wrote in the early 'twenties, 'is not so much because of color as of condition; we have built no nation, no government; because we are dependent for our economic and political existence.' The Negroes of America still have no nation, no government and therefore still remember the Back to Africa dream.

* One of these, Stokeley Carmichael, comes from the West Indies, where Garvey's son is also a black militant.

PART FIVE

Chapter One

The train for Bo
She no agree for go
The engine she done tire
For lack of plenty fire
The train for Bo
She no agree for go

(The Sierra Leoncan troops serving in Burma in the Second
World War sang this nostalgic song which then grew popular
with other Allied troops who may never have heard of Bo, or
indeed of Sierra Leone.)

With the opening of the railway line from Freetown to Bo, in the
palm-oil country, the economy of Sierra Leone passed into the
hands of British big-businessmen. As each stretch of the line was
opened, the traffic increased in volume and value, for palm products were much in demand in the first decade of the century.
Glycerine for explosives was produced out of the oil; margarine
was made from the kernels; the Lever soap company cried out for
more supplies. The narrow-gauge railway was always noted for
safety rather than speed, as the words of the ditty above make
clear, but the boost it gave to the trade of the colony can be seen
from the soaring figures for exports from 1900.

Until the Hut-Tax War in 1898, the trade into the interior was
controlled by Freetown Creoles, whose know-how was unequalled by the whites. The opening of the railway offered the
British the chance to squeeze out the Creoles. 'With few exceptions,' wrote T. J. Allridge in 1910, 'the European's cry is: "trade,
trade, trade! Bring us palm-oil and palm-kernels".' Large British
companies, such as Lever, now sent young Englishmen to the

interior as buyers. Thanks to their massive capital, they could advance credits to chiefs to get a monopoly of the area, they could buy in bulk to undersell smaller competitors, and were confident that the up-country officials would take their side against Creole traders. The ships returning from Liverpool brought cheap manufactured goods to sell up country. 'With the march of so-called civilisation,' Allridge went on, 'the paradox is presented of asking the natives on the one hand to grow cotton for the English market, while on the other hand the English manufacturers are sending out, as an article of trade, manufactured yarns in all colours for people to use in place of their own country-grown cotton which they have cultivated and spun as far back as we can get at their history.' Shoddy singlets and trousers replaced the dignified gowns of the hinterland; earthenware bowls were exchanged for tin basins; beer bottled in Lancashire was preferred to palm wine.

The expansion of trade to the interior was especially bad for the Creole middlemen. The big British companies shipping to Africa followed the practice then common in Britain of entering into the retail as well as the wholesale trade. Companies that had dealt in hogsheads of tobacco now sold it in pound packets over the counter. The wealthier people in the colony now ordered direct by cable from England, while even the poor could purchase by mail order from temptingly lavish catalogues. Everything appeared to conspire against the Creole traders. Once they had done good trade with the Mandingoes of the savannah country who came south to Freetown with ivory, gold, bullocks and sheep. The Creoles would entertain them, bargain with them and, if possible, swindle them. Then, early in the century, the border with France was sealed just south of Mandingo territory, so that most of their trade went to Konakry.

The gravest threat to the Creole traders came from the competition of Syrians, who had first drifted to Freetown around the turn of the century. Most of these came from what is now Lebanon and are now generally called Lebanese, although some come from Syria proper, Jordan and Palestine. Like their ancestors, the Phoenicians, these Syrians were consummate merchants, prepared to venture into the wild for the sake of a few per cent profit. The Phoenicians had traded for tin from the savages of Cornwall; the Syrians, during the nineteenth century, opened up savage West Africa. By 1910 there were nearly two hundred Syrian traders in Freetown alone. Another less trustworthy report said that in 1916 there were three thousand Syrians in and around the capital. Their effect on the economy was enormous. Beginning as street-traders or stall-holders, the Syrians worked long hours, sold cheap and were ready to travel rough for the sake of a bargain.

There is argument as to how and why the Syrians superseded the Creoles as traders. Some blamed it on the tendency of intelligent Creoles to seek a job in government or the professions. Yet this could be the result as well as the cause of their economic failure. The historian Christopher Fyfe points out that the Syrians, just like the former recaptive street-traders, would club together to beat the market, while Creoles competed fiercely among themselves. This explanation salves the pride of the Creoles for having been pushed out of trade. Most Englishmen at the time blamed Creole laziness for the rise of the Syrian traders. Allridge, who half admired them, wrote:

The Syrians live on country chop. Both men and women work desperately hard; everything with them is work and money. You never see them drinking ... The commercial success of the Syrian baffles the understanding of the Sierra Leonean trader. The Sierra Leonean men and women (especially women), who are all born traders, are struck with amazement that these Syrians are succeeding where they are barely living; for it was always thought that if any one could do business, they could. He is indeed a very serious competitor, but if the Sierra Leonean were wise he might perceive that his rival presents a very striking object lesson if only he would learn it. The Syrian saves where the Sierra Leonean squanders. He professes nothing; he makes no show; he attends strictly to business. He does not use the parcel post for getting himself an up-to-date costume quite unsuitable

281

for the climate, the height of his Sierra Leonean neighbour's ambition.

Most of the money the Syrians saved was remitted to the Levant to pay for a hard-earned retirement. Contributing little to the economy of Sierra Leone, they were also a source of social rancour. Envied and hated by the Africans, despised and snubbed by the Europeans, the Syrians, like the Jews whom they so much resemble, retreated into a ghetto life consoled by hard work, perhaps by a plump Syrian wife, and always by the dream of a villa among the cedars or down by the Mediterranean.

Both whites and Creoles resented the Syrian newcomers, but tended, as well, to draw apart from each other. The discovery that malaria was carried by mosquito bites had encouraged the Europeans to live at an altitude where mosquitoes were seldom found, but racial as well as medical motives prompted the founding of Hill Station, eight hundred feet up on Wilberforce Hill. By 1910, most of the white community had moved to this bungalow colony, which was blatantly closed to Creole or Syrian residents. The Creoles down in Freetown, who had always invested their savings in property, saw rents collapse when their British tenants departed. Just as the railway to Bo was the symbol of Creole economic decline, the Hill Station railway, opened in 1904, marked the end of their social pretensions. Every morning at half-past eight, the train left from the hill with the governor and his senior staff at the front, and the rest of the white officials and businessmen ranged in importance behind. Each afternoon at half-past three they returned from the town to the agreeable cool of the mountainside. The station of the town terminal was beside the enormous cotton tree in whose shade, more than a hundred years earlier the Nova Scotian settlers had proclaimed their independence.

As the colony grew more healthy, more Europeans brought their wives and children to live with them in the Hill Station. The women, as in British India, proved less inclined than the men to mix in society with the natives. Cut off already by five miles of railway track, the Europeans tried to extend their colour bar. A hospital was founded for Europeans only. Creoles were not made welcome in white clubs and the one hotel. Allridge wrote with approval of the new 'European ice company' as though he assumed that only the Europeans could want their food fresh or their drinks cold. The tone of the Europeans when speaking or writing about the Creoles acquired a new condescension. 'Fourah Bay [College] has been doing very well this term,' wrote the Bishop of Sierra Leone in his diary in 1911, 'and I like the look of the men. I played cricket for them on Saturday against the customs men—native. There was a bit of trouble at the end and I had to intercede. They are so like children; they are quite amenable, and in the end took a beating by two runs in very good part: the trouble was really between the umpire and the other side.'

Governors in the twentieth century continued Cardew's policy of appointing whites instead of Creoles to government jobs of responsibility. This applied particularly in the protectorate where Creoles were always looked upon with suspicion and could not get more than a clerical job, however impressive their qualifications. Even in Freetown, Europeans were given quite junior jobs, such as deputy customs inspector, which always before had been held by a Creole. In 1900 and again in 1907, a European called Phillip Lemberg won the election for Mayor of Freetown. Although he was popular with some of the Creole voters, his choice was typical of the trend.

Sometimes the British excused their discrimination by saying that there were no Creoles suitable for the job. Occasionally they revealed an explicit racial prejudice. In 1909, for example, the Secretary of State for the Colonies ruled that no coloured doctors could get a post in the recently formed West African Medical Service. The committee that recommended this change did not believe

that in professional capabilities West African native doctors are on a par, except in very rare instances, with European doctors, or that they possess the confidence of European patients on the coast. Social conditions, particularly in

283

Southern Nigeria, where European officers live together and have their meals in common under the 'mess' system, and in Northern Nigeria, where a large proportion of the European staff consists of officers of the regular army, make it extremely undesirable to introduce native medical officers in the Protectorates.

In cruder language, the British officers refused 'to have a damned nigger in the mess'.

The Creoles were furious, and with reason. During the nineteenth century, twenty Creoles had qualified from medical schools in Britain. The Creole doctor James Africanus Horton had not only served for twenty years as a medical army officer, but had written one of the best early books on how to keep healthy in Africa. A coloured West Indian army doctor had actually served for a year as governor of the colony and had earned wide praise from the whites. The Creoles in 1909 understood the racial prejudice behind the decision to ban coloured doctors. They compared it, accurately, with the growing hostility towards Creole lawyers and Creole graduates in the Civil Service.

Is it not a very sad matter [wailed the *Sierra Leone Weekly News*] that English rulers, of all rulers, in West Africa should initiate a policy of repression among natives when they could find no cogent—no sufficient, no *reasonable* reason for this policy, except this perhaps utterly unworthy one, viz.—that they alone, as being masters, might enjoy the good things of the country which they never created ... We don't like to learn the white man in these his present ways among us. It depresses us greatly to have to do this. We like to be able to retain the ancient belief which obtained among our fathers— due to the righteous ways of Victorian England—that the white man, nay the Englishman, is an embodiment of the best conscience—of justice—of mercy, righteousness and kindliness. Times are changing: and with the emergencies of life, so pressing, we do not quarrel with the white man because of a show of less kindliness on his part. But is justice, too, becoming difficult, if not impracticable, for the English-man?

Frustrated in commerce and the professions, many Creoles joined ratepayers' associations, akin to political parties. The Civil Servants, and Bar Associations were formed to protect Creole interests in the professions. In the nineteenth century merchants had taken the leadership of the Creole elite, but after the Hut-Tax War and the inroads of British big business Creoles turned instead to careers in law and government. Their political parties were not anti-government and certainly not anti-colonial but rather pressure groups to resist racial discrimination.

Christopher Fyfe has calculated that Creoles, in 1892, held eighteen out of some forty senior government posts, but in 1912 held only fifteen out of ninety-two. Discrimination against the Creoles was even more marked in the protectorate, where the British preferred to employ the more tractable, less well-educated people from tribal society. Even the Freetown police came increasingly, to be recruited from the protectorate. The Creole newspapers accused the British of exercising a policy of 'divide and rule' to play off the protectorate against the colony. Certainly many white administrators of the early twentieth century, not only in Africa but also in Britain's Asian territories, felt a preference for the savage and martial tribesmen over the troublesome, carping townsmen. The British officers respected 'your Pathan, a first class chap', while feeling contempt for the politicians and 'typewriter wallahs' of Bombay, Calcutta or Freetown. This attitude found expression in Lugard's Nigerian policy of 'indirect rule' through the chiefs. The sheiks and emirs of the north were encouraged to keep their tribesmen in the traditional feudal ignorance while the southern Ibos and Yorubas, with their utterly different social systems, grabbed eagerly at the white man's ideas. The policy of the British of playing off north and south while at the same time welding them in a federation, was to result in the hideous tragedy of the Biafran War.

The theories of 'indirect rule' were expressed with candour in the prospectus for Bo School, founded by Governor Probyn in 1905 for the sons and nominees of protectorate chiefs. 'By locating the school in the Protectorate,' wrote James Proudfoot, the proud first principal, 'the pupils will not be removed to any serious or injurious extent from their environment.' He goes on to make clear that this 'injurious' influence comes from the Creole ways and example. 'Under existing conditions, pupils educated in Freetown almost invariably return home with a feeling of contempt for their native Towns, and even for their nearest relatives. To prevent this, both the native teachers and the pupils will be expected to wear country clothes, and their lives outside of school hours will be spent in a small town, the government of which will be upon ordinary native lines.'

The emphasis of the teaching at Bo was on practical skills, above all farming, as much as on academic subjects. The pupils were to be taught that Labour, spelled with a capital 'L', was paramount in education. The former missionary, Proudfoot, devoted much of his prospectus to the teaching of moral qualities such as habit, truthfulness, work and self-control, and the dangers of sloth, slander and lack of self-control. The prospectus indicates what kind of man the school was meant to turn out. He should be diligent, dignified, modest, hard-working, not over-clever and steeped with respect for his tribe and land. It also indicates what sort of man the school was meant not to turn out. He would be indolent, over-dressed, rootless, lying, slanderous and averse to agriculture—in short the caricature of a Creole, as represented by Burton, Reade and their many later disciples. Because the Creoles aped the British, the boys at Bo School would be taught pride in their African tribal inheritance. 'Mendi pupils', says the prospectus, 'will be taught in such a manner as to make them prefer Mendi land to any other country, so with Temenes and all the various tribes represented in the school.' These ideals were realized during the 1960s when politicians of independent Sierra Leone, many educated at Bo School, tore the country apart to seize the spoils of office on behalf of the Mende or Temne tribes. The fragmentation of Africa, so piously deplored by recent British governments, is very largely a product of 'indirect rule' and the foolish encouragement of tribalism.

The Bo School boys would be permitted to follow their own religion, but Governor Probyn, knowing that most came from Muslim homes, insisted that special lessons be given to foster respect for women. The prospectus promised a series of lantern lectures showing the principal incidents in the lives of Florence Nightingale, Elizabeth Fry and the late Queen Victoria. A petition assembled in Freetown suggested with logic that the pupils should study the lives of Khadya, Fatimah, the Virgin Mary and Asiyah, wife of Pharoah, who had been named by Mohammed as the four perfect women.

The Creoles, in their wounded dignity, got no comfort from Edward Blyden, who spent the last years of his life in the colony. Obstinate and cantankerous as ever, he mocked Creole pretensions to being Englishmen, and deplored the effects of foreign culture on Africans—except, one assumes, himself. Five years before his death in 1912, Blyden published a series of articles in the *Sierra Leone Weekly News*, in which the Creoles found themselves scorned not by Burton or Reade or scurrilous English journalists, but by Africa's greatest writer.

Sierra Leone greeted the First World War with patriotic enthusiasm. For several days before Britain entered the fray, rumours of 'war palaver' had spread round the protectorate, and scores of reservists drifted to headquarters at Daru. The Sierra Leone Battalion of the Royal West African Frontier Force was too late to take part in the lightning Togo campaign, but helped to expel the Germans from the Cameroons. Unemployment, as well as military zeal, explains why thousands of Sierra Leonean men went to serve as carriers in East Africa and the Middle East. During the war years, Freetown became an important naval base and the sales of alcohol doubled; otherwise the economy suffered. Most of the colony's exports and almost all its export of palm kernels had gone to the German market which, inevitably, was cut off. The shortages and perils of war-time shipping bumped up the cost of freight and caused inflation. So great was the increase in the price

287

of Manchester cotton that women in the protectorate reverted to country cloth.

The First World War still further strengthened the big British companies in the colony. With the disappearance of German ships, the Elder Dempster Line held a monopoly of the shipping, and, through it, a produce monopoly. The Chamber of Commerce fixed the price to be paid for local palm kernels and oil, and although, in theory, others were free to outbid the monopoly price, those in the ring could control a rebel by getting the dockers to black his goods, or by other nefarious methods. The British wholesalers, with no competition from foreigners, exploited the opportunity of the war to squeeze still harder on African middlemen. They stopped giving the Creoles wholesale prices for goods, and employed 'selling girls' of their own to compete with and undercut opposition. The Africans, pushed out of a trade that had been theirs for more than a century, took out their wrath, not on the guilty British, but on the weaker and more vulnerable Syrians. Savage riots took place in 1919.

Sierra Leone between the two wars was a sad and neglected colony. Britain's capital and its intellectual talent were drawn to Nigeria and the Gold Coast. Too small to build up her own manufacturing industries, Sierra Leone still had to rely on the export of crops and, later, of iron ore and diamonds. There were, of course, signs of progress. A new constitution was given in 1924, setting the colony on the way to self-government and eventual independence. Electric lighting was introduced to Freetown streets and houses in 1927. A full-time scoutmaster joined the colony's pay-roll. During the 'thirties, Freetown was linked to the outside world by the B.B.C. service and by air flights via the Gambia to Great Britain. Motor cars grew so prevalent that the Hill railway was stopped in 1929, having run for twenty-five years without an accident. Yet outsiders were critical of the colony. A Commission of Inquiry into the affairs of the Freetown Municipality reported in 1926 that the 'City Council has failed to provide the town with services of even moderate efficiency'. The markets and the slaughter-houses it categorized as deplorable, the cemeteries were

288

ill-kept and the fire brigade offered no real protection against fires. Raymond Buell, the American writer, compared Sierra Leone unfavourably with Liberia. 'Whatever may be the defects of administration in Liberia, one does not find there the chasm separating the rulers from the ruled which existed in Sierra Leone.'

The Creoles, between the two wars, fought a stubborn but losing battle against the British and the protectorate chiefs. Their first stand was made over the Constitution of 1924 that gave members from the protectorate equal voice with the Creoles in the Legislative Council. The Creoles claimed that as educated men with a long tradition of government, they could legislate in the interests of the backward and ignorant natives. The political leaders from the protectorate wanted a voice in the council to air the demands of their underdeveloped region. They argued that since taxes were paid in the protectorate, it was only fair that representative chiefs should vote on what to do with the money.

The Creoles argued their case with characteristic pedantry, claiming that people in the protectorate were aliens who therefore had no right to legislate for the British. One Creole spokesman, Shorunkeh-Sawyerr, suggested solving the problem by making these aliens British subjects and therefore, or so he secretly thought, putting the whole protectorate into the hands of the colony Creoles. He and the other Creole leaders spoke slightingly of the protectorate people. When a bill was introduced in 1923 to replace Creole policemen on the island of Sherbro to the south-east, Shorunkeh-Sawyerr complained that arrest by these new court messengers instead of by Creole constables would be an indignity for 'people of refinement' and 'people of standing'. These superior airs offended the more advanced men from the protectorate, who accused the Creoles of wanting to keep them back.

Why is the thorough education of the Protectorate Aborigines neglected? [asked one manifesto of a Protectorate Party]. If the Colonial Africans really considered them their kith and kin, and expected them to take their place amongst them in

matters concerning the welfare of Sierra Leone in general...
After all these have been accomplished, and the Protectorate
can literally march with the colony in every sphere of life
then, but not till then, will a new era dawn on Sierra Leone.

Although the Creoles complained of their dwindling role in
government, this was still immense when compared to that of the
Africans in the other British colonies. In Kenya about this time, the
white population rose in revolt at the threat of allowing an Indian
into the Legislature; black politicians were not even imaginable.
The Creoles had far more power than the Africans in Rhodesia
then, or indeed in Rhodesia now. Their bitterness was that of the
proud man suddenly forced into dependence.

> Tu proverai si come sa di sale
> Lo pane altrui, e come e duro calle
> Lo scendere e 'l salir par l' altrui scale.

Sierra Leonean delegates took an important part in the National
Congress of British West Africa, which was formed in 1920 to
agitate for greater power and to protest against the splitting of
Africa among the European empires. Their first petition was
nothing if not loyal. It placed on record 'their unfeigned devotion
to throne and person of His Majesty the King Emperor' and
announced their wish 'to preserve ... inviolate the connection of
the British West African Dependencies with the British Empire'.
The Freetown Creoles, as we shall later see, were to prove loyal
to Britain when most West Africans were eager for independence; but in the 'twenties and 'thirties they flirted with radical
notions.

Most Creoles, however bourgeois in outlook, supported the
1926 railway strike. A shocked British official was so displeased by
this 'unworthy behaviour' that he wanted to suspend the Creole
elected element in the Legislative Council. The governor thought
this was going a bit too far.

In my opinion [he wrote to the Secretary of State for the
Colonies] the harm that demagogues of the type of Dr

Bankole-Bright and Mr Deoku-Betts can, and undoubtedly do, cause is to some extent mitigated rather than accentuated, by the fact of their membership of the Council. Their sense of responsibility as legislators is, it is true, painfully low but it is occasionally discernible ... In my judgment, to oust from the Legislative Council the members who were chosen of the people less than two years ago would, by making martyrs of them, increase their power for harm far more than continued tolerance of their presence can do ... It would tend to drive underground the disorderly and undisciplined elements always unhappily present in the Colony of Sierra Leone and thereby gravely enhance the danger arising from such elements ... At the same time ... the events of the last few months have supplied Government with abundant reasons for proceeding at a much slower pace with Africanisation of the Service.

The punishment was as foolish as it was cruel. Discrimination against the Creoles in a government that had once been theirs produced the bitterness that had led them to back the strikers. More discrimination could only make them more bitter. In the 1930s many Creoles supported a hot-headed young journalist who had been to Moscow's People's University. Isaac Theophilus Akuna Wallace-Johnson—the very name proclaimed him Creole —started a West African Youth League whose support came from the Freetown workers. But having been elected to the Legislative Council in 1938, he was clapped in prison during the war under the 18B Regulation.

Until the Second World War there was little overt hostility between the Creoles of Freetown and the natives of the protectorate. More and more people from the protectorate came to Freetown for work or from curiosity; mosques arose; Muslims were no longer jeered at for wearing their up-country clothes; the educated of both groups intermarried and sometimes worked for an intellectual understanding. Whereas in the nineteenth century people from the protectorate had assumed Creole (and frequently double-barrelled) names, now Creoles occasionally changed to African names to express their brotherhood with the aborigines. However, it was more normal for people from the protectorate to imitate Creole ways and manner of speaking; having mastered which, they frequently called themselves Creoles. In the debates leading up to the Constitution of 1924, it was widely predicted that quarrels between Creoles and up-country chiefs would mar the quiet decorum of the council chamber. This danger was never realized in the years before the Second World War. Indeed rude language was used by Creoles against their fellow Creoles as when, for example, the Tory Bankole-Bright referred to the followers of the Socialist Wallace-Johnson as 'ragamuffins' and 'hoi polloi'.

The Creoles, in their slow decline, had first blamed the rivalry of the Syrians, but had trusted still in the British. By the Second World War, this trust had begun to dwindle. They began to blame their decline in power on the economic rivalry of the big British firms as well as on the ambition of British officials. The lawyer E. S. Beoku-Betts accused the Government of having, from racial discrimination, closed down Creole factories. He referred to the case of 'the late D. B. Curry [who] manufactured lots of local foodstuffs and also ventured into chocolate making, selling them at a penny a bar, locally. That was enough to stir a great firm in England, like Cadbury's, to send representatives out here to see what Curry was doing, and following their report, Cadbury's produced chocolate which they placed on the market here at halfpenny a bar. How can we compete with a millionaire firm?' Chocolate, soap, margarine and cotton clothing are all produced from materials grown in West Africa yet almost every-where on the coast people bought the end product from British manufacturers. Small wonder that Beoku-Betts and other Creole leaders felt bitter against the British.

The Second World War brought a second bout of inflation and falling trade. Since Sierra Leone lies in the part of Africa nearest to South America, its off-shore waters became a hunting ground for U-boats hoping to sink Allied ships as they passed between the north and south Atlantic. The Royal Navy feared that German spies might be sent to Freetown to report on movements of ships to the U-boat captains, and the British counter-intelligence outfit, M.I.5., sent one of its temporary agents to Freetown to take charge of security in the colony. This period is the background for Graham Greene's novel *The Heart of the Matter*, without doubt the best book on Sierra Leone and to my mind the best novel set in Africa.* Greene had stopped in Freetown in 1934 to pick up provisions and porters for the trek through northern Liberia that he described in his travel book *Journey without Maps*. His description of Freetown before the war was sardonic, with hints of the old Burton prejudices. Like every visitor he praised the setting of tree-covered hills but thought it

> powerless to carry off the shabby town ... Freetown had a Bret Harte air without the excitement, the saloons, the revolver shots or the horses ... This was an English capital city; England had planted this town, the tin shacks and the Remembrance Day posters, and had then withdrawn up the hillside to smart bungalows, with wide windows and electric fans and perfect service ... They had planted their seedy civilisation and then escaped from it as far as they could. Everything ugly in Freetown was European ...

Greene looked with pitying humour at the Creoles—their flowery language, their uniforms, their double-barrelled names, 'their votes and city councils, their shadow of self-government; they were expected to play the part like white men and the more they copied white men, the more funny it was to the prefects.'

Although Greene understood that the Creoles 'had been educated to understand how they had been swindled' he did not understand that before this swindle, when the Creoles had more than 'their shadow of self-government', they were not regarded as ludicrous by all Englishmen. Some of Greene's comments upon the Creoles are uncharacteristically vulgar and even banal. 'It

* Conrad's magnificent *Heart of Darkness* is really a long short story.

would be so much more amusing', he wrote, 'if it was all untrue, a fictitious skit on English methods of colonisation. But one cannot continue long to find the Creole's painful attempt at playing the white man funny; it is rather like the chimpanzee's tea-party, the joke is all on one side.' A Creole writer, Davidson Nicol, has given an interesting insight into Greene's anti-Creole remarks:

> In his novels and journals, Greene does not show any particular affection for educated Africans. This is not so however in his personal life in Europe where he is known to be capable of striking up pleasant acquaintanceships regardless of race and colour. This fact in a writer of his depth and sincerity makes one wonder whether the African *evolué* or the educated African is *really* an unattractive creature. My detached view is that he probably was in the colonial context. The educated African was insecure in the presence of Europeans and the latter made him more so. He reacted badly, as frightened people do. He showed either servility or brashness, mendacity or unctuousness. He knew that he had been condemned before even opening his mouth because of his shirt and necktie, his pressed trousers, his cheap shoes, his fountain pen and the odour of his nervous perspiration.

Writing a preface in 1946 to the second edition of *Journey Without Maps*, Greene looked back with a certain regret to the hard words he had used about Freetown, for Freetown was now one of the homes where he had lived and worked in all seasons. After a year in Sierra Leone he had learned to recognize in himself the inertia he had condemned in others. 'If I were writing of Freetown now,' Greene stated in 1946, 'how unnaturally rosy would my picture be, for I begin to remember mainly the sunsets when all the laterite paths turned suddenly for a few minutes the colour of a rose, the old slavers' fort with the cannon lying in the grass, the abandoned railway track with the chickens pecking in and out of the little empty rotting station, the taste of the first pink gin at six o'clock.'

At about the time that he wrote that preface, Greene began work on *The Heart of the Matter*, which gives anything but a 'rosy picture' of Freetown. Many Greene books have been set in wretched or sleazy cities like Saigon, Havana and Port-au-Prince, which critics have jokingly lumped into a special country called 'Greeneland'. Freetown, as described in *The Heart of the Matter*, is outstandingly horrible even for 'Greeneland'.

The descriptions of Freetown in *The Heart of the Matter* are just as unflattering as those in the earlier travel book. Greene's fascination with Freetown's natural life had increased to the point of obsession. 'Only the vultures were about—gathering around a dead chicken at the edge of the road, stooping their old men's necks over the carrion, their wings like broken umbrellas sticking out this way and that...' 'they sat in the hollow room holding hands, listening to the vultures clambering on the iron roof'; '... disturbing a rat that had been couched on the cool rim of the bath, like a cat on a gravestone...'; 'a dead pye-dog lay in the gutter with the rain running over its white swollen belly...'; 'The lizard pounced upon the wall, the tiny jaws clamping on a moth. Something scratched outside the door—a pye-dog?' '... In the bathroom a rat moved, and once the iron roof crumpled as a late vulture settled for the night.'

The hero, Scobie is 'an abscure policeman in an unfashionable colony' who has been refused promotion because of the gossip that he has slept with black girls and taken bribes from the Syrians. Except for Scobie, who is kind and intelligent, the whites in the novel are most unattractive. Wilson, a Secret Service man who spies on Scobie and tries to seduce his wife, is a jealous snob who conceals his liking for poetry so as not to be thought stuck-up. The white community, isolated by colour pride, is yet riven by envy and backbiting. Bored, homesick, lonely and drunken, they hate the city, Africa and the Africans. Only Scobie likes the country but cannot at first explain why, except that 'it's pretty in the evening'.

The Africans who appear are mostly policemen and plaintiffs—the former corrupt and the latter cantankerous. The women, especially, 'would sit quietly all day in a white man's backyard in order to beg for something he hadn't the power to grant, or they would shriek and fight and abuse to get served in a store before their neighbours.' Only Scobie's houseboy, a Mende, is thoroughly loyal and honest, and for this, by the logic of tragedy, he is murdered.

The Creoles, who had been held up to so much ridicule in Greene's earlier book, play only a bit-part in the novel, and are then transformed into West Indians. ' "They aren't real niggers",' says one of the Englishmen. ' "Just West Indians and they rule the coast. Clerks in the stores, city council, magistrates, lawyers—my God! It's all right up in the Protectorate. I haven't anything to say against a real nigger. But these—my God! The Government's afraid of them. The police are afraid of them… "' Elsewhere the Creoles are mentioned but Greene does not give them a role in the book in any way comparable to their role in Freetown.

Sierra Leoneans are proud that Greene should have written a book on their country but they are not very flattered by the result. The general view is that Greene has overdone the horrors; the flavour is right but the brew is too strong. Several Englishmen who met Greene when he came out to help with the filming were puzzled to find that the author of such a sad book was a genial companion who liked nothing more, in the words of a District Officer, 'than enjoying a joke over a drink'. Certainly Sierra Leone is not so unremittingly grim as *The Heart of the Matter* suggests. The African women laugh and sing as well as raise palavers; whites are not all so backbiting nor the Syrians so avaricious; there are other creatures than rats, pye-dogs, vultures and cockroaches. Greene's emphasis on the evil and squalid is explained in a passage of meditation by Scobie, the hero. 'Why, he wondered, swerving the car to avoid a dead pye-dog, do I love this place so much? Is it because here human nature hasn't had time to disguise itself? Nobody here could ever talk about a heaven on earth. Heaven remained rigidly in its proper place on the other side of death, and on this flourished the injustices, the cruelties, the meanness that elsewhere people so cleverly hushed up.' Greene the moralist is

296

drawn to those parts of the world that most clearly reflect his pessimistic idea of the human condition. Like Conrad's *Heart of Darkness*, whose mood as well as whose title it echoes, *The Heart of the Matter* sets a personal tragedy in a tragic and suffering continent. Greene knows what Conrad called 'the fascination of the abomination'.

Some politicians in Sierra Leone now talk of their independence 'struggle'. In fact the first impetus towards self-government came not from Freetown but London. The Labour Government elected in 1945 believed in progress towards independence for all Britain's then still-enormous empire. The new constitution for Sierra Leone, which was pressed through in 1947, did not arouse any excitement in the colony. In the protectorate there was still little political awareness, while the Freetown Creoles feared that independence would put them into the power of protectorate chiefs. A group of Creoles in 1948 sent a petition to London protesting against the new powers given to 'foreigners' (i.e. protectorate people) under the new constitution. Another petition in 1950 reaffirmed the Creoles' desperate loyalty to Britain:

The Humble Petition of the Inhabitants of the Colony of Sierra Leone under the aegis of The Sierra Leone National Council Sheweth:

That your Majesty's petitioners are British Subjects and Descendants of the Settlers, Nova Scotians, Maroons and Liberated Africans for whom this Settlement was acquired in 1788, (hereafter described as The Council);

2 That The Council would humbly seize the opportunity of expressing their loyalty, devotion and attachment to Your Majesty's person and throne;

3 That as mother of The West African Colonies, Sierra Leone with her invaluable Atlantic Sea-Board, and with a history whose romantic nature no other Colony could surpass, has been subjected to many vicissitudes and unfortunate official measures since the earliest days of her annals ...

The British Government, faced with so many claims for independence throughout the restless empire, was no doubt touched and amused by the Creoles' desire to stay British; but history was against the petitioners. The politicians in the protectorate were scornful of this Creole pride, and their leader, Dr Milton Margai, said in one angry outburst how much he regretted that 'our forefathers had given shelter to this handful of foreigners'. A Creole spokesman, Otto During, answered this with a hurt oration late in 1950:

> I take strong objection to this speech in the Assembly by a man who says we are to cooperate together. Furthermore he says we in the colony are apeing at Western civilisation ... Our forefathers were taken from this land of Africa into bondage for many, many years. In their bondage they came across Western civilisation, and they have handed it down to us. Woe to this country if we do not keep what has been handed down to us. Woe to us if we send our boys to the United Kingdom and after gaining education, when they return they squat on the floor to eat with dirty fingers from calabashes and bowls with a bevy of women around them.

Such spiteful jibes at protectorate ways were alternated with ringing appeals to history. The Creole Bankole-Bright said in 1952 that the Sierra Leonean Government

> has by its action brought into existence a cleavage between the people of this Colony and this Protectorate by abrogating the ethical principles governing British law and order in attempting by legislation to create unconstitutionally an Executive and Legislative Council controlled by a majority of Protectorate people who are not British subjects, inimical to the fundamental principles laid down in the acquisition of this colony in 1788 ...

The member for Bo, the Hon. R. B. S. Coker, answered this argument with derision: 'In the 1788 Treaty or Agreement it is stated that the free settlers were to be under the protection of King Naimbana, and that if they want to govern themselves, the best thing to do is to return the land which they had been living in, under protection, to their former owners. And take shelter in the sugar-cane plantation where they came from ... .' These reminders that the Creoles were the descendants of slaves were well received in the protectorate, where slaves were traditionally criminals to be looked upon with contempt.

In the years before Independence, which came in 1961, Sir Milton Margai's Sierra Leone People's Party often played on anti-Creole feelings to rally support in the protectorate. In the colony, however, the S.L.P.P. pleaded for unity; even its candidates were usually chosen from Creoles. Sir Milton himself, after the anti-Creole outburst mentioned already, was always anxious to calm Creole fears in the interests of harmony. He could afford to be conciliatory to such weak opponents. The 25,000 Creoles were outnumbered a hundred to one by tribal Africans, and even the Creoles were split by political differences. While the old guard, such as Bankole-Bright, petitioned London and discussed 1788, many younger Creoles wanted harmony with the protectorate. Some joined the S.L.P.P. and adopted African names, so that it grew increasingly difficult to distinguish between the Creoles and the elite of the protectorate. They studied together at Fourah Bay College, lived in the same parts of Freetown, worked together and intermarried. The new generation of Creoles was bored with the old settler myths, preferring rather to identify with the new anti-colonial movement then symbolized by Nkrumah's Ghana. Like most West Africans, the Creoles still felt a sympathy and regard for Britain but no longer regarded themselves as transplanted British. The Christian piety that had once distinguished the Creoles had dwindled since the Second World War. The Creole pretensions had grown not only embarrassing but irrelevant. The issues that mattered now were those facing other countries in West Africa, such as the struggle for power between the chiefs and the new elite, the drift of peasants into the towns, unemployment and government graft. With Independence in 1961, the old distinction between the colony and the protectorate was swept away by a new Constitution that finished off Creoles as a political entity. The political parties grouped round Mende and Temne factions, while the Creoles looked on with indifference.

Sierra Leone, the White Man's Grave, once so written about and discussed and praised and abused, has declined at last into obscurity. The coup of 1967 brought it a flicker of fame, as soldiers and politicians, most with double-barrelled names, engaged in obscure and laughable wrangles. But few foreign businessmen stop off in Sierra Leone on their aeroplane trips around Africa. Few writers and journalists consider it worth their attention. Ian Fleming tried with no success to wring some excitement out of the diamond smugglers. Elspeth Huxley included Sierra Leone in a travel book on West Africa which, of course, praised the scenery and regretted the lack of farming. A photograph of a man in a hammock was captioned, with almost a Burton touch, 'The favourite posture of Sierra Leone.'

Chapter Two

In all Africa,
Tubman is a shining star.
The future of Liberia will always be gay
As long as President Tubman has his way.
(From a calypso heard on Liberian radio in 1967)

The European colonial Powers disliked the Firestone agreement with Liberia. Not only had the United States intruded into a continent which Europeans thought their preserve, but the production of rubber by an American company was a blow to the Europeans' monopoly. Imperial jealousy played a part in the sad if comical scandals that shook Liberia in the 1930s. From 1929 until 1934, Liberia, which had been founded by freed slaves, stood accused by the League of Nations, the press and public opinion of the world of condoning slavery at home and of selling young men into forced labour abroad. It was the first and, so far the last, time that Liberia has been front-page news, and no Liberians today want a recurrence of such publicity.

In most West Coast towns until very recent times, there was gossip of slavery in the interior. The apprentice system and, still more, the pawning of labour were widespread in this part of Africa and, however they seemed to Europeans, were considered acceptable by most Africans. Another practice that lent itself to more serious abuse was the recruitment of young men in one part of West Africa for labour along the coast. Liberia had always been a principal source of this labour, since the Krus, normally known as Krumen, came from this part of the coast and have worked for centuries as the sailors, deckhands and porters of West African shipping. Some Krus and their neighbours from other Liberian tribes would contract themselves as lumberjacks in French Gabon, as cocoa pickers in the Gold Coast, but above all for work on Fernando Po, the small Spanish island in the Bight of Biafra.

Fernando Po had a bad reputation. In the 1860s, Sir Richard Burton, the new British Consul to Fernando Po, remarked on the difficulty of recruiting men to work there. ' "Nanny Po" was a word of fear to the Krumen; they had been made to work in gardens and on the roads and they complained—most falsely, I afterwards found—of *puoco comer mucho trabajo*.* Some of them had been engaged for one year, not two, and had been kept for three—the usual time—to the great sorrow of their mammies and to the abiding resentment of themselves.' However, as Burton was first to contend, Fernando Po was a feverish hole where many Africans as well as whites died after only a year or two. A more reputable historian states that many Liberian workers in Fernando Po during the closing years of the century contracted tuberculosis and venereal disease which they afterwards spread through Liberia.

Liberians, acting as Spanish Consuls, recruited the labourers and took a commission for each man hired. When the labourers returned from Fernando Po they would hand the consul a voucher for the balance of their wages. Dishonest consuls, as many undoubtedly were, would steal part or all of this money on fabricated pretexts. The Acting British chargé d'affaires wrote from Monrovia in 1923 that 'it is not the conditions of labour in that island but the frauds practised on the labourers in Liberia prior to their departure and after their return that render the traffic so undesirable'. In 1923, under pressure from the American economic adviser, the Liberian government banned the recruitment of boys for Fernando Po. The trade was resumed after the Spanish Consul had 'fixed' the Liberian legislature for the moderate price of £150.

Serious accusations of slavery started during the 1920s. Some itinerant journalists published the second-hand talk that they heard in Monrovia. The same rumours appeared, now at third-hand, in a feeble study of *Slavery* by Lady Simon, the wife of

* Little food, much work.

Sir John Simon, a British Cabinet Minister. The family name and her husband's illustrious job gave an air of authenticity to the book which it certainly did not deserve. After repeating the vague charges of slavery that she had read in the other books and in newspaper articles, Lady Simon made an attack on Liberia and its ruling classes. She advanced as proof of their incompetence that the population of Liberia was one million greater than that of Sierra Leone, while its volume of trade was only a quarter as great. Unfortunately for Lady Simon's argument, the trade figures were unreliable, while the population of Liberia was certainly less than half that of Sierra Leone.

The strongest attack on the Liberian Government came from Thomas J. Faulkner, the unsuccessful candidate in the presidential election of 1927. Faulkner and his People's Party had real grounds for disgruntlement, since the ruling President King and his True Whig Party had managed to win 243,000 votes from a qualified electorate of a mere 15,000. The defeated Faulkner, an American Negro who owned a hotel-cum-icecream-parlour, sailed in a rage to the United States where he gave a series of newspaper interviews denouncing the members of the Liberian Government. He claimed that they used forced labour, amounting almost to slavery, that they kidnapped young men for labourers in Fernando Po, and that they refused to investigate charges of brutal floggings by government officers. These accusations, and Lady Simon's books, caused much concern in Britain and the United States. In June 1929, the American Secretary of State, Henry L. Stimson, sent a message to his counterpart in Liberia referring to reports that the 'so-called "export" of labour from Liberia to Fernando Po have resulted in the development of a system which seems hardly distinguishable from organised slave trade and that in the enforcement of this system the services of the Liberian Frontier Force and the services and influence of certain high Government officials are constantly and systematically used.'

The sudden concern shown by the United States Government over an export of labour that had been practised for almost a century may in part have been influenced by economic interest.

The Cape Palmas area of Liberia from which most of the labourers went to Fernando Po, was also the main recruiting ground for the Firestone Company. In April 1928, the company's manager went to Cape Palmas and 'was by no means sanguine about the sufficiency of labour of which, it is alleged, an actual shortage exists'.

The Liberian President, King, denied the truth of the allegations and asked the League of Nations, of which Liberia was a member, to send a commission to his country to investigate the question. The League appointed an Englishman, Dr Cuthbert Christie to head the investigation. He was a dentist, a shy and reticent Scot, who had lived in Nigeria, which apparently was his main qualification for the job, but who proved an able and open-minded investigator. His assistants were Dr Johnson, a Negro academic representing the U.S. Government, and Arthur Barclay, a former Liberian president. During the four months that the commission spent in Liberia, it interviewed 250 witnesses of whom 145 were outside Monrovia. The British and American representatives made several visits down the coast to the Cape Palmas area, from where it was said that forced labour was sent to the Gabon and Fernando Po. The commission admitted its difficulties in collecting facts, which was not surprising when one considers the shortage of time, assistants and proper communication. The Scot and the American worked well in harmony, while Mr Barclay, a true Liberian lawyer, spent most of his energies objecting to evidence on the grounds that it dealt with matters outside the terms of reference. An African writer, Nnambi Azikiwe, who was later to become the first President of Nigeria, complained in 1934 that none of the commissioners had experience in cultural anthropology, African ethnography or colonial administration. Yet the report, read today, has a definite ring of authority.

The commission's report, published in 1930, found the Liberians innocent of most of the charges brought against them. Slavery, as defined in the Anti-Slavery Convention, did not exist. Government ministers did not possess domestic slaves and discouraged others from the practice. There was widespread pawning of labour

304

and misuse of forced labour on public works but that could be said of all West African territories. The peculiar and sensational finding of the commission was that 'a large proportion of the contract labourers shipped to Fernando Po and French Gabon from the southern counties of Liberia have been recruited under conditions of criminal compulsion scarcely distinguishable from slave raising and slave trading, and frequently by misrepresenting the destination'. The grossest instance of this had occurred at Wedabo Beach, in the south-east of Liberia where, so the commission reported:

> Vice-President Yancy and other high officials of the Liberian Government as well as County Superintendents and District Commissioners have given their sanction for the compulsory recruitment of labour for road construction for shipment abroad and other work, by the aid and assistance of the Liberia Frontier Force; and have condoned the utilisation of this Force for purposes of physical compulsion on road construction, for the intimidation of villagers, for the humiliation of Chiefs, for the imprisonment of inhabitants, and for the conveying of captured Natives to the coast, there guarding them till the time of shipment.

Vice-President Yancy and his colleagues, who took a fat commission for each labourer they provided, pretended that the Wedabo chiefs were legally bound to provide this labour for the Liberian Government. If they refused, Yancy persisted, each chief would have to pay a ten-pound fine for each man less than the sixty demanded. Paramount Chief Broh of Frenropo replied that his boys did not want to go to Fernando Po because thirty boys had gone some years ago, but none had yet returned. Moreover, some men whom he had sent for government road work were taken instead to the Firestone plantation. No doubt suspicious of Yancy's good faith, Broh sent a message to Monrovia asking President King whether the government really ordered him to send men to Fernando Po. King replied that he had not given this order, whereupon Yancy, assisted by the county superintendent and two Senators acting for him as lawyers, arrested Chief Broh and had him flogged as an example to his people. Yancy then imposed colossal fines on the Chief and further insisted that he pay fees of one hundred dollars to each of the politician lawyers.

The commission called this process the 'pressure of fines':

The Wedabo Beach incident narrated serves the Commission as an example of the use of governmental authority in a manner not distinguishable to the natives, from the Government itself. Exploitation of the tribal relationship of natives to their chiefs has been a most effective means of getting the semblance of consent to shipment, throwing the burden of force upon the chief. When the chiefs have resisted as in the case cited they can be urged to terms by the gradual process of impoverishment of the whole of the people.

No wonder the Wedabo women sang:

> We were here when trouble came to our people,
> For this trouble Jeh was imprisoned and fined,
> For this reason Yancy came to our country—
> He caught our husbands and our brothers,
> Sail them to Nana Poo
> And there they die (repeat).
> Tell us
> Yancy, why (repeat).
> Wedabo women have no husbands,
> Yancy, why?
> Wedabo women have no brothers,
> Yancy, why?
> Mothers, fathers, sons have died,
> Waiting for the return,
> Yancy, why?

The commission blamed the Liberian Government for the use of forced labour on public and private works, the forcible methods used in recruiting labourers for abroad, and for exercising insufficient control on the Liberian Frontier Force. It recommended, among other things, that the present District Commissioners

306

should be replaced by Americans or Europeans, and suggested strengthening Liberia by immigration from America 'of the best type of persons of African descent'.

The Christy Commission report appeared in September 1930 and caused an immediate uproar. The United States Government sent stern notes to Liberia; Lady Simon seethed with joyful indignation while Sir John, her husband, plotted with other statesmen to bring Liberia under foreign, and preferably British, mandate. The first response in Liberia had been to appease the League. President King criticized aspects of the report but agreed to accept its recommendations. The Liberian Legislature began an impeachment of Yancy; the Representatives accused by the report were ordered to be expelled from the House; the lawyers named in the Wedabo Beach affair resigned their seats in the Senate. Although many foes of the True Whig Party made capital from the report, the crowd in Monrovia and the other towns was indignant against the League. At the end of 1930, Yancy resigned, followed the next day by President King, although he had not been criticized in the report. King was succeeded by the Secretary of State, Mr Edwin Barclay.*

Both the British and the Americans refused to recognize the new government in Liberia. The British Foreign Secretary, Arthur Henderson, wanted Liberia to ask the League of Nations for a Governing Commission, or in other words, for a mandate. He instructed the British chargé d'affaires in Monrovia to inform the Liberian Government 'that failure on their part to make the request [for a Governing Commission] would be viewed by His Majesty's Government with grave concern, and could not but have the most serious reaction on the friendly relations at present existing between the two countries.' In short, Britain ordered Liberia to appeal for the removal of her independence. The British further insisted that Liberia should accept a loan under League auspices, thereby putting her into an international receivership and obliging

* Edwin Barclay, who stayed in office from 1930 to 1944, was the nephew of Arthur Barclay, the 'Grand Old Man' of Liberia who had been President from 1904 to 1912, and one of the League's Commissioners.

her to renege on the Firestone agreement. President Barclay was unhappy about these threats to his country's sovereignty but he agreed in principle to adopt the recommendations of the Christy Commission, and he made a formal request to the League for help in solving Liberia's financial problems. Representatives of the League met in London in March 1931 to appoint a three-man committee under the chairmanship of a Frenchman, Henri Brunot.

For the next three years there was a complicated three-way wrangle involving Liberia against the Firestone Company; Britain and France against the Firestone Company; Britain and France against the United States. The three Great Powers, under the leadership of Great Britain, wanted Liberia to agree to a form of League of Nations control, and the assistance of foreign 'advisers'. The Liberians wanted to keep their independence and they hoped for an improvement in their finances. Time was on Liberia's side. An improvement in the world economy after the slump of 1929–1931 gave a boost to the production of rubber and therefore Liberia's revenue from the Firestone plantation. The British case for exercising a mandate was much improved in 1932 when reports reached the outside world of a massacre of the Krus by Liberian troops. Without waiting for information, Sir John Simon expressed himself satisfied that 'the proceedings of the Liberian Frontier Force... in the Kru country... were tyrannical and high-handed in an inexcusable degree'. He hinted again without evidence, that the killings were a reprisal against the Krus for having given evidence to the Christy Commission. However, the British Vice-Consul went from Monrovia to the Kru country and found that what the Liberians claimed was true. The rising was caused by a tribal dispute having nothing to do with the Christy Commission and although Colonel Davis, the officer in charge, had acted high-handedly and with cruelty, there was no evidence of a planned or deliberate massacre. Critics of the British case were quick to point out an equally bad uprising that took place at about this time in the neighbouring protectorate of Sierra Leone.

The files of the Foreign Office for the early 1930s reveal at last, what contemporaries had suspected, that British policy to Liberia was influenced by jealousy of the Firestone Company. The dispatches to London from Mr C. Graham, the British Chargé d'Affaires in Monrovia, carry frequent and sometimes justified complaints against the Firestone loan and Firestone plantation officials. His argument was supported by the Dutchman, Mr Lighthard, one of the three-man League of Nations Committee, who was knowledgeable on rubber from his experiences in the Dutch East Indies. After a tour of the Firestone plantations in June 1931, Mr Lighthard told Graham that 'the gravest problem facing the Firestone rubber enterprise in Liberia will undoubtedly be that of labour as soon as extended harvesting operations begin; i.e. in the course of three years ... ' He estimated that Firestone would need between 150,000 and 200,000 labourers out of a total population of 800,000 or less. M. Brunot, a Frenchman and head of the league's committee, added that Firestone, the largest agricultural enterprise in West Africa, was run on a system 'quite unsuited to West African conditions'. Mr Lighthard told Graham that 'the local heads of the Firestone enterprise cannot work without forced labour, and he is satisfied that they are bound to have the intention of ultimately employing such labour.'

The local Firestone officials, so Graham believed and reported, were interested not in the welfare of Liberia, but in maintaining their own jobs and salaries. He thought they were plotting a comeback for President King, as a very amenable politician through putting pressure on C. E. Mitchell, the American Minister to Liberia. The Foreign Office agreed with Graham in wishing that Mitchell 'had been of Anglo-Saxon stock' instead of a weak and timid Negro. Although Graham quite liked Mitchell—much preferring him to another diplomat who was so decrepit as to be 'mentally imbecilic'—he feared him to be under the Firestone influence. 'Numbers, energy of character (at least in some cases), and race predominance are all on the side of the Firestone officials... I am convinced that Firestone interests have been decisive in preventing Mitchell from co-operating with me.' The Firestone people according to Graham, were responsible for removing the Bank of British West Africa from Liberia—'an incredible number of cheques were constantly drawn for petty amounts on Liberian Loan account. Sometimes a cheque for a few pence was drawn.'

The press and politicians in Britain remained hostile towards Liberia but, as so often, their outrage was matched by ignorance. The Lords debate on Liberia of March 16th, 1932, had a truly breathtaking fatuousness. Viscount Cecil, who had been heralded by Lord Snowden as 'having the most intimate knowledge of these matters', and who, indeed, had been chairman of a League of Nations Committee on Liberia, began his address to his peers:

> My Lords, Liberia is a country, as your Lordships probably know, on the West Coast of Africa. It is of considerable size. As far as I can make out from the figures I have seen* it is at least as large as this country, and it consists of a strip of land on the sea coast occupied mainly by the Americo-Liberians— that is to say the Americans, who in 1845 or some date of that kind, were sent over from the United States... Some years ago an American company called the Firestone Company conceived the idea of creating a big plantation there—I think it was a rubber plantation—and they did so...

Lord Lugard, the creator of Nigeria, spoke with more coherence than Lord Cecil, but his judgments were just as harsh. He accused Liberia of permitting slavery and he claimed that two million natives had been reduced to a state of misery by a handful of foreign Negroes.

British businessmen with an interest in West Africa were particularly critical of Liberia, revealing a jealousy of the Firestone Company and a greed for Liberia's wealth. These attitudes are mirrored in a special symposium on Liberia in *Elder's West African Review*, the magazine of the Elder Company, published in August 1931. One contributor, a former colonial officer, wrote that a black republic in Africa would never be successful. 'England certainly has no desire', he continued, 'to add to her responsibilities

* The boundaries of Liberia had been fixed for thirty years so that its size, in square miles, could be found in any atlas or almanac.

in Africa, but her interests in connection with commerce and shipping on the Liberia coast are very large.' Sir William Geary, another contributor, claimed that the Liberian officials were aliens and had no rights in Liberia. A former British consul-general, R. C. F. Maugham, who had once published a friendly account of *The Republic of Liberia* now claimed his experience of the country to state that Liberians 'were hopelessly incapable of governing either themselves or the country which, by a deplorable error of judgment, was committed about eighty years ago, to their corrupt and futile rule'. Like most of the writers in this symposium, he wanted a British mandate under the League of Nations. A chairman of the United Africa Company, the Unilever subsidiary that still handles most of the palm produce in British West Africa, suggested that most Liberians would prefer to live under a mandate, while Robert L. Holt, another big West Coast trader, thought that there was no doubt that the Liberians wanted this mandate to be British.

Even in Britain there were apologists for Liberia. Left-wing writers detected British big-business enmity to the rival Firestone interest. *West Africa* magazine compared the plight of Liberia with the Balkan countries. 'One of them was the scene of the immediate cause of the Great War. In others political murder is as common as sanitation is uncommon. We do not recollect Lord Cecil's advocacy of the annexation by "some civilized country".' Even Dr Christy, the author of the League's report, was relatively gentle in his attitude to Liberia and he deplored the resignation of President King.

The British Government never succeeded in getting a protectorate over Liberia. By 1934 the American State Department reached the view that Liberia was still capable of self-government and it sent Colonel Harry McBride, a diplomat with experience in Monrovia, to see what could be done to meet her problems. The most pressing of these was the failure of Liberia to pay the interest on her loan from the Firestone Company's Finance Corporation. Now, with more rubber coming into production and therefore more revenue into the country's coffers, Liberia could begin to pay back some of the interest due, so that relations grew more friendly again between Firestone and its host. The American businessmen had the sense to compromise on a deal; President Barclay of Liberia was reasonable and patient; in 1934, the government of Liberia was once more recognized by the United States and two years later, if grudgingly, by Great Britain.

Liberia's trial before the world was a newspaper sensation that died away and is now wholly forgotten. On re-examining the case, the evidence and the judgments given, one is struck not so much by the wickedness of the accused as by the ignorance and hypocrisy of the accusers. Domestic slavery, forced labour and forced shipment of labourers were common practice in Liberia but so they were in the colonies of the European Powers. Some journalists remarked on this at the time. In reply to Lord Buxton who had attacked Liberia, an article in *West Africa*, March 26th, 1932, asked: ' ... But have the Lords' speakers read Dr Leys' extracts from the labour laws of the British colony of Kenya? And do any of them, does Lord Buxton, an ex-Governor-General of South Africa in particular, innocently imagine that the vast African labour force of the Rand gold mines is free, voluntary, independent? Do they think it reaches the Rand of its own accord?'

In the protectorate of Sierra Leone, domestic slavery was not merely practised but actually permitted by law until 1928. An Austrian traveller in the protectorate in the 1930s reported that pawning of labour was widespread. Forced labour for public works was common in most African colonies. Its gross abuse only came to light when a famous writer like André Gide reported cases of flogging and murder. All the colonial Powers used pressure of some kind to gather labourers for railway gangs, cocoa plantations, mines, ranches and lumber depots. The Portuguese would arrest as a vagrant any African who was not under contract for work. The British and French forced Africans into work by imposing a poll or hut tax that had to be paid in cash. The conditions of work on Fernando Po were no worse and almost certainly better than those enjoyed by labourers in the French and British

312

colonies. During the building of the railway from Brazzaville to Pointe Noire, which was under way during the height of the argument over Liberia, it was estimated that 17,000 workers died in order to lay eighty-five miles of track.

Of all the territories on the continent at this time, the grossest instances of forced labour, the worst brutality by employers and the basest exploitation of natives by an alien minority were to be found in South-West Africa, which was a League of Nations mandate.

In the fourteen years of President Barclay's administration, the reputation of Liberia changed from the sinister to the preposterous. Journalists would stay two or three days to gather material for an article, or two or three weeks if they planned to write a book. Most of these offered tit-bits from the League of Nations report, warmed up and served as fresh, when spiced with comic details of life in Monrovia. Two journalists, Roland Wild and Harry J. Green-walls, noted during their interview with Barclay that 'the President's trousers were hanging out to dry in a far more prominent place than the republican flag'. They criticized the young officials, who travelled in hammocks carried by sweating forced labourers, and they claimed that the last of the country's admirals was resident in the lunatic asylum. Both of them, in a book published after Hitler's advent to power, proposed a German mandate for Liberia.

A comical but less sneering account came from Mrs Elizabeth Furbay, whose husband, John, was President of the Liberia College and had once offended his pupils by going to work in his shirt-sleeves. From her account it would seem that Liberia had surpassed even Sierra Leone as the most litigious country in West Africa.

If I wished to dismiss a boy from my service [she wrote] I should give as a reason only that I was 'not satisfied'. I should never tell a cook that he could not cook or any other domestic that he did not do his work well, for either could sue me, under American–Liberian law, for ruining his reputation and his chance of finding further employment... I soon wondered if all Americo–Liberians were lawyers. Here in Liberia we foreigners say when we part, 'I'll be suing you'.

The novelist Graham Greene chose to ignore this risk when writing about Liberia, with the result that sales of *Journey Without Maps* were stopped by an injunction from Monrovia. Admitting that it was easy to make fun out of Monrovia, Greene was most severe about the European community, with their after-breakfast beer, their whisky at four in the morning, and their iced crême de menthe throughout the day. 'They had every reason to drink; you couldn't read much in a climate which rotted your books; you couldn't even deceive yourself that you were there for some good, ruling the natives, for it was the natives in this case who ruled you and presented, so far as the Cabinet Ministers were concerned, a depressing example of sobriety and attention to business.' Graham Greene was accompanied on his long walk through the hinterland by his cousin, Barbara Greene, who also published a book about the experience.* They both met President Barclay whom Barbara Greene described as looking as if he had just left the fifty-shilling tailors. She wrote sparingly of the President's 'intimate friend' and only said that Barclay had made her father a judge. Graham Greene, on the other hand, called this intimate friend 'the loveliest thing I saw in Liberia'. Both writers found Barclay an affable, talkative man with a ham-actor's, Tammany Hall style of politics. Yet Graham Greene considered Barclay a man of courage and energy who was 'something new on the Coast'.

Even writers like Graham Greene, who tried to be fair to Liberia, implied that its condition had always been one of decadence, that even a man like Barclay was 'something new on the coast'. Yet the most friendly descriptions of Liberia in the 1930s are less favourable than the most hostile description of Liberia in the 1860s. It is hardly fair to the country of Roberts or even of Arthur Barclay, the uncle, to say that Edwin Barclay was 'something new on the coast'. The country that had produced

* The British Chargé d'Affaires, A. E. Yapp, who was host to the Greenes in Monrovia, guessed that 'they found conditions in Liberia so normal that they were disappointed'.

Blydens' essays and Anderson's *Narrative of a Journey* was governed now by a President who could write such drivel as this:

Break! Break! Break! On my rugged shore, O Sea!
Dash in furious madness to windward and (to) lee!
But ne'er canst thou daunt the spirit Ethiopia breathes within
Whilst thou bringst from proud Europa her violence and sin ...
Sing well the white man's burden! ay, sing her pleasures too!
The pleasures are his portion, the burdens others rue!
Yea, others pour their life-blood to quench his sordid greed,
While he lives on unconscious, unmindful of their need ...

Liberia was ridiculous—but she had not always been so.

The wealth of Firestone and the influence it exerted through the terms of its loan made Liberia almost dependent on the United States. 'Ole Mammy' coins, so called because of Victoria's head, were withdrawn from circulation and replaced by American dollars and cents. The ties with the United States were still further tightened during the Second World War. Liberia, in the part of West Africa closest to America, was an obvious site for one of the chain of airports planned to link the United States with Cairo. The same Colonel McBride who had formerly solved Liberia's economic problems returned in 1942 to negotiate for an air base. Some Liberians, recalling the German bombardment during the First World War, were wary of an agreement, especially since it was not yet clear that America was on the winning side. However, McBride was able to argue that in return for letting a base, the Liberians would acquire a large airfield, a long stretch of new road and even a harbour for good measure. Cynics then and since have pointed out that the new Robertsfield airport was built next to the offices of the Firestone rubber plantation, but twenty-five miles from the capital that it serves.

I shall close this history of Liberia with the accession in January 1944 of President William Vacanarat Shadrach Tubman, a lawyer and former Supreme Court Justice, who is still, at the time of writing, in office. President Tubman's international fame goes far back, further indeed than most of his friends care to remember; he was one of the Senators who had served as a lawyer for Vice-President Yancy in the Wedabo Beach affair. As late as 1943, a foreign author complained that slavery was 'the law in practice in Liberia—the law which supports Supreme Court Justice W. V. S. Tubman, partner and attorney for the slavers'. No harsh remarks of this kind appear in the recent, official biographies of the President, which ignore any reference to the unsavory affair. The handbook *Liberia. Open Door to Travel and Investment* recalls that Tubman, as a young lawyer, 'quickly won fame as the "poor man's friend" because he pleaded gratuitously and won many cases for his impecunious client'. In the following final chapter on Liberia and Sierra Leone today, I shall discuss what progress has been made in the country of Tubman, 'the poor man's friend'.

316

Chapter Three

In this study of the Back to Africa movement, I have tried as much as was possible not to intrude any judgments I might have formed as to whether the movement was worth while. I have left the appraisals of Sierra Leone and Liberia to those residents and visitors of the two little countries who have proved so eloquent in their praise or, more often, abuse. In this final chapter I shall advance a few ideas of my own on Sierra Leone, Liberia and the Back to Africa movement.

Freetown today* is so like the caricatures by Sir Richard Burton that it is hard to make a description sound true. Its ugliness, both spiritual and physical, would be difficult to exaggerate. The rotting old houses, blotched with sweating mould, are now interspersed with grotesque, stark office blocks in the South Bank or Festival of Britain style. The multitudinous vultures perch impartially on the tin roofs of the shacks and the cement roofs of the office buildings. The open storm-drains that line every street are cluttered with rubbish during the dry season and swollen with water, drowned pye-dogs and sometimes drowned children during Freetown's legendary wet season. Sundays are still rife with hymns which have inspired an 'Ancient and Modern Rice and Grinding Mills' on Krootown Road. The enormous cotton tree beneath which the Nova Scotians gathered to pray still serves as a memory of historic achievement, but most of the man-made monuments have rotted with damp, neglect or old age. There is still an inscription over the 'King's Yard Royal Hospital and Asylum for Africans rescued from slavery by British Valour and Philanthropy', but the near-by flight of steps built by MacCarthy, the greatest

---

* I was there during the unpopular military dictatorship. People say that Freetown now is much improved.

governor, is cracked and fenced off with barbed wire and almost buried beneath a pestiferous scree of filth thrown from the buildings above. St George's Cathedral has been preserved in all its historic hideousness, with the wall plaques recording the scourge of the coast: 'Sacred to the memory of Peyton Blakiston Esq., R.N., Commander of H.M.S. *Sparrow*. Who died on board the *Isis* of Fever on the 21st December, 1865. Aged 55 years. And was buried at sea. Also William Lot his steward. Who died from the same cause the same day. In the midst of life we are in death.' Down the road is the statue of Edward Blyden, who in life was so proud of his pure black skin but whose effigy, by some quirk of the climate, has gained a complexion of red, laterite clay.

Historic Freetown is symbolized by the City Hotel, where Graham Greene lodged during his year in the colony and which he re-named the Bedford. The building was once a private nursing home and therefore has catered for both the illness and thirst notorious in Sierra Leone. Between the two wars, so I was told by its elderly patrons, the City was popular with the officers of the garrison, whose broad backs blocked the bar to the milder civilian customers. Since Independence in 1961, the City Hotel has tended to decline. The outer gate that leads into the hotel courtyard is picketed by a rabble of beggars, thieves, pimps, whores and taxi-drivers. The front of the building is blotched, mottled and gangrened by the incessant ravages of damp. The two palms that stand in the courtyard act as the daytime doss-house for a multitude of fruit-bats that drop from the trunks each dusk like specks of ash from a burning brand.

Most of the Europeans who go to the City Hotel are veteran 'Coasters': men who have worked or traded for years here or in Gambia, Ghana and Nigeria; men grown sallow and old for their years. 'We're remittance men. We're here in Sierra Leone because they wouldn't take us anywhere else,' one Englishman joked. They both love and loathe 'the Coast' with its squalor and heat and lethargy—and its moments of strange beauty. The short-term men, the two-year bankers, the economic advisers and high-school teachers, prefer the cool of Hill Station and the remoter European suburbs; but Coasters respond to the curious charm of Freetown. At dusk on the first-floor balcony of the city hotel drinking pink gins and gossiping with an African lady, and watching the colours return to the rich red earth and the sea in the bay and the rust in the tin roofs on which the familiar vultures perch, the 'Coaster' will tell you that he is quite content to be buried one day 'in the laterite'.

The manager, Freddy, is an Italian Swiss who has spent thirty years in the City Hotel and looks on its customers with the weary, forgiving smile of a prison priest. He and the customers do not talk much of the Greene book although one trader, from Manchester, said; 'Quite frankly I didn't like it, just as a piece of writing. I'd say it was written in prose.'

One day an American lady, writing a thesis on something or other, came to examine the place where Greene stayed and was loudly abused by a drunk white trader. Undaunted, she turned to an even more drunk Creole lady, who had not heard of Greene but accepted a Guinness and gawped in bewilderment when the American lady pulled out photographs of her children back in Ohio. One day Freddy showed me the manuscript of a novel written by one of the customers, who had been a diamond miner and an adventurer. It was a short, lyrical story of beer, sweat, mining and beautiful black girls. A friend who had known the author said the story was true to life: 'He died on the job of a ruptured aorta. But the girl he cracked up wasn't really so beautiful. To my mind she looked like a half-dead kipper.'

Many Sierra Leoneans who go to the City are Creole, or call themselves Creoles. 'Everyone is a Creole,' one Englishman said with a sneer. 'They tell you "me na Krio" even though they've got tribal scars all the way down their face.' In contrast to Ghana and Nigeria, even people of some education speak the tiresome pidgin English that Creoles claim as a special language. In a tailor's shop on my second day I was much impressed by the linguistic skill of a European customer: 'You got one suit for me, na so. You get him one time. Why for you go rubbish me? ... ' and so on. That customer must have spent long on the coast, I thought, but the tailor informed me afterwards: 'He from da Russian

Embassy. Big man, too much.' The genuine Creole, the heir of the settlers, the Nova Scotians, Maroons and recaptured slaves, is today rather a sad but likeable survivor. The touchiness and pomposity, so cruelly mocked by every visitor from Burton to Greene, now seem more pitiable than offensive. 'Look at that Lebanese over there,' says an elderly Creole in the City Hotel. 'He's a very rich man but almost illiterate. Do you see how the Europeans he's with are laughing at him because of the bad English he speaks. Truly, "a little learning is a dangerous thing".' The same man loves to recall the days of the great Creole politicians whose scorn and eloquence made them feared and respected even by the British:

'In a Leg. Co. debate on sanitation Bankole–Bright said; "I am the only one qualified to talk on this subject. You are all swimming in a pool of ignorance." Once he said to the Colonial Secretary: "Who are you but a paid clerk?" and another time he said to the governor: "If you want me to leave the country, we shall leave on the next boat—together." Then there was Sharunka-Sawyerr. He told the governor who was going to get on the Bo train during a strike, that he would have him put under arrest ... Wallace-Johnson was much loved in Freetown. Even some Europeans cried at his funeral. And the coffin came all the way from Russia, they said.'

When the Creoles are out of earshot, the Coasters recount all the old tales of Creole cantankerousness. 'One of my workmen spat at me last week. He was trying to get me to hit him and make me liable for a court case. There was an Englishman the other day who was fined fifty pounds for giving a man a light slap. If you want to deal with one of these jokers you've got to get him alone, give him a good hiding and say he has fallen downstairs.' Freetown, after, say, Accra or Abidian or Dakar, is indeed a quarrelsome place. Almost every day I heard Creole men and more frequently women in hideous, blood-curdling palavers. The words 'shrew', 'scold' and 'jade' appeared for the first time in my diary and my vocabulary. The courtesy and the dignity which one meets almost everywhere else in West Africa were rare in Freetown—and rarer still in Monrovia.

Crime, born of poverty, is manifest in the centre of the town. The policemen, as in Graham Greene's day, are scared to patrol the streets in the dark, although sturdy policewomen, with big bums and highly starched uniforms, sometimes passed on patrol. Thieves broke into the City Hotel several times a week. The many ineptly forged coins that circulate in Sierra Leone are constantly offered for drink at the City bar. One evening I heard a commotion up the street and found a crowd kicking a man almost to death. A European, claiming the privilege of his race, had been given the best place and plenty of room, and was kicking the other man in the head. The man, who bore the name of a famous C.M.S. missionary, had entered a pools office and bashed the lady clerk with a mason's hammer but failed to make away with the loot. A few days later there was a mass battle inside the courtyard of the City Hotel between some of the taxi-drivers and the crew of a South Korean fishing-vessel.

The City Hotel is at its best on Saturday mornings when, by tradition, the 'Coast' assembles to drink. A Ghanaian minstrel wearing a harlequin suit plays the guitar as he sings such favourites as 'My Bonny Lies Over the Ocean', 'I'm Forever Blowing Bubbles', 'We're Going to Hang Out the Washing on the Siegfried Line' and, most popular of all with the European expatriates, that doleful lament 'I Wanna Go Home'. During the morning a tumbler arrives, a muscular acrobat who balances a glass of water on his hand and then turns somersaults up and down the bar. Everyone drinks a lot of beer, sitting in cane chairs, under slowly turning fans, enjoying the ritual of Saturday on the Coast. One day some Germans tried to teach the minstrel to play the Horst Wessel Song, the Nazis' militant anthem. They sang all the verses over and over again, but the minstrel refused to add this new song to his repertory.

The Europeans will often tell you that Freetown, a squalid corrupt city, is not the real Sierra Leone. For Europeans, especially the two-year man with a house and car and expenses as perks of his job, the country is typified by Hill Station and grander suburbs even farther away from town, or by the 'real Africa' of the interior, where the protectorate used to be. It is true that political power no longer depends on Freetown. The politicians who ruled the country before the military coup of 1967 drew their support from the Mende people who live in the south and east. The politicians who regained power at the end of the military government drew much support from the Temne people who live in the north and west. But Freetown, just like other West African capitals, has attracted thousands of unemployed and ambitious men from the interior. 'Up country depends on foreigners,' a German engineer remarked. His company had advertised for a secretary to work more than a hundred miles from Freetown at a salary of eighty pounds a month, with an air-conditioned bungalow, servants, the use of a swimming pool and free transport to Freetown every other week-end. They could not find a girl to accept the job. Young American and British volunteers do most of the teaching work, even in Freetown. As Dr Davidson Nicol, then Vice-Chancellor of the University, warned his Sierra Leonean students:

> University-educated Africans like ourselves should cease to regard themselves as a privileged class entitled to a car, furnished quarters, refrigerators and servants, as soon as they graduate. These things must be earned. Again, we cannot, as a nation, keep hoping that young American and British citizens, as Peace Corps or V.S.O.s [Voluntary Service Overseas] will continue to do the less glamorous work of our country's development.

Most of these volunteers that I met were bitterly critical of their treatment, complaining that in their work of 'chiefdom development' (the lunatic phrase the Americans use to describe giving advice to a village) they are obliged to pay much of their meagre allowance in 'dashes', or bribes, to the chief.

A Peace Corps couple said that the most dreaded appointment in the country was 'beating-master' at a certain school whose whole

322

first football eleven had once been thrashed for losing an important match.

Moreover, the vices of Freetown flourish in the interior. The commissions set up in 1967 to delve into malpractices of the former regime found an orgy of corruption in the Mende diamond country. Chiefs had salted away fortunes in Swiss accounts. Officials of the United Mineworkers Union boasted of having embezzled the dues: 'We shaib (shared) the money on chop chop am.' The famous Bo School is now shabby and strongly ridiculous. The boys are divided into 'towns' or what, in English schools, are called houses. The teacher who showed me around said: 'The towns are Manchester, Liverpool, London and Paris. Although some people might think this an anachronism, they have so much sentimental value to us who think of ourselves as Old Londoners, or Old Mancunians or Old Parisians ... —A Bo School boy who goes to any part of the country is sure to find himself friends.' The night-clubs and the casino of Freetown are among the likeliest places to meet Old Londoners, Old Mancunians or Old Parisians. Even Bo School is better than the establishment at Kenema, where the pupils recently rioted because no expenses were paid to the football team. Two of the boys that night started to smash the windows of the house of the umpire, a local council official, who rushed out and hospitalized them both with a broken beer bottle.

Reluctantly one is forced to see that the 'old' Sierra Leone, the dingy, woebegone, pious, drunken, poor, litigious, yet somehow charming city of Freetown is much more real than the 'new' Sierra Leone of Englishmen in starched white shorts and of chiefs' sons with smart suits and shabby degrees, enriching themselves in personnel management, public relations or politics. I once met a girl who had gone to Ghana by ship and stopped at Freetown to get a first look at West Africa. After a brief stroll she burst into tears.

Monrovia, after Freetown, looks a go-ahead, even prosperous city, but this illusion cannot survive more than the first few days of a visit. There is more a display than the substance of progress.

323

There are glittering great banks—but much of their money leaves the country. A gigantic hotel stands on the hill where the first settlers defied the unfriendly natives—but the hotel staff, the descendants of those natives, are just as unfriendly today. In the downtown streets, named after pious pioneers such as Ashmun, Gurley and Lott Carey, there are night-clubs where black girls strip in the dark. One hostess whom I met off duty sneezed a great deal and complained of the cold at work. 'Those Americans, they want the air-conditioner up, up, up. I get gooseflesh all over my arms because we aren't allowed to wear anything more than the bunny costume.' There are fine government buildings but no proper government. There are huge air-conditioned limousines but holes in the road almost big enough to engulf them.

In most West African cities poverty is relieved by charm. Monrovia is unique in its overwhelming nastiness. The ruling class of Americo-Liberians, or 'A.L.s' as they are unfondly called, tend to be vain, ostentatious and quarrelsome. The venality and sheer knavery of the Liberian ruling class is impossible to describe, not from any lack of good evidence but because of those shark Liberian lawyers who live by spurious libel claims. Liberia's police are the laughing-stock of the continent. They will arrest and demand bribes from any foreigner on any trumped-up charge. A friend of mine was arrested one day for taking a constable's picture and the following day for not taking the same constable's picture. The police constantly flag down and board passing cars then demand five dollars in cash as a fine for an 'infringement'. Once, when we could stand this no longer, we drove our arresting policeman two miles out of town, told him untruthfully that we were personal guests of President Tubman, ordered him out of the car and left him to walk back. A sergeant, who had not been given a sweetener by our small hotel, arrived in a rage one night, brandished his pistol and nightstick, and announced to the puzzled guests his intention of shooting the landlord. One visitor to Monrovia, Professor Stanislav Andreski, was arrested in front of the presidential palace on a charge of trying to get information about the building.

The behaviour of the police in Monrovia is modified by their exposure to publicity. In the hinterland, where there is no publicity, the ruling class can plunder and graft with impunity. President Tubman and his public relations men claim to have ended the old distinction between the original settler class, the Americo-Liberians, and the natives of the interior. The newspapers constantly praise the wisdom of Tubman's 'interior policy'. In fact, power remains in the hands of a very few families of Americo-Liberians—the Barclays, Shermans, Tolberts, Coopers and now, above all, the Tubmans. Those native chiefs who have married into the aristocracy of the coast have soon acquired the flamboyant, sub-American way of life. The Americo-Liberians now control not only Congress, the Civil Service, the judiciary, the churches and the Freemasons, but have taken over leadership of the natives' tribal Porro societies, thus adulterating the forest culture with cheap American vulgarity.

In Liberia, more than anywhere else in Black Africa, one is struck by the gross contrast of rich and poor, of ruler and ruled. The peasants pay a hut tax, euphemistically called a Real-Estate Tax, but get scarcely any services in return. The Peace Corps volunteers who carry the burden of teaching in schools complain, even more angrily than their colleagues in Sierra Leone, of the government's indolence and corruption.* The wages offered to labourers on most of the country's rubber estates are so low that many Liberians, even when hungry, prefer to loaf in Monrovia or to emigrate down the coast. The President's well-known horror of communism discourages militant trade-union leaders. He did, however, permit and settle a strike led by his son Shad Tubman, the son-in-law of Vice-President William Tolbert. In contrast to Ghana or the Ivory Coast, there are few farmers of cash crops in Liberia. A group of Nationalist Chinese experts established a rice farm in the north of the country on which Liberians were encouraged to raise crops. The farming had been successful but the

* The disgruntlement of the Peace Corps is the subject of a novel, *The Zinzin Road* by Fletcher Knebel (W. H. Allen, 1967), in which Liberia is disguised as 'Kalya', and the Americo-Liberians as 'The Family'.

farmers did not seem happy. They complained rather timidly that they had not yet been paid for the rice they had sent off down to the coast. The consignee was a very important person.

It is no longer possible to maintain that Liberia is a colony of the United States. Although Firestone is still the largest exploiter and still controls the country's finances, the Europeans have joined in the feast. The Swedes are dominant in the LAMCO consortium that is extracting iron ore at Nimba, close to the Guinea frontier. They have built a harbour at Buchanan and a fine fast railway between the sea and the mountain of iron. The company town of Yekepa has Swedish shops with Swedish sales-girls, Swedish bankers and banks, Swedish schools and a Swedish arts centre, where the Swedish child artists display their paintings of Swedish hippies and Swedish demos but none, that I noticed, of Africa. The company has created a fine town with magnificent streets like Tubman Ridge and President W. V. S. Tubman Avenue. They look after the health and happiness of the workers. 'The tribes are mixed together,' I was informed, 'and that causes problems and constant palavers. That's one reason why the company is making a Christmas gift to the workers of two "palaver houses" with round, thatched roofs. We build them in the native style but with civilized materials such as concrete blocks and instead of wooden poles, steel pipes.' Palavers, however, are not encouraged on company matters. The *Lamco News* of August 1966 carried a 'Workers' Apology to Management', in which J. Benjamin Duncan, Vice-President of the National Mine Workers Association of Liberia, deeply regretted the illegal strike that had taken place, professed the innocence of the association's board, and voiced his hope that the labour–management relationship would 'long exist in a good atmosphere'. Copies of this letter were sent to the Secretary of Commerce and Industry, the superintendent of the country and, of course, to President W. V. S. Tubman. The Swedes will depart when the mountain of iron has been flattened; but few Liberians will have learned their skills. Not only do Swedes do most of the management, but other Africans take the skilled manual jobs. 'If you find a good carpenter or mason,' said an executive, 'and you ask him where he comes from, he'll almost certainly say Guinea, Senegal or Sierra Leone. There are many skilled craftsmen specially recruited from Ghana, Nigeria and Sierra Leone to do the skilled jobs like running the mechanical shovels.'

The country that was founded to bring civilization to Africa now has to rely for its artisans on Nigeria and Ghana, which, only a hundred years ago, were still primitive societies. The country where Blyden lectured and wrote is now an intellectual desert. In the newspapers, only the horoscopes are of interest: 'You will notice some weakness in the first half of the day. It isn't malaria. It is caused by the reflection of the moon on your star. Love is favoured for negligible period. Find a preacher to solve your religious doubts.' That was my horoscope for December 2nd, 1967. The same issue and every issue of every journal in Liberia was crammed with adulation for the President.

> Williams Tub is a fountain of progress,
> And of wealth unbounded, and of happiness for all.
> More regard for tribal welfare; redress
> For wrongs to tribal people, are the principal
> Points of the Interior Policy
> Flowing from this tub with accuracy.

Nobody now remembers that 'this tub', so solicitous for the tribal people, resigned from the Senate after the League of Nations Commission had named him for helping to sell tribal people as labourers in Fernando Po.

President Tubman, who received me at his country estate, has a huge vivacity and charm. A devotee of cigars, the fair sex and whisky, a glad-handing, cornball, crackerbarrel philosopher, he is like a stage caricature of a Southern Senator—blackened. His energy is astounding. He countersigns all government cheques for amounts of one hundred dollars or more and he interviews scores of people each day. While we were talking to him on his farm he was approached by a lawyer just returned from the United States and by a peasant, in country clothes, who had a complaint over a land claim. Restless and curious, he likes to keep on the move both

327

inside Liberia and around the world. He is, however, frightened of flying, and used to travel around by sea until the presidential yacht was sunk in a rather mysterious accident. The President collects animals on his foreign trips, and he loves to potter about his private zoo. 'What's that?' he inquired at one cage. 'It looks like a bag of wool. A lama? It must have been from Bourguiba. Get it sheared.' The lama, like almost everything else, reminded the President of the Bible. 'As it says in the Bible ... 'the lamb before the shearer' ... I was in Kenya the other day and I saw the lambs being sheared and they weren't opening their mouths. Those old fellows in the Bible, they must have seen that.' When asked to pose for his photograph, the President smiled and agreed: 'I am a child of sorrow, and acquainted with grief.'

Sierra Leone and Liberia have not fulfilled the hopes of their founders. The fault lay in the concept of 'Back to Africa'. The plan failed in its first and most important purpose of easing the lot of the blacks in England and America. The 'colour problem' in England during the second part of the eighteenth century was to melt away during the next hundred years; but this was not due to the founding of Sierra Leone. Only three hundred black people left England to settle in Africa, or about one in a hundred of the estimated total. Years after the settlement in Sierra Leone there was a large black community in this country. There is no way of deducing exactly how this community died out during the next few decades. Some possibly went to Canada or the United States or, after the ending of slavery, to the West Indies.Perhaps many died of disease and cold. The majority, one can only guess, married white people, whose children in turn married white people until their descendants were no longer regarded as Negro or coloured but rather as dark English. Those anti-Negro polemicists who had predicted a mongrelization of England, the breeding of a dusky race such as the Portuguese, misunderstood the workings of genetics and heredity. When one race in any community is not only larger but more admired, that race will tend to predominate in succeeding generations. The Portuguese, it is true, tended to take

328

on the dark appearance of the Muslim Africans who had conquered them; but as Dr Gilberto Freyre has pointed out, the Portuguese had grown to admire the appearance of their rulers. In Portuguese stories and legends, 'the Moorish brown girl is regarded as the supreme type of beauty and of sexual attractiveness; the Moors are considered superior, and not inferior, to the purely white Portuguese.'

In the United States, where there were hundreds of thousands of Negroes, the emigration to Africa had even less effect. For every Negro who left to live in Liberia, ten or twenty more were bred to slave on the Southern plantations. The colonization movement, far from easing the misery of the freed black poor, only inflamed the passions of friends and critics of slavery. The Marcus Garvey movement gave the Negroes a new pride in their African heritage; but it sent only a handful of Negroes to Africa.

Colonization by Negroes from England and the United States failed in its second purpose of bringing civilization to Africa. Sierra Leone and Liberia never expanded deep into the hinterland of West Africa. The influence of the settlers, until the twentieth century, did not really extend beyond the towns and villages of the coast. This failure, once again, should not be blamed on the colonists. The Liberians and the Freetown Creoles during the nineteenth century had neither the manpower nor the capital to open up the interior. The 'civilization' of Africa by the Western Imperialist Powers was to require armies, railroads and teams of officials, backed by the financial might of trading and manufacturing companies. These capitalists, during the present century, have tried to oust the settlers from influence even in Freetown and Monrovia, where they had once exercised power. The redemption of Africa hoped for by Sharp and the American Colonization Society had to wait until the time was ripe for Unilever, Firestone and the Liverpool Chamber of Commerce.

Considering all their handicaps, the Negro settlers in Sierra Leone and Liberia made worthy achievements during the nineteenth century. Both Freetown and Monrovia were prosperous well-run cities. Trade and the professions flourished. Creole

329

businessmen, missionaries and officials carried the ways of civilization right along the West Coast. The careers of men like Blyden, Crowther and Lewis seem all the more remarkable when one considers that they were former slaves or the descendants of slaves. Both colonies, during the nineteenth century, were ample proof, for those ready to see the truth, that the Negro race was capable of self-government. The decline of the two countries into their present shoddy condition is to be blamed not on the citizens but on European imperialism. Yet Sierra Leone and even Liberia are today more pleasant places than most of the Southern United States, the black districts of New York and Chicago, or the wretched Negro areas of north-east Brazil, and the Republic of Haiti.

Jewish Zionism was to succeed decisively after two thousand years only when millions of Jews had died in Hitler's extermination camps. The impetus to return to Palestine came from the shocked survivors. The American Jews, although giving money to Israel, have shown little desire to emigrate. If, God forbid, the Negroes in their diaspora should be the victims of an extermination policy, their survivors, too, might demand to return to their homeland. Meanwhile, a return to Africa offers no cure for the sufferings of the Negro race. The evangelicals and the colonizationists hoped that the Back to Africa movement would recompense for the cruelty of the slave trade to America. It did not and could not. There can be no recompense, as long as western civilization survives, for the white man's crime against Africa.

Source Notes

Most of the material for this book comes from secondary sources. Scholars, working on books or theses, have well explored most of the history of Sierra Leone and Liberia, concentrating their efforts on one aspect or period of each country. To have re-ploughed those furrows would have taken a lifetime for someone intending, as I did, to write an interpretative history. Where I did so, I found little that had not already been found by scholars like Christopher Fyfe. In writing about Liberia in the 1930s I studied the recently opened files of the Foreign Office. Here again, although I found evidence in the documents, I frankly found nothing to make me change my thesis. The documents served only to prove what I had already guessed; that Britain's policy towards Liberia was dominated by its jealousy of the Firestone Company. The part of this book that I venture to claim is both original and surprising concerns the Negro problem in England two hundred years ago. The evidence for this comes from secondary but forgotten sources. The following are some bibliographical notes for each chapter. I append a fuller bibliography of sources consulted during the preparation of this book. Books not cited in full are given with all details in the bibliography.

Part One. Chapter One

For this and every chapter about Sierra Leone until the present century I am overwhelmingly indebted to Christopher Fyfe's *A History of Sierra Leone*. A former acting archivist to the government of Sierra Leone, Mr Fyfe spent years on this monumental yet elegant history. His bibliography and notes were an invaluable guide to further research and reading. I delved at length through Treasury and Admiralty papers referring to the foundation of

Sierra Leone, in the hope of finding some evidence Mr Fyfe might have missed on the mystery of the white prostitute passengers. The search was fruitless. The study of *Continental and Colonial Servants in Eighteenth Century England* by J. Jean Hecht is interesting. Both the above books put me on the track of some little-known tracts and chapbooks about the eighteenth-century colour problem. Other main sources for this chapter are Granville Sharp and his biographer Prince Hoare.

Part One. Chapter Two

Anna Falconbridge's *Two Voyages to the Sierra Leone River*, recently reprinted, are racy but reasonably reliable. Sharp's writings are again important. The Chatham and Admiralty papers record the enmity between the settlers and the slave traders.

Page 29, line 4 Hoare II 86; line 27 Hoare II 97–8. **Page 30,** line 9 Hoare II 95. **Page 32,** line 12 Hoare II Appendix xiii. **Page 34,** line 3 Porter 24 ff. **Page 35,** fn MacKenzie-Grieve *passim.* **Page 37,** line 13 Hoare II 163–4. **Page 38,** line 7 Hoare II 166–8.

Part One. Chapter Three

The Clarkson papers in the British Museum and the extracts from his diary quoted in Sierra Leone Studies, March 1927, are both valuable.

Page 42, line 12 Add MSS 41262 B. **Page 43,** line 34 Halliburton 21–2, quoting Clarkson's diary. **Page 47,** line 3 *Substance of the Report* ... 58; line 26 *Substance of the Report* ... 61. **Page 49,** line 25 Add MSS 12131. A letter from James Strand, an official of the Sierra Leone Company. **Page 50,** line 2 Falconbridge 140; line 20 Add MSS 41262 A. Thornton to Clarkson September 14th, 1792.

Part One. Chapter Four

Macaulay's journals, quoted in the biography by Baroness Knutsford, give an intriguing impression of this unpleasant man. The originals are in Los Angeles.

Page 54, line 12 Knutsford 7; line 27 Knutsford 8. **Page 55,** line 9 Knutsford 11. **Page 58,** line 19 Booth 48. **Page 59,** line 3 Afzelius 9; line 13

Ingham 93. **Page 60,** line 8 Knutsford 65; line 22 Fyfe, *Sierra Leone Inheritance* 124. **Page 61,** line 2 Hoare Appendix; line 10 Kirk-Greene 118; line 20 Knutsford 68; line 26 Knutsford 77. **Page 62,** line 2 Knutsford 85; line 18 Knutsford 86–7; line 32 Knutsford 87. **Page 64,** line 35 Knutsford 122. **Page 66,** line 11 Trevelyan 17.

Part One. Chapter Six

Governor MacCarthy's dispatches are disappointingly flat. One could not say the same of the quarrel between the Macaulays and their detractors that raged in books, pamphlets and newspapers. Robert Thorpe and Kenneth Macaulay were fiercest in debate.

Page 77, line 17 CO/267/47 MacCarthy to Bathurst, June 11th, 1817. **Page 78,** line 30 Rankin 126. **Page 83,** line 33 Memoir of the Rev. W. A. B. Johnson 53. **Page 85,** line 20 Rankin 178.

Part Two. Chapter One

Political and Legislative History of Liberia by C. H. Huberich is encyclopaedic but pretty dull. Moreover it stops in the mid-nineteenth century. Sir Harry Johnston's *Liberia* goes up to this century. Although he did not have recourse to much of the relevant material, his conclusions are sound and his style a delight. There is a first-class recent book, *The African Colonization Movement, 1816–65* by P. J. Staudenraus. Readable and scholarly, it is also a good guide to further reading. I read widely on the Negro question in early nineteenth-century America, as well as many books by or about contemporary politicians and divines.

Page 89, line 11 Jefferson 253. **Page 90,** line 6 Beloff 66. **Page 92,** line 6 Clay II 265–6. **Page 93,** line 11 Hoare II 125–9. **Page 95,** line 14 Beloff 95; line 30 Jefferson 253–4. **Page 96,** line 20 Cresson 175.

Part Two. Chapter Two

Documents quoted by Huberich supplement the biographies of Mills and Bacon. I also read through the *African Repository*, journal of the American Colonization Society: partisan, but illuminating.

Page 101, line 22 Spring 14. **Page 103,** line 16 Spring 186. **Page 104,** line 2 Spring 173. **Page 105,** line 22 Spring 228. **Page 107,** line 4

Ashmun, *Bacon* 111; line 28 Huberich quoting Coker's journal for February 19th, 1820. **Page 108,** line 7 Ashmun, *Bacon* 253; line 22 Ashmun, *Bacon* 257. **Page 109,** line 14 Ashmun, *Bacon* 265.

Part Two. Chapter Three

Ashmun's *History of the American Colony in Liberia* and Gurley's *Life of Jehudi Ashmun* are the main material for this and the following chapter. There is much further material in the *African Repository*, Huberich and Staudenraus.

Page 113, line 5 Gurley, *Ashmun* 122–3; line 33 Marchais 120. **Page 121,** line 7 Ashmun, *History* 25. **Page 122,** line 10 Ashmun *History* 28–9. **Page 123,** line 6 Ashmun, *History* 37; line 13 Ashmun, *History* 35.

Part Two. Chapter Four.

Page 127, line 11 Gurley, *Ashmun* 178. **Page 128,** line 16 Gurley, *Ashmun* 192. **Page 129,** line 6 Gurley, *Ashmun* 197. **Page 130,** line 28 *African Repository* I 24. **Page 134,** line 24 Gurley, *Ashmun* 267. **Page 136,** line 2 Gurley, *Ashmun* 366; line 18 Wilkeson 50; line 22 Wilkeson 51. **Page 137,** line 28 *African Repository* V 10.

Part Two. Chapter Five

Books by and about Garrison supplement the fine analysis by Staudenraus of the quarrel between colonizationists and abolitionists. The topic provoked a mass of literature on both sides of the Atlantic.

Page 140, line 11 Innes 107. **Page 144,** line 35 Staudenraus 214. **Page 146,** line 7 *African Repository* IX 65. **Page 147,** line 13 Merrill 72; line 20 Garrison, W. P. and F. J., *Garrison* 374. **Page 148,** line 5 Merrill 66; line 12 Merrill 73. **Page 149,** line 8 Staudenraus 227; line 35 Gurley, *Colonization* 17.

Part Two. Chapter Six

Huberich has much good material on the coming of independence. Sir Harry Johnston was critical in a friendly way.

Page 152, line 22 Huberich 753; line 30 Huberich 755. **Page 153,** line 13 Huberich 739. **Page 154,** line 8 Johnston, *Liberia* I 219; line 25 *Africa Redeemed* 242.

Part Three. Chapter One

Arthur T. Porter's *Creoledom* gives a good analysis of the rise and decline of the 'black gentlemen'. J. D. Hargreaves's *A Life of Sir Samuel Lewis* is most valuable. *The Black Bishop. Samuel Adjai Crowther* by Jesse Page is a bit uncritical. Unfortunately there is not yet a biography of James Africanus Horton, but his own books are fascinating.

Page 161, line 19 S. A. Walker 328. **Page 163,** line 25 Fyfe, *History* 437. **Page 166,** line 15 Page 15. **Page 167,** line 10 Page 382; line 26 Fyfe, *Sierra Leone Inheritance* 140. **Page 171,** line 2 Poole 30; line 12 Poole 33; line 36 Porter 52. **Page 172,** line 24 *Special Report of the Paris Anti-Slavery Conference* 49.

Part Three. Chapter Two

There are many accounts of Sierra Leone in the nineteenth century by both residents and visitors. Rankin's *The White Man's Grave* is the most readable; Poole's *Life Scenery and Customs in Sierra Leone and the Gambia* is unconsciously the most funny.

Page 175, line 22 Rankin 44. **Page 176,** line 25 Johnston, *The Gay-Dombeys.* **Page 177,** line 4 Hoare 400; line 32 *Thompson in Africa* 22. **Page 178,** line 14 *African Repository* IX 209. **Page 179,** line 18 Holman 86–96. **Page 180,** line 4 Rankin 175. **Page 181,** line 12 *A Residence ...* 86; line 22 Rankin 191. **Page 182,** line 36 Johnston, *The Gay-Dombeys.* **Page 183,** line 13 Carnes 71. **Page 185,** line 17 *A Residence ...* 243; **Page 186,** line 2, Rankin 15. line 15 Fyfe, *Sierra Leone Inheritance* 292–4; line 20 Fyfe, *Sierra Leone Inheritance* 290; line 31 Rankin 139; line 35 Rankin 179.

Part Three. Chapter Three

Burton, Reade and Kingsley speak for themselves. Of the Burton biographers, Farwell is marginally better than Brodie. Both are excellent.

Page 188, line 5 Chamier, *The Life of a Sailor.* Burton quoted this passage from memory, and got it substantially wrong. He repeated the error in his second book referring to Sierra Leone. **Page 190,** line 5 Burton, *Wanderings in West Africa.*

335

Part Three. Chapter Four

N. A. Cox-George's *Finance and Development in West Africa* is an excellent study of the Sierra Leone economy. More general books of great interest on the 'scramble for Africa' are those of Mary Kingsley and E. D. Morel. Also *Africa and the Victorians.*

Page 202, line 9 Kingsley, *Travels in West Africa* 656; line 22 Fyfe, *Inheritance* 234. **Page 203,** line 11 Easmon, *Paramount Chief* 195. **Page 205,** line 25 Harris 5. **Page 206,** line 3 Harris 5. **Page 208,** line 32 Porter 125. **Page 210,** line 27 Wallis 40. **Page 211,** line 6 Wallis 2; line 26 Wallis 119. **Page 212,** line 34 Morel, *Affairs* ... 277. **Page 213,** line 9 Wallis 36. **Page 214,** line 19 Kingsley, *West African Studies* 283. **Page 216,** line 1 Bonner 27. **Page 217,** line 4 Parliamentary Papers, Chalmers Report; line 10 Stewart.

Part Four. Chapter One

Brown's *The Economic History of Liberia* is important. Benjamin Anderson's *Narrative of a Journey to Musardu* is to be republished by Cass (London), in the spring of 1971.

Page 222, line 5 Stockwell 232.

Part Four. Chapter Two

Blyden's *Christianity, Islam and the Negro Race* has recently been re-published with an introduction by Christopher Fyfe. There is a first-rate recent biography, *Edward Wilmot Blyden* by Hollis R. Lynch which provides an illuminating insight into Liberian politics in the nineteenth century, particularly the importance of the Black versus Mulatto controversy.

Page 238, line 1 Add MSS 44395/223. Blyden to Gladstone January 25th, 1861; line 12 Add MSS 44398/301 Blyden to Gladstone May 11th, 1862. **Page 243,** line 14 Pope-Hennessy to Blyden December 10th, 1872. Among typewritten copies of Pope-Hennessy letters in library of Fourah Bay University, Freetown. **Page 244,** line 13 Blyden, *Christianity, Islam and the Negro Race* 315; line 18 Blyden, *Christianity, Islam and the Negro Race* 169; line 31 Blyden, *Christianity* ... 50. **Page 245,** line 27 Lynch 144. **Page 246,** line 2 Lynch 145 fn. **Page 247,** line 2 Blyden, *Christianity* ... 266; line 26 Blyden, *Aims and Methods* ... 24. **Page 250,** line 13 Blyden, *Thee Needs* ... 1; line 22 Blyden, *Three Needs* ... 6, 1. **Page 251,** line 5

Blyden, *West Africa Before Europe* 23; line 30 Blyden, *West Africa Before Europe* 2.

Part Four. Chapter Three

For Liberia's economic decline see Brown, and also Azikiwe—who is a much better historian than he is a politician. Sir Harry Johnston's role in Liberia is described moderately well by himself; better by his biographer Roland Oliver in *Sir Harry Johnston and the Scramble for Africa*. Harvey Firestone and his biographers have contributed towards our understanding of the establishment of the rubber plantation.

Page 255, line 24 Johnston, *Liberia* 368. **Page 257,** line 19 Firestone 254. **Page 258,** line 11 Lief 228; line 36 FO/458/92. A report on the Liberian Cabinet meeting, March 3rd, 1925. **Page 259,** line 23 Young 53; line 35 FO/458/9 Ledger to Vansittart, September 9th, 1926. **Page 260,** line 4 Azikiwe 146; line 8 Azikiwe 155.

Part Four. Chapter Four

Black Moses, by Edmund David Cronon, is a full, sympathetic but fair study of Marcus Garvey, whose own *Philosophy and Opinions* contains more rant than reason. Books by DuBois are better than those, so far, about him.

Page 262, line 28 Garvey, *Philosophy and Opinions* II 125. **Page 263,** line 11 Cronon 17. **Page 264,** line 34 Garvey II 71. **Page 266,** line 8 Garvey II 279. **Page 267,** line 3 Cronon 65, 66. **Page 268,** line 22 Rudwick 229; line 29 Garvey II 311. **Page 270,** line 3 Nembhard 86; line 17 Garvey II 365; line 29, Garvey II 399; line 35 Garvey II 399. **Page 271,** line 16 Garvey II 400. **Page 272,** line 6 Garvey II 378; line 11 Cronon 128; line 23 Garvey II 389. **Page 273,** line 3 Azikiwe 95; line 31 Garvey II 239. **Page 274,** line 15 Drake II 752; line 22 Du Bois, *Dusk of Dawn* 125. **Page 275,** line 5 Garvey xxv; line 14 Garvey I 16.

Part Five. Chapter One

Martin Kilson's *Political Change in a West African State* gives a sound account of Sierra Leone's not very exciting history in this century. Cox-George is once again illuminating on economic development. The works by American sociologists remain lost to

337

me in the obscurity of a learned language. Graham Greene returned to Freetown a few years ago to spend his Christmas at the City Hotel. His account was published in the *Weekend Telegraph* magazine.

Page 279, line 27 Allridge, *A Transformed Colony* 78. **Page 282,** line 2 Allridge, *A Transformed Colony* 83 **Page 283,** line 2 Allridge, *A Transformed Colony* 53. line 12 Walmsley 43. **Page 284,** line 5 Fyfe, *Inheritance* 302; line 35 Fyfe, *Inheritance* 302. **Page 286,** line 10 Fyfe, *Inheritance* 305. **Page 288,** line 32 Buell, *The Native Problem in Africa* 886. **Page 289,** line 3 Buell, *The Native Problem in Africa* 890–91. **Page 290,** line 2 Kilson 129. **Page 294,** line 32 Greene, Graham, *Journey Without Maps* v–vi. **Page 297,** line 31 Fyfe, *Inheritance* 326–7. **Page 289,** line 16 Sierra Leone Legislative Council Debates December 18th, 1950; line 27 Sierra Leone Legislative Council Debates July 29th, 1952; line 34 Sierra Leone Leglislative Council Debates July 29th, 1952.

Part Five. Chapter Two

Merran Fraenkel's *Tribe and Class in Monrovia* is a sociological work —but well written and keenly observed. R. Earle Anderson gives a good account of Liberia during and after the Second World War in *Liberia, America's Friend*. *Les Héros Sont Fatigués* is an impressionistic account that rings true.

Page 302, line 12 Burton, *Wanderings* ... 2; line 28 CO/267/602 Paterson to Foreign Office May 30th, 1923. **Page 303,** line 33 Anderson, R. Earle, 108. **Page 304,** line 6 FO/458/100 Bernard to Foreign Office April 25th, 1928. **Page 307,** line 30 Greenwall and Wild 212. **Page 308,** line 24 Anderson, R. Earle 124. **Page 309,** line 12 FO/458/117 Graham to Foreign Office July 8th, 1931; line 17 FO/458/117 Graham to Foreign Office July 8th, 1931; line 21 FO/458/116 Murray (Foreign Office) to Graham; line 28 FO/458/119 Memorandum from Murray, Foreign Office. **Page 310,** line 20 Parliamentary Debates, House of Lords. March 16th, 1932. **Page 316,** line 5 Buell, *A Century of Survival* 13.

Part Five. Chapter Three

This chapter is based on my own two months' stay in Sierra Leone and Liberia.

Page 322, line 26 *West Africa* September 30th, 1967.

Bibliography

BOOKS CONSULTED

Abel, Annie Heloise and Frank J. Klingsbury, *A Sidelight on Anglo-American Relations 1839–1858* (New York, 1927)

Address to the Public on the Subject of the African School ... (New York, 1816)

Africa Redeemed (London, 1851)

Afzelius, Adam, *Journal*, Ed. A. P. Kup (Upsala, 1967)

Alexander, James Edward, *Narrative of a Voyage* ... (London, 1837)

Allridge, T. J., *A Transformed Colony* (London, 1910)

—— *The Sherbro and its Hinterland* (London, 1901)

An Answer to the Rev. Mr Clarkson's Essay (London, 1789)

Anderson, Benjamin, *Narrative of a Journey to Musardu* (New York, 1870)

Anderson, R. Earle, *Liberia, America's Friend* (New York, 1952)

Andreski, Stanislav, *The African Predicament* (London, 1968)

Ashmun, Jehudi, *History of the American Colony in Liberia* (Washington, 1826)

—— *Memoir ... of the Rev. Samuel Bacon* (Washington, 1822)

Azikiwe, Nnamdi, *Liberia in World Politics* (London, 1934)

Bacon, Leonard, *A Discourse Preached at the Funeral of Jehudi Ashmun* (1828)

Baker, John, *Diary*, Ed. Philip C. Yorke (London, 1931)

Balandier, Georges, *Afrique Ambigue* (Paris, 1957)

Banbury, G. A. Lethbridge, *Sierra Leone or the White Man's Grave* (London, 1888)

Bancroft, Frederic, *Colonization of American Negroes* (University of Oklahoma Press, 1957)

339

Banton, M., *West African City* (London, 1957)

Barnes, Gilbert Hobbs, *The Anti-Slavery Impulse 1830–1844* (New York, 1933)

Beloff, Max, *Thomas Jefferson and American Democracy* (London, 1848)

Blyden, Edward Wilmot, *Africa and the Africans* (London, 1903)

—— *The African Problem* (London, 1890)

—— *Aims and methods of a Liberal Education for Africans* (Cambridge Mass., 1882)

—— *The Arabic Bible in the Soudan* (London, 1910)

—— *Christianity, Islam and the Negro Race* (Edinburgh, 1967)

—— *The Problems before Liberia* (London, 1909)

—— *Proceedings at the Banquet in honour of Edward Wilmot Blyden* (London, 1907)

—— *The Three Needs of Liberia* (London, 1908)

—— *A Voice from Bleeding Africa* (Monrovia, 1856)

—— *West Africa before Europe* (London, 1905)

—— *The West African University* (Freetown, 1870)

Bonner, Sir George, *An Assize in Sierra Leone* (Sierra Leone Studies, November 1933)

Booth, Charles, *Zachary Macaulay* (London, 1934)

Brawley, Benjamin, *A Social History of the American Negro* (New York, 1921)

Bridge, Horatio, *Journal of an African Cruiser* (New York, 1853)

Broderick, Francis L., *W. E. B. Du Bois* (Stanford, 1959)

Brodie, Fawn M., *The Devil Drives* (London, 1967)

Brown, George W., *The Economic History of Liberia* (Washington, 1941)

Brown, Ina Corina, *The Story of the American Negro* (New York, 1936)

Brown, Isaac V., *Biography of the Rev. Robert Finley* (Philadelphia, 1857)

Buell, Raymond Leslie, *A Century of Survival* (Philadelphia, 1947)

—— *The Native Problem in Africa* (New York, 1928)

Burns, Edward McNall, *James Madison* (Rutgers University Press, 1938)

Burton, R. F., *Abeokuta and the Cameroons Mountains* (London, 1863)

—— with V. L. Cameron, *To the Gold Coast for Gold* (London, 1883)

—— *Wanderings in West Africa* (London, 1863)

Butt-Thompson, F. W., *The First Generation of Sierra Leoneans* (Freetown, n.d.)

Campbell, Olwen, *Mary Kingsley. A Victorian in the Jungle* (London, 1957)

Campbell-Maclachlan, A. N., *Memoir of Sir Neil Campbell*

Carnes, J. A., *Journal of a Voyage from Boston* ... (Boston, 1852)

Chamier, F., *The Life of a Sailor* (London, 1832)

Church, R. J. Harrison, *West Africa* (London, 1961)

'Church, Mary', *Sierra Leone or the Liberated Africans* (London, 1835)

Claridge, W. Walton, *A History of the Gold Coast and Ashanti* (London, 1915)

Clarkson, John, *Extracts from Diary* (Sierra Leone Studies, March 1927)

Clarkson, Thomas, *Essay on Slavery* (Dublin, 1786)

Clay, Henry, *Papers* (University of Kentucky Press, 1961)

Colton, Calvin, *A Voice from America to England* (London, 1832)

Conton, William, *The African* (London, 1960)

Corry, Joseph, *Windward Coast of Africa* (London, 1807)

Coupland, Reginald, *Wilberforce* (London, 1945)

Cox-George, N. A., *Finance and Development in West Africa* (London, 1961)

Cresson, W. P., *James Monroe* (University of North Carolina, 1946)

Cronon, Edmund David, *Black Moses* (Madison, 1955)

Crouch, A. P., *On a Surf-bound Coast* (London, 1887)

Dallas, R. C., *History of the Maroons* (London, 1803)

Davidson, Basil, *Africa in History* (London, 1968)

Davis, R. P. M., *History of the Sierra Leone Battalion of the Royal West African Frontier Force* (Freetown, 1932)

Davis, Stanley A., *This is Liberia* (New York, 1953)

341

Drake, St Clair and Horace R. Cayton, *Black Metropolis* (New York, 1962)
Du Bois, W. E. B., *Black Folk* (New York, 1939)
— — *Dusk of Dawn* (New York, 1940)
— — *The World and Africa* (New York, 1947)
Duffy, James, *Portugal in Africa* (London, 1962)
Easmon, M. C. F., *Paramount Chief Bai Kur, M.B.E., M.L.C.* (Sierra Leone Studies, June 1957)
— — *Sierra Leone Cloths* (Freetown, 1924)
— — *Sierra Leone's Connection with Royalty* (Sierra Leone Studies, June 1962)
Eaton, Clement, *Henry Clay and the Art of American Politics* (New York, 1957)
Eberl-Elber, Ralph, *Westafrika's Letztes Rätsel* (Salzburg, 1936)
Eminent Sierra Leoneans (Freetown, 1962)
Evans, Ifor L., *The British in Tropical Africa* (Cambridge, 1929)
Falconbridge, A. M., *Two Voyages to the Sierra Leone River* (London, 1967)
Farwell, Byron, *Burton* (London, 1963)
Figaniere e Morao, J. C. de, *Descripcao de Serra-Leoa ...* (Lisbon, 1822)
Firestone, Harvey S., with Samuel Crowther, *Men and Rubber* (London, 1926)
First, Ruth, *South West Africa* (London, 1963)
Fitch-Jones, B. W., *Hill Station* (Sierra Leone Studies, November 1932)
Fleming, Ian, *The Diamond Smugglers* (London, 1957)
Flickinger, D. K., *Ethiopia or Twenty Years of Missionary Life* (Dayton, 1877)
— — *Sketches in Africa* (Dayton, 1857)
Flickinger, R. E., *The Flickinger Family in the United States of America* (Des Moines, 1927)
Floyd, Barry, *Eastern Nigeria* (London, 1969)
Fowler-Lunn, Katharine, *The Gold Missus* (London, 1938)
Fraenkel, Merran, *Tribe and Class in Monrovia* (London, 1964)
Franck, Frederick, *African Sketchbook* (London, 1962)

342

Franklin, John Hope, *From Slavery to Freedom* (New York, 1956)
Freetown Vademecum, Compiled by Hans M. Zell (Freetown, 1966)
Freyre, Gilberto, *New World in the Tropics* (New York, 1951)
Fuess, Claude M., *Daniel Webster* (Boston, 1930)
Furbay, Elizabeth Dearman, *Top Hats and Tom-Toms* (London, 1946)
Fyfe, Christopher, *A History of Sierra Leone* (London, 1962)
—— *Obituary of Charles Rhodoway Morrison* (Sierra Leone Studies, December 1961)
—— *The Sierra Leone Press in the Nineteenth Century* (Sierra Leone Studies, January 1957)
—— and E. D. Jones, *Freetown* (London, 1968)
Fyfe, Christopher (ed.), *Sierra Leone Inheritance* (London, 1964)
Fyfe, C. H., *Thomas Peters: History and Legend* (Sierra Leone Studies, December 1953)
Garnier, Christine, *Les Héros Sont Fatigués* (Paris, 1953)
Garrison, William Lloyd, *An Address delivered at the Broadway Tabernacle, Boston* (1838)
—— *An Address delivered ... in Philadelphia* (1831)
Garrison, W. P. and F. J., *William Lloyd Garrison* (New York, 1885)
Garvey, Marcus, *Philosophy and Opinions*, compiled by Amy Jacques Garvey (London, 1967)
George, Claude, *The Rise of British West Africa* (London, 1904)
Green, Lawrence G., *White Man's Grave* (London, 1954)
Greene, Barbara, *Land Benighted* (London, 1938)
Greene, Graham, *The Heart of the Matter* (London, 1962)
—— *In Search of a Character* (London, 1961)
—— *Journey Without Maps* (London, 1962)
Greenwall, Harry J. and Roland Wild, *Unknown Liberia* (London, 1936)
Gunther, John, *Inside Africa* (London, 1955)
Gurley, Ralph Randolph, *On the Colonization and Civilization of Africa* (London, 1841)
—— *Life of Jehudi Ashmun* (New York, 1835)
Gwynn, S., *The Life of Mary Kingsley* (London, 1932)

Halliburton, G., *The Nova Scotian Settlers of 1792* (Sierra Leone Studies, December 1957)

Hargreaves, J. D., *African Colonization in the Nineteenth Century* (Sierra Leone Studies, June 1962)

—— *A Life of Sir Samuel Lewis* (London, 1958)

—— *Prelude to the Partition of West Africa* (London, 1963)

—— *Sir Samuel Lewis and the Legislative Council* (Sierra Leone Studies, December 1953)

—— Ed., *France and West Africa* (London, 1969)

Harris, John M., *Annexations to Sierra Leone* (London, 1883)

Hayman, Arthur I., and Harold Preece, *Lighting up Liberia* (New York, 1943)

Hecht, J. Jean, *Continental and Colonial Servants in Eighteenth Century England* (Northampton Mass., 1954)

Henries, Doris B., *The Liberian Nation, A Short History* (New York, 1954)

'Hereditary Planter', *Observations upon the Oligarchy ...* (London, 1816)

Historical Statistics of the United States (U.S. Department of Commerce, 1960)

Hoare, Prince, *Memoirs of Granville Sharp Esq.* (London, 1820)

Holman, James, *Travels in Madeira ... etc.* (London, 1840)

Horton, James Africanus, *Physical and Medical Climate and Meteorology of the West Coast of Africa* (London, 1867)

—— *West African Countries and People* (London, 1868)

Huberich, Charles Henry, *Political and Legislative History of Liberia* (New York, 1947)

Hutchinson, Thomas, *Diary and Letters*, Ed. Peter Orlando (London, 1886)

Huxley, Elspeth, *Four Guineas* (London, 1957)

Industrial Exhibition at Sierra Leone (London, 1866)

Ingham, E. G., *Sierra Leone. After a Hundred Years* (London, 1894)

Innes, William, *Liberia* (Edinburgh, 1831)

Jackman, Isaac, *The Divorce. A Farce* (London, 1781)

Jaeger, Muriel, *Before Victoria* (London, 1967)

Jay, William, *Slavery in America* (London, 1835)

Jefferson, Thomas, *Notes on Virginia* (1782)

Johnson, L. G., *General T. Perronet Thompson* (London, 1957)

Johnson, Oliver, *William Lloyd Garrison and his Times* (Boston, 1881)

Johnston, Harry H., *The Gay-Dombeys* (London, 1916)

—— *Liberia* (London, 1906)

Kilham, Hannah, *Present State of the Colony of Sierra Leone* (London, 1832)

Kilson, Martin, *Political Change in a West African State* (Harvard, 1966)

Kingsley, Mary, *Travels in West Africa* (London, 1897)

—— *West African Studies* (London, 1901)

Kirk-Greene, Anthony, David George. *The Nova Scotian Experience* (Sierra Leone Studies, December 1960)

Knutsford, Baroness, *Life and Letters of Zachary Macaulay* (London, 1900)

Kuczynski, R. R., *Demographic Survey of the British Colonial Empire* (London, 1948)

Kup, A. P., *A History of Sierra Leone 1400–1787* (London, 1963)

Lardner, H. H., *The Agricultural Question* (London, 1880)

Lascelles, Edward, *Granville Sharp* (London, 1928)

Latrobe, John H. B., *Maryland in Liberia* (Baltimore, 1885)

Lawrence, A. W., *Castles and Forts of West Africa* (London, 1963)

League of Nations Document C.658M.272. Commission's Report (Geneva, 1930)

Legum, Colin, ed., *Africa Handbook* (London, 1961)

Leonard, Peter, *Voyage to the Western Coast of Africa* (Edinburgh, 1833)

Lethbridge, Alan, *West Africa the Elusive* (London, 1921)

Lewis, Roy, *Sierra Leone* (London, 1958)

Liberia. Open Door to Travel and Investment (Monrovia, 1967)

Lief, Alfred, *Harvey Firestone. Free Man of Enterprise* (New York, 1951)

Long, Edward, *Candid Reflections …* (London, 1772)

—— *History of Jamaica* (London, 1774)

Lynch, Hollis R., *Edward Wilmot Blyden* (London, 1967)

Macaulay, Kenneth, *The Colony of Sierra Leone Vindicated* (London, 1968)

Macaulay, Zachary, *A Letter to ... the Duke of Gloucester* (London, 1815)

MacKay, Claude, *Harlem* (New York, 1940)

MacKenzie-Grieve, Averil, *The Great Achievement* (London, 1953)

Marchais, Chevalier de, *Voyage en Guinée* (Paris, 1830)

Marteroy, P. H., *Freetown 1899–1938* (Sierra Leone Studies, January 1939)

Martinelli, Lawrence A., *The New Liberia* (London, 1964)

Matthews, John, *A Voyage to the River Sierra Leone* (London, 1788)

Maugham, R. C. F., *The Republic of Liberia* (London, 1920)

Memoir of the Rev. W. A. B. Johnson (London, 1852)

Memorials of John Bowen. Late Bishop of Sierra Leone (London, 1862)

Merrill, Walter M., *Against Wind and Tide* (Harvard, 1963)

Metcalfe, G. E., *MacLean of the Gold Coast* (London, 1962)

Mills, Samuel J. and Daniel Smith, *Report of a Missionary Tour* (Andover, 1815)

Milne, A. H., *Sir Alfred Lewis Jones* (Liverpool, 1914)

Moore, Bai T., *Murder in the Cassava Patch* (Holland, 1968)

Morel, E. D., *Affairs of West Africa* (London, 1902)

—— *The Black Man's Burden* (London, 1920)

Munford, Beverley B., *Virginia's Attitude towards Slavery and Secession* (New York, 1910)

Myrdal, Gunnar, *An American Dilemma* (New York, 1944)

The Negro Servant (Edinburgh, 1804)

Nembhard, Len S., *Trials and Triumphs of Marcus Garvey* (Kingston, 1940)

Newland, H. Osman, *Sierra Leone* (London, 1916)

Nicol, Davidson, *Africa—A Subjective View* (London, 1964)

Nye, Russel B., *William Lloyd Garrison and the Humanitarian Reformers* (Boston, 1955)

Oliver, Roland, *Sir Harry Johnston and the Scramble for Africa* (London, 1957)

The Origin and Purpose of African Colonization (Washington, 1883)

Page, Jesse, *The Black Bishop. Samuel Adjai Crowther* (London, 1908)

Pares, Richard, *A West Indian Fortune* (London, 1950)

Parrish, John, *Remarks on the Slavery of the Black People* (Philadelphia, 1806)

Peterson, John, *Province of Freedom* (London, 1969)

Pfeffer, Karl-Heinz, *Sierra Leone und Gambia* (Bonn, 1958)

Phillips, Hilton Alonzo, *Liberia's Place in the Sun* (New York, 1946)

Poole, Thomas Eyre, *Life, Scenery and Customs in Sierra Leone and the Gambia* (London, 1850)

Pope-Hennessy, James, *Verandah* (London, 1964)

Porter, Arthur T., *Creoledom* (London, 1963)

President Tubman on African Unity (Monrovia, n.d.)

Proceedings of the Royal Geographical Society (London, 1860)

Rainy, William, *The Censor Censured* (London, 1865)

Rankin, F. Harrison, *The White Man's Grave* (London, 1836)

Reade, W. Winwood, *Savage Africa* (London, 1863)

—— *The African Sketch-Book* (London, 1873)

Record, Wilson, *The Negro and the Communist Party* (North Caroline, 1951)

A Residence at Sierra Leone, by 'A Lady' (London, 1849)

Ricketts, Major, *A View of the Present State of Sierra Leone* (London, 1831)

Robinson, Ronald and John Gallagher with Alice Denny, *Africa and the Victorians* (London, 1965)

Rosenthal, Eric, *Stars and Stripes in Africa* (London, 1938)

Rudwick, Elliott M., *W. E. B. DuBois* (Philadelphia, 1960)

Rydings, H. A., *Prince Niambana in England* (Sierra Leone Studies, June 1957)

Seddall, Henry, *The Missionary History of Sierra Leone* (London, 1874)

Segal, Ronald, *African Profiles* (London, 1963)

Seligman, C. G., *Races of Africa* (London, 1957)

Sharp, Granville, *The Just Limitations of Slavery* (London, 1776)

—— *Short Sketch of Temporary Regulations* (London, 1786)

347

Silliman, Benjamin, *A Journal of Travels* ... (New Haven, 1820)
Simon, Lady, *Slavery* (London, 1929)
Smeathman, Henry, *Plan of a Settlement* (London, 1786)
Special Report of the Directors of the African Institution (London, 1815)
Special Report of the Paris Anti-Slavery Conference (London, 1867)
Spilsbury, F. B., *A Voyage to the Western Coast of Africa* (London, 1807)
Spring, Gardiner, *Memoirs of the Rev. Samuel J. Mills* (New York, 1820)
Stamp, Kenneth M., *The Peculiar Institution* (New York, 1956)
State Visit of the President of Liberia, Dr W. V. S. Tubman and Mrs Tubman to Sierra Leone. June 1959 (Freetown, 1959)
Staudenraus, P. J., *The African Colonization Movement. 1816–65* (New York, 1961)
Stewart, Lt J., *Extracts from a Diary Written on Active Service* (Sierra Leone Studies, February 1932)
Stock, Eugene, *History of the Church Missionary Society* (London, 1899)
Stockwell, G. S., *The Republic of Liberia* (New York, 1869)
Substance of the Report delivered by the Court of Directors of the Sierra Leone Company ... On Thursday the 27th March 1794 (London, 1794)
Thompson, George, *Thompson in Africa* (Dayton, 1857)
Thompson, Virginia and Richard Adloff, *The Emerging States of French Equatorial Africa* (Stanford, 1960)
—— *French West Africa* (London, 1958)
Thorpe, Robert, *A Letter to William Wilberforce* (London, 1815)
—— *A Reply 'Point by Point'* ... (London, 1815)
Torrey, Jesse, *American Slave Trade* (London, 1822)
Trevelyan, G. O., *The Life and Letters of Lord Macaulay* (London, 1881)
Tubman, William V. S., *Aphorisms*, Ed. John Bolton Williams (Monrovia, 1968)
Tucker, St George, *A Dissertation on Slavery* (Philadelphia, 1796)
Van der Laan, H. L., *The Sierra Leone Diamonds* (London, 1965)

348

Wadstrom, C. B., *An Essay of Colonization* (London, 1794)
Walker, Samuel Abraham, *The Church of England Mission in Sierra Leone* (London, 1847)
Walker, Thomas H. B., *History of Liberia* (Boston, 1921)
Wallis, C. Braithwaite, *The Advance of our West African Empire* (London, 1903)
Walmsley, John, *Diary*, arranged by E. G. Walmsley (London, 1923)
Ward, W. E. F., *The Royal Navy and the Slavers* (London, 1969)
Wauwermans, Colonel, *Libéria. Fondation d'un État Nègre Libre* (Brussels, 1885)
Welch, Galbraith, *The Jet Lighthouse* (London, 1960)
Welcome to our Capital (Monrovia, 1963)
Whitehead, Thomas, *Original Anecdotes of the late Duke of Kingston* (London, 1792)
Wilkeson, Samuel, *The American Colonies in Liberia* (Washington, 1839)
Williams, Gomer, *History of the Liverpool Privateers* (London, 1897)
Wilson, H. S., *The Changing Image of the Sierra Leone Colony in the works of E. W. Blyden* (Sierra Leone Studies, December 1958)
Woodson, Carter G., *Negro Orators and their Orations* (Washington, 1925)
Yancy, Ernest Jerome, *Historical Lights of Liberia* (Xenia, Ohio, 1934)
—— *The Republic of Liberia* (London, 1959)
Young, James C., *Liberia Rediscovered* (New York, 1934)

MANUSCRIPTS

Public Record Office
  Adm. 1 Admiralty in-letters
       3 Admiralty Board Minutes
      51 Captains' Logs
      53 Ships' Logs
     106 Navy Board in-letters
  C.O. 267 Governors of Sierra Leone to Colonial Office

F.O. 47 Foreign Office relating to Liberia
H.O. 7 Convicts, miscellaneous
P.R.O. 30/8 Chatham papers
British Museum
    Add. MSS 41262 John Clarkson papers
             41263 John Clarkson papers
             12131 Papers relating to Sierra Leone
             44393 Gladstone Papers. Containing
                   correspondence with E. W. Blyden
             44394 Gladstone Papers. Containing
                   correspondence with E. W. Blyden
             44395 Gladstone Papers. Containing
                   correspondence with E. W. Blyden
             44398 Gladstone Papers. Containing
                   correspondence with E. W. Blyden
             44420 Gladstone Papers Containing
                   correspondence with E. W. Blyden
Sierra Leone Archives Local Letters

PUBLISHED DOCUMENTS

Parliamentary Papers
House of Commons and Lords' Debates
Sierra Leone Legislative Council Debates
Newspapers and Periodicals
    African Repository (Washington)

Blackwoods Magazine	The *New Statesman*
Christian Observer	*Palm* (Monrovia)
Daily Mail (Freetown)	The *Spectator*
Daily Star (Monrovia)	The *Sunday Times*
Daily Telegraph	The *Times*
Elders West African Review	*Time*
Illustrated London News	*Unity* (Freetown)
John Bull	*West Africa*
Listener (Monrovia)	

Index

Dew, Thomas R., 139
Diagne, Blaise, 272
Dilke, Sir Charles, 207
Divorce, The (Jackman), 15–16
Dossen, Chief Justice James D., 271
Du Bois, W. E. Burghard, 267–8, 269, 273, 274, 275
Du Chaillu, Paul, 225
Dumas, Alexandre, 15, 237
Duncan, J. Benjamin, 326
During, Otto, 298

Elder's West African Review, 310–11
Elder Dempster line, 288, 310
Elizabeth (American ship), 107–9, 112
Elliot, A., 29–30
Essay on Slavery (Clarkson), 18
Ethiopia, 155, 274
Ethiopian Church, 261
Evangelicals, American, 91, 93–4, 98, 100, 138, 160
'Evangelicals' (Clapham Sect), 16–17, 21, 76, 83, 84, 102; *see also* 'Saints'
Ezzidio, John, 162–3

Falconbridge, Alexander, 34–7, 45
Falconbridge, Anna, 24–6, 35, 36, 37, 45, 49, 51, 58
Faulkner, Thomas J., 303
Fergusson, William (only coloured Governor of Sierra Leone), 170–71
Fernando Po, 302, 303, 304–5, 312, 327
Findlay, Governor, 180, 182
Finley, Rev. Robert, 93, 98, 100
Firestone, Harvey, 257–8, 259
Firestone Rubber Company, 257–60, 301, 304, 308, 309–11, 315, 325, 329
First World War, 256, 263–4, 287–8
Fleming, Ian, 300
Flickinger, Daniel, 202
Fort Stockton, 131
Fourah Bay, 111, 161; College, 166–7, 172, 242–3, 283, 299
Frazer, Patrick, 24, 25, 27, 29
Freetown, 56, 64, 76, 79, 170, 173, 185, 252, 288, 329; original settlement, 27; Nova Scotians in, 44–50, 73, 282; St

George's Cathedral, 84, 174, 177, 193, 197, 199, 318; recaptives in, 162, 169; descriptions of, 175–6, 192–3, 317–23; religion and morals, 177–8; Burton and, 197, 222; expansion and trade, 202–5, 280, 282, 290–92; in First World War, 287; in Second World War, 292–3; Greene and, 293–5, 319; City Hotel, 318–21
Freetown-Bo railway, 279, 282
French Guinea, 212
Freyre, Dr Gilberto, 328
Frontier Police, 207, 213, 216, 218, 256
Fugitive Slave Law, 236, 238
Furbay, Mrs Elizabeth, 313
Fyfe, Christopher, 163, 186, 281, 285

Gallinhas territory, 224
Gambia, 159
Garcia, Elie, 270–71
Garrison, William Lloyd, 140–48
Garvey, Marcus, and 'Back to Africa' movement, 262–75
Garvin, John, 65, 66
Geary, Sir William, 311
George, David, 61
Georgetown, 73
Georgia, 84
Ghana, 156, 327
Gide, André, 312
Gladstone, W. E., 200, 201, 235–6, 237, 246
Gold Coast, 159, 169–70, 199, 200, 207, 210
Goldie, Sir George Taubman, 207
Graham, C., 309
Grant, William, 197
Granville Town, 27–32, 36, 44
Greene, Barbara, 314
Greene, Graham, 293–7, 314, 318, 319
Greenwall, Harry J., 313
Griffiths, Elliott, 36–7
Grigg, Jacob, 65
Gurley, Ralph R., 129–30, 131, 137, 139, 142, 144–5, 148–9

Haensel, Charles L. F., 166–7
Haile Selassie, Emperor, 274

353

Haiti, 155
Hall, G. W., 222
Hanway, Jonas, 22, 23
Hargreaves, J. D., 217–18
Harlem rally (1920), 265–7
Harris, John M., 205–6, 224–5
Hastings, 161
Hatter, Mrs, 136
Heart of Darkness (Conrad), 293 n, 296
Heart of the Matter, The (Greene), 293, 294–6
Heddle, Charles, 182
Heighway, Thomas, 83
Henderson, Arthur, 307
'Heritage' (Cullen), 261
Hill Station, 282, 318, 321
Holt, Robert L., 311
Hopkins, Samuel, 92–3
Horton, Dr James Africanus, 163–5, 185, 284
Huberich, Charles Henry, 111 n
'Hut-Tax War', 209–18
Huxley, Elspeth, 300

IBO TRIBE, 79, 83, 161, 162, 164, 190, 239, 285
Independence, American Declaration of, 89–90, 94
Interior, Ministry of, Liberia, 247, 248
Irwin, Joseph, 24, 25, 28, 29
Ivory Coast, 155, 156, 250

JACKMAN, ISAAC, 15
Jackson, Henry, 139
Jaeger, Muriel, 17
Jarrett, Dr Michael, 181
Jay, William, 145
Jefferson, Thomas, 89–90, 95, 96, 97, 248
Jemmy, King (Temne sub-chief), 32, 36
Jews, 262, 264, 273, 330
Johnson, Colonel Elijah, 116, 154
Johnson, Dr (in Christy commission), 304
Johnson, Gabriel, 266
Johnson, H. R. W., 248 n
Johnson, Dr Samuel, 16
Johnson, William, 75, 83
Johnston, Sir Harry, 154, 254–5

Journal of Travels in England, Holland and Scotland in the Years 1805 and 1806 (Silliman), 13
Journey without Maps (Greene), 293, 294, 314

KENEMA SCHOOL, 323
Kennedy, Governor Sir Arthur, 171, 180
Kent, Edward, Duke of, 70
Kentucky, 94, 97
Kenya, 156, 200, 201, 290
Key, Francis Scott, 98
King, President C. B. D., 266, 271, 272–3, 303, 304, 305, 307, 309, 311
Kingsley, Mary, 198–9, 201–2, 206, 214, 216, 218, 251
Kizell, John, 103, 108, 109
Knox, Rev. and Mrs John P., 362
Kru tribesmen, 113, 176, 180, 301–2, 308
Ku Klux Klan, 264

LAFAYETTE, MARQUIS DE, 59
Lagos, 165, 169, 249
LAMCO consortium, 326
Lark (Liberia's only naval vessel), 155, 256
League of Nations, 301, 304–7, 308–9, 313, 327
Leeke, Admiral Sir H., 169
Legislative Council, Sierra Leone, 171, 173, 208, 209, 213–14, 217, 289, 290–91
Leicester Mountain, 102
Lemberg, Philip, 283
Leopold II of the Belgians, 201
Letter to William Wilberforce (Thorpe), 80
Lever soap company, 279
Leverhulme, Lord, 260
Lewis, Sir Samuel (first black knight), 160, 172–4, 204, 209, 217–18
Liberator, 141–2
Liberia (Johnstone), 254–5
Liberia College, 224, 240, 247–8, 255
Liberian Development Company, 255–6
Liberian Herald, 133, 238
Liberian Rubber Corporation, 254
Lighthard, Mr, 309
Lincoln, Abraham, 150
Lisle, David, 19, 20

054239